M000006624

DOES JUDAISM CONDONE VIOLENCE?

Does Judaism Condone Violence?

HOLINESS AND ETHICS IN THE JEWISH TRADITION

{⟨━━◝◞◜◟━━⟩}

Alan L. Mittleman

PRINCETON UNIVERSITY PRESS

PRINCETON & OXFORD

Copyright © 2018 by Princeton University Press

Published by Princeton University Press,
41 William Street, Princeton, New Jersey 08540

In the United Kingdom: Princeton University Press,
6 Oxford Street, Woodstock, Oxfordshire OX20 1TR

press.princeton.edu

Jacket art: Yoram Raanan, *Mount Sinai II* / Raanan Art, Ltd.

All Rights Reserved

ISBN 978-0-691-17423-5
Library of Congress Control Number: 2017963020

British Library Cataloging-in-Publication Data is available

This book has been composed in Miller

Printed on acid-free paper. ∞

Printed in the United States of America

10 9 8 7 6 5 4 3 2 1

CONTENTS

DOES JUDAISM CONDONE VIOLENCE?

WHAT IS HOLINESS? How is it related to morality? How is it implicated in that breakdown of morality that we call violence? These three questions motivate this book.

We are used to thinking of holiness as intimately related to morality. A holy person, say, Mother Teresa, is distinguished by her moral excellence—her compassion, her self-sacrifice, her humane beliefs and persistent dedication to human betterment. As moderns, we are comfortable with the idea that holiness maps onto goodness. But what then are we to make of holy places or times? Of holy objects? These do not seem to have anything to do with morality. Indeed, the power of holy places—for example, the Temple Mount in Jerusalem—can motivate people to do immoral things. A "Jewish underground" in the 1980s plotted to blow up the Dome of the Rock so as to spark an apocalyptic war after which the Third Temple would be built and the messianic age would begin.[1] An intense fixation on the holy can lead to ethical derangement. How then can we parse the distinctions between holiness and morality, as well as keep them both conceptually and normatively integrated? This is a philosophical task. In this book, we will use the resources of Jewish philosophy to answer these questions.

Lest these issues seem overly abstract, readers should keep in mind that they are meant to facilitate an analysis of religious violence in Judaism. What do I mean by violence? As in the earlier example, our concern is with violence motivated by religious belief, by convictions held to be so compelling that they give license to actions that override conventional morality. Examples include the murder, by Dr. Baruch Goldstein, of twenty-nine Muslim worshippers in the Cave of the Patriarchs in Hebron, before he was beaten to death, in 1994, and the assassination, by Yigal Amir, of Prime Minister Yitzhak Rabin in 1995. Goldstein was inspired by the extremist Rabbi Meir Kahane, who believed that in order for the holy people (the Jews) to achieve redemption in the holy land (Israel), the unholy (Arabs) had to be banished. Kahane's was a wrathful God who required vengeful measures. Amir came to believe, with indirect support from the preaching of militant rabbis, that Rabin was a *rodef* (in Jewish law, a pursuer intent on murder who could be killed to defend the innocent from his depredations). In these cases, imagined religious duty mixes with political beliefs, subordinating ethical constraints for "higher" purposes. This kind of violence has a political context. Religious violence, of course, can be more diffuse. It can pervade daily life, oppressing women, children, or sexual (and other) minorities in the name of some allegedly God-given holy way. Although I am not directly concerned with such phenomena here, they have a common source in misguided construals of the holy and, further upstream, in theological misprisions of God.

Of course, many books have been written, especially since 9/11, about "terror in the name of God" or "terror in the mind of God." This has become a burgeoning field for scholars of religion, political scientists, journalists, and others. Fine books exist on violence in Jewish thought. The present book uses some of this scholarship but departs from it as well. As a work of Jewish philosophy, its contribution is neither historical nor sociological, but normative and constructive. I want to argue for a concept of holiness in Judaism that is true to its biblical roots—that is not simply reducible to moral categories but that is nonetheless allied with morality. I want to argue for a concept of God that has been purged of violence. This book therefore works in the idioms of philosophical theology and ethics. Its emphasis is more on the critique of religious violence than on its description. To do so, I advance an original theory of holiness, a "natural history of holiness," and explore the connections among holiness, ethics, and violence in light of the theory.

Part of what motivates this inquiry is a confrontation with some highly problematic texts. The Bible sometimes presents God as wrathful. It also enjoins violent conduct toward perceived enemies, such as the Canaanite nations that occupy the land promised to the Israelites. These texts raise fundamental problems about holiness, ethics, and violence. The biblical characters themselves seem to struggle with them. King Saul, for example, balks at the seeming irrationality of God's command to obliterate the livestock along with the people of Amalek (I Samuel, chapter 15). He loses his kingship for following his own judgment, which falls short of the prescribed genocide. Such texts invite philosophical reflection on how the presumed goodness and justice of God can be reconciled with the cruelty of his commands. Why should a holy will fail at times to be a moral one? Far from a parochial project, the philosophical idiom opens up this hermeneutic reflection to readers of all religions or of none. The subject matter is primarily Jewish, but the problem of a gap between contemporary moral beliefs and ancient religious ones is universal.

The gap between moral beliefs and religious ones, however, is not a problem just for moderns. The ancients felt it, too. Bridging the gap involves a struggle to purge immoral elements from the concept of God, disallowing the concept to serve as a warrant for unworthy behavior. Socrates works on a version of this problem in Plato's *Euthyphro*. In that dialogue, Socrates encounters a young man, Euthyphro, who believes himself to be expert in matters of holiness. Holiness or piety, *hosion*, refers to what the gods prescribe for or permit human beings to do.[2] The gods want human beings, for example, to do justice—that is part of holiness or piety. Indeed, Euthyphro, out of a fanatical devotion to what he understands justice and the divine will to be, is in the midst of bringing an indictment against his own father, whom he holds accountable for the murder of an underling. Socrates, and everyone else, thinks that this is madness. In Socrates's Athens, a lawsuit against a murderer was brought by the family of the victim. Here, Euthyphro is taking the victim's side against his own family. He believes that such extreme devotion to justice is what holiness or piety demands. After all, Zeus—the most just of the gods— imprisoned his own father, Kronos, who had in turn, castrated his own father, Ouranos. Euthyphro holds to a version of *imitatio dei*—do as the gods do. He believes that the holy and the good are defined by reference to what the gods desire or abhor. As Socrates presses Euthyphro, he comes to realize that, given polytheism, the gods disagree as to what is desirable. Merely following traditional religious beliefs about what the gods endorse can provide no criterion for what is truly just or good. A higher criterion, which the gods themselves must take into account, is needed. To the incisive Socratic question whether the gods love the holy because it is (intrinsically) holy or because their act of loving it makes it so, Euthyphro has no answer. He is now perplexed about the relationship between holiness and ethics.

Although not completed in this dialogue, Socrates works up toward a vision of the gods and the good in which the famous question loses its dilemmatic character. The gods (or God) will only the good. The mythological stories of Homer and Hesiod about the gods are unworthy of the gods. Socrates favored, in the words of a leading interpreter, a "philosophical religion founded on a rationalist psychology and theology that devalued the old, publicly observable, external standard of piety that connected capricious all-too-human gods to humanity through the system of burnt sacrifice. In its place, Socrates advocated an internal standard of virtue and human happiness that emphasized the rational purification of the soul through elenctic argument and a viewpoint that presupposed the existence of benevolent rational deities who loved justice but were relatively indifferent to sacrifice."[3]

The *Euthyphro* shows how matters of holiness, ethics, concepts of God, and the place, if any, of violence in a life devoted to God are bundled together. The tack that Socrates takes, one of rational or contemplative religion, departs from traditional piety but also infuses that heritage with new significance. It rescues inherited religion from being beholden to mere ipse dixit and elevates it to accord with intellectual and moral virtue. It is part of the axial age revolution of deepening the ethical character of received religion. This is all to the good, and yet a sense of the uncanny must remain. A God domesticated to purely human categories would be a diminished divinity. Socrates's contemporary, Sophocles, captures the element of awe, fear, or uncanniness in our dealings with the holy in *Antigone*: "Nothing that is vast enters the life of mortals without a curse."[4] No holiness without danger nor awe without terror.

The modern discourse on the nexus of awe and terror begins in the late seventeenth century with English travelers to the Alps. It continues in the eighteenth century with the work of Edmund Burke. The key term in the discourse is "sublimity," or the "sublime." For Burke, the beautiful may please us, but the sublime, the incomparably majestic, overwhelms and astonishes, filling us with awe: "Astonishment is that state of the soul, in which all its motions are suspended, with some degree of horror. . . . Astonishment . . . is the effect of the sublime in its highest degree."[5] Sublimity, astonishment, and horror are linked. In the presence of vast vistas and massive objects, we are transfixed. Our reason is arrested. A deep, uncanny fear takes hold of us, even as we are transported by an irresistible force. That which transfixes and transports us could as easily crush and destroy us. Burke captures the duality of the sublime, its ability simultaneously to ennoble and disconcert us.

The emphasis on the sublime is a reaction to an overly rational, bourgeois, ordered view of human nature and purpose. It gave a vocabulary to the attempt to resist a "too-rosy picture of the human condition, shorn of tragedy, irreparable loss, meaningless suffering, cruelty and horror."[6] But the sublime also became, for our early modern ancestors, a substitute for the holiness of God. Writers like Burke and his predecessors no longer speak of the uncanny, numinous quality of divine presence or of its lingering traces—the phenomena that "holiness" in one of its senses describes. They displace the holy onto nature, specifically onto what is majestic and awe-inspiring in nature. The aesthetic experience of the grandeur of nature becomes a kind of religious experience, with natural sublimity taking the place of God. There is some justice in this transposition. I shall return to it in chapter 3.

Nature can certainly threaten us. Even the gentle trout stream where I fish can (and does) turn into an angry torrent after many days of rain. The nexus of beauty, sublimity, and terror makes some sense here. But to turn back from this modern ersatz to God, does God also threaten us? If we have veridical experiences of God, do they too come with some quotient of terror? Should the very thought of God include an attitude of fear? Thomas Jefferson wrote that he feared (for his country) when he reflected that God is just. But what if God's justice is a post hoc consideration? What if we should just fear God as such, before moral criteria are introduced against which we may find ourselves wanting? What if the moral criteria themselves—the attempt to pin God to ethically intelligible norms—are an evasion? What if, to put it abstractly, holiness and violence are simply concomitant?

A paradigm case for the Bible is Isaiah, chapter 6. Isaiah has an encounter with God and His angelic retinue in the Temple. God is seated on a high throne, the "skirts of His robe filled the Temple." Six-winged fiery angels (*seraphim*) stood about Him calling to one another "Holy, holy, holy! The Lord of Hosts! His presence fills all the earth!" The Temple filled with smoke and shook. Isaiah cried: "Woe is me; I am lost! For I am a man of unclean lips and I live among a people of unclean lips; yet my own eyes have beheld the King Lord of Hosts." Isaiah is terrified; he knows that he is unfit to stand in God's presence. A seraph then flies to Isaiah and touches his lips with a burning coal taken from the altar of the Temple. The angel exhorts him: "Now that this has touched your lips, your guilt shall depart and your sin be purged away." The physical contact of burning coal, taken from the holy altar, to the prophet's unclean lips purges impurity, guilt, and sin—all of this in a quite tangible, not quite metaphorical way. Isaiah, now transformed and emboldened, finds the strength to answer God's call. "Whom shall I send? Who will go for us? . . . And I said, "Here I am; send me."[7]

In this story, astonishment and awe are mingled, as we would now expect, with fear. God appears in a physical, embodied way. He is announced, described, lauded by his retainers as holy (*kadosh*), a term suggesting separateness, purity, and power in the sense of energetic and potentially explosive force. It is as if Isaiah entered into the core of a nuclear reactor. How could he not be overwhelmed by terror? He is unclean (*tamé*), a term bearing both ritual and moral significance. Before he can endure the divine presence, his uncleanness must be purged. He thus undergoes a mysterious ordeal. We next learn that he is able to respond to God, as Abraham responded long before: *Hineni!* Here I am! His life, like Abraham's, now takes a new direction. Isaiah, commissioned, has a mission to teach, adjure, and castigate his people for their disloyalty to the divine King. Isaiah's terrifying experience of holiness ultimately serves a moral purpose. The prophet's life is now given over to a kind of moral instruction; he is to remind Israel of its covenantal obligations, of the rectitude with which it is supposed to live.

Although it is not the first point made by the story, the eventual conjunction of holiness and morality is important. Even so strong a defender of the mysterious, metarational otherness of the Divine as Rudolf Otto refused to decouple divinity entirely from morality.[8] Although there is nothing *inherently* ethical about God's theophany, its lasting impact on human lives occurs (or ought to occur) in a moral register. Conduct should change. The holy is *conceptually* distinct from the good and the right but *practically* entangled with them. The experience of the holy is uncanny, but the consequences of experienced holiness are not. They are transparent to practical (that is, moral) reason. In part, the moral consequences authenticate the experience of holiness. If experienced holiness led to carnage and savagery, would the experience not thereby forfeit its claim to have been an experience of the holy? As much as I believe that the answer to that question is yes, the answer is not self-evident.

Indeed, God still seems to trade in terror. He reveals himself to Abraham, only to demand that he sacrifice his son. He reveals himself to Moses and Israel in a theophany so dreadful that God warns Moses to keep the people away. Mount Sinai is covered in fire and smoke, trembling as if in an earthquake; mere physical contact with it will incinerate the very people that God had just liberated. Why these terror-inducing displays?

Why the violence or threat of violence? Are these necessary to establish God's sovereignty over a refractory and stubborn people?[9] God could have approached Isaiah as he did Elijah, to whom he was present as a "soft, murmuring sound" (I Kings 19:12). In that revelation, God deliberately chose *against* appearing in a mighty wind that split mountains and shattered rocks, or in the earthquake that followed the wind, or in the firestorm that followed the earthquake. God chose against the vast and terrible as the means for his disclosure in favor of the small but insistent, the "still, small voice," as the King James translation has it. Those sublime phenomena are presented by the text as *from* God, but God was not *in* them. God seems to know the terror that he can bring but restrains himself from using it. God does not want to be associated too intimately with violence or the threat of violence. So too with the private theophany that Moses experiences. He turns to see the astonishing sight of a bush burning yet enduring through the flames. A voice issues forth from it, telling him not to approach further and to remove his shoes—for the ground he stands on is "holy" (Exodus 3:5). When God announces his identity, Moses "hid his face, for he was afraid to look at God" (Exodus 3:6). The bush, the voice, and whatever Moses saw are dramatic— they are astonishing—but they are modestly scaled. They do not overwhelm. Nonetheless, they still inspire fear. Moses like Isaiah and Elijah soon finds his footing and, after negotiation, accepts his commission.

These cases connect the holy with displays of power that cause fear, to one degree or another. God is not overtly violent, but he could be. Fear, dread, and terror are appropriate human responses to his self-disclosure.[10] The vastness that enters the lives of mortals does not bring a curse, but it does bring danger. Holiness and terror are paired in the Bible's vivid poetry.

That they eventually issue into a moral orientation toward action in the world is crucially important, but it does not detract from the initial eruption of power and ensuing human panic.

These considerations help orient the inquiry into holiness, ethics, and violence that is the aim of this book. They point in two directions, upstream and downstream, so to speak. Upstream lies the divine source of holiness; downstream indicates how an idea or ideal of holiness shapes our conduct, whether for good or ill. As we can see from the Isaiah citation, holiness has to do with God. God and holiness are mutually implicated. When we talk about holiness, our use of words such as "holy," "sacred," "profane," "pure," and "impure" occurs in a framework in which God, as a concept, plays a crucial role. If God were not thought to have a presence in the world, in the burning bush or the ancient Tabernacle and Temple, or if God were not thought to command a unique ("holy") way of life or worship, these words would have little traction. The occasion for their use would not arise. The holiness "language game" is mostly played by theists.[11]

Metaphysically, an inquiry into holiness and violence leads us to ask about the nature of God, about God's character and conduct—to the extent that any of this can be known. That extent, including the prior matter of whether God exists, may be very slight. God is, in a way, an empty vessel into which we pour our notions of ultimacy, finality, and value. Religious traditions, such as Judaism, often claim a privileged knowledge, vouchsafed by a revelation of divine presence and will. At Mount Sinai, so Jews have held, God made himself known to an entire nation. God shared information as to his thought, character, and desire. Epistemically, I cannot help but see such narratives as stories that human beings have told to fill that empty vessel. Our own appraisals of what life means, of what our highest purposes are or should be, or what, in the case of the Jews, a national life should embody contribute to our concept of God. Yet, I cannot also help but think that God pushes back. The true God does not allow our false ideas to stand. God qua concept is not just an "empty vessel" but a normative imperative, an idea of the good that brooks no compromise. Perhaps the pressure on reason that the highest ideas of God exert is a sign of the divine as such. The entanglement of holiness with goodness seems to me such a sign. What follows is an essay on its implications. This book is written from the point of view of a contemplative piety, akin to the stance earlier ascribed to Socrates. The stance may be called rational mysticism. This form of piety is decidedly heterodox. It is both critical of inherited doctrinal claims and open to whatever truth they might contain. The "rational" part implies openness to science and a broadly naturalistic perspective. The "mystical" part knows, with Wittgenstein, that when science has answered all of its questions, the problems of life have not been touched at all (*Tractatus* 6:52). Most of all, it seeks an ethical moment. It finds the form of life licensed by the belief in the God of Israel to have its own practical excellence regardless of the constraints that a post-Kantian metaphysics puts on claims about the divine as such.

The question about holiness and violence is a question about how we ought to conceive of God. Abstractly, it is a question about whether the Highest One is synonymous with the Good; whether God should be thought of as a Perfect Being whose nature excludes anger, vengeance, and the capacity to harm. Or is it rather the case that the main character of the Hebrew Scriptures, who is a portrayed as a Person with a tumultuous emotional life, is indeed God. On this view, Goodness, Perfection, Simplicity, and the other characteristics ascribed to God by classical theism are Greek-inspired distortions of a far more personal deity. Divine anger and the violence to which it leads make sense on this personalist conception.[12] But whether there are any good reasons for holding such a view, other than to preserve the appearances of the biblical text, is an important philosophical-theological question.

Downstream, concepts of holiness influence how human beings live. To believe that there is a way of life prescribed by the holy God is to believe that its concerns, foci, and preoccupations cannot be reduced to a "profane" way of life. Coming from the Highest One, it is higher than other ways of life. Denizens of the world that holiness engenders may look askance at the lives of others; they may come to consider the others a lower form of life, not fully or exemplarily human.[13] That is certainly true of the Canaanite pagans, toward whom the biblical God demands complete extirpation (*herem*). Later, in postbiblical Judaism, there are theologies, typically derived from mystical sources, in which Jews and gentiles are thought to have different kinds of souls. Gentiles are trapped by their embodiment and animality more than Jews (allegedly) are. Jews who believe such things might value gentile lives less than Jewish ones. They might be treated more roughly under certain circumstances, as advocated by a horrific contemporary Jewish legal (*halakhic*) work, *Torat ha-Melekh* (*The King's Torah*). These are painful things to say, not because they are true but because they are true of some strands of Jewish tradition, both ancient and modern. They should rightly be shunned and quarantined; Jews who continue to embrace such views should be challenged morally and theologically. Nonetheless, it is not immediately clear on what basis such a challenge should come.

If the basis for the challenge is contemporary, Enlightenment-derived morality, such as Kantian ethics, then what claim should that have on observant, traditional Jews? Does such a morality have so unimpeachable a pedigree that moralities internal to ancient—in this case, religious—traditions are by comparison less cogent? If the basis of the challenge is a moral stance internal to Judaism, one that uses some preferred sources to offset the baleful influences of other sources, then what is the basis for the preference? If one prefers an inclusive, generous attitude toward humanity in all of its expressions, isn't one simply constraining the tradition to accord with contemporary secular democratic norms? Where is the criterion that allows one to accept some moral views and reject others?

Questions such as these always arise in Jewish ethics. (Indeed, the term "ethics" implies a rational, universal perspective that can immediately generate tension with traditional Jewish norms, which are thought to be revealed by God at Sinai and inscribed in the Torah. Even to use the term "ethics" signifies a subtle if fatal distancing from tradition on this view.[14]) Yet even in a normative approach that hews closely to halakhic texts and decision-procedures, fundamental matters of selection and weighting—moves that presuppose value commitments—come into play. *Torat ha-Melekh*, which advocates the possibility of killing young gentiles in wartime because they will grow up to be adult anti-Semites, employs a "meta-halakhic" stance based on the presumed higher value of Jewish life, given the supposed higher value of the Jewish soul.[15] Another halakhic work, which was written to repudiate *Torat ha-Melekh*, *Derekh ha-Melekh* (*The King's Way*), appeals to rational, "natural" ethical norms to offset the former's racist ones.[16] In both cases, there is no such thing as a purely procedural halakhah; legal decision making takes place in a context of value-laden choices. Jewish law is never aloof, the pretensions of some of its positivist practitioners aside, from ethical considerations.

The best relation between religious and secular normativity is dialectical; the two sources should challenge, supplement, check, reconfigure, and enrich one another.[17] That is the stance I take in this book. Nonetheless, there are some inherited religious normative claims that ought not to be appropriated. The idea that the Jews are a holy people in a putatively *biological* way seems to me a clear case of an irredeemable view. I would argue that constructions of holiness that push Jewish morality in chauvinist, racist, and overall violent directions are a disgrace to Judaism, however ancient their textual pedigree. Descriptively, one could call Judaism a religion (to the extent that "religion" is apt for something as multifaceted as historic Judaism) of peace as well as a religion of violence.[18] But normatively, I want to make a constructive case for severing the link between holiness and violence. To do this, we shall have to dig deeply into the roots of holiness, morality, and violence. These three topics are *seriatim* the foci of the book's three chapters.

This book will therefore attend both to our understandings of holiness as well as to the ethical consequences that flow from those understandings. There is a normative argument to be made—that any correct conception of the Highest One excludes violence—but there is also much descriptive work to be done. First, the concepts of holiness at work in biblical religion and subsequent Judaism need to be clarified and analyzed. Our usage of words on the semantic "holiness spectrum" is tentative today. "Holy," "profane," "sacred," and so on have gauzy meanings and sentimental associations. We need to get a firm grip on what these terms meant in their biblical and Jewish contexts as a prologue to constructive theorizing about holiness (and its relation to both morality and violence) in Judaism.

Chapter 1 tries to secure that grip. It reconstructs the meanings of holiness from representative texts of the Jewish tradition. The chapter is primarily descriptive but is organized around two claims, which the texts, in my reading, support. The first is that biblical thought does not divide the world into a neat dualism of sacred and profane. The most prevalent contrary of "holy" is "unclean." This has important consequences for the nature of the world and for human conduct within it. The second claim is that the Bible and subsequent Judaism conceive of holiness in three different ways. Holiness sometimes refers to what might be called a property. It describes a physical force, which is energetic, dangerous, and powerful. It is as if holiness were a form of energy, radiating out from a place where divine disclosure occurred. Objects, places, and persons can absorb this force—hence the notion of property. This is perhaps the aspect of holiness most alien to contemporary thought. Second, holiness indicates a status. When something belongs to God and is thereby set aside from ordinary things and given special treatment, it is or becomes holy. Objects, places, times, and persons thought to be holy have a special status. Third, holiness is a value or project: it indicates a norm; it exerts pressure on our will and choice. Holiness can be thought of as an ideal, an aspiration, a normative way of life. These three characteristics of holiness can coalesce or separate. To try to boil down holiness to one of them distorts the complex way in which the tradition conceives of the holy. I am especially concerned in this chapter with the ideas of the holiness of the people Israel and the holiness of the Land of Israel. Both of these foci are morally problematic and will figure into the later concern with violence in the name of the holy.

Chapter 2 theorizes the relation of holiness and ethics or, in shorthand, the holy and the good. I seek the origins of both in our primordial encounters with nature and with one another. The Enlightenment was not wrong to look to nature for the experience of the sublime and mutatis mutandis of holiness, although nature is not, in the end, a substitute for God. I propose a natural history of holiness in which the human experiences of love and awe, of goodness and holiness arise together against our evolutionary background as social primates. The inspiration here is less Burke than Maimonides. That is, I follow Maimonides in the belief that, given the absolute gap between Creator and creature, the closest we can get to God is through scientifically oriented reflection on the natural world, conceived as God's Creation. We cannot know God, but if we permit ourselves to see the world as God's world, we can take our bearings from the beauty, order, and goodness of the whole. To underwrite that, I argue the case for moral realism as a philosophical way of taking seriously the Bible's affirmation that Creation is good. Values are not a residue of human subjectivity spread over the surface of valueless reality. Value emerges quite naturally in our dealings with the world. This gives grounds for a retrieval of the "alien" sense of holiness as a property of things, with the qualification that property is best taken as a value-property. Cherishing the newborn baby is as close as we come to experiencing goodness and holiness as value-properties of an "object" in the world.

I do not see ethical naturalism and biblical theism as antagonists. I use the former to offer an origin story compatible with some of the core convictions of the latter. The Bible has a vision of the goodness of Creation; ethical naturalism—the reality of natural goodness—supports a comparable meta-ethics. In a very different idiom, the twentieth-century Jewish mystic, Rabbi Abraham Isaac Kook, writes of a natural morality (*ha-musar ha-tivi*) on which the morality of the revealed Torah builds. Natural morality remains in force ("in all the depth of its glory"; *b'khol omek hodo*) even after the revelation of the Torah.[19] But if one does not permit oneself Rav Kook's imaginative metaphysics, what place does holiness have in a robustly naturalistic story? Holiness, I argue, fixes natural goodness in a symbolic way. Making and interpreting symbols is a uniquely human capacity. The elaborate symbolization of extraordinary value in religious traditions such as Judaism gives holiness a public framework. It should not obscure, however, its natural, experiential origins. As a property, holiness is dispositional and emergent. It begins in nature but requires human subjectivity for its full expression. The same is true of goodness.

The relation between holiness and goodness is not one of simple identity. That the cosmos, *pace* Genesis, chapter 1, is good is a generality. "Good" here is a rather thin term.[20] Moving toward greater specificity and thickness, there are intrinsic goods, such as friendship or knowledge, that win wide affirmation among human beings. There are even more specific goods of an instrumental character that might suit certain characters or lives but not others. (I love the quiet contemplative experience of fly fishing; one of my sons likes the boisterous excitement of amusement parks.) Over and against this range of goods, are foci of extraordinary value. These are hard to characterize in general terms: the face of an innocent child, the look in the eyes of a vulnerable person pleading for protection, an ancient shrine or statue, the flag of a beloved country. The political theorist George Kateb distinguishes between (ordinary) "moral values" and (extraordinary) "existential values."[21] We ought, ordinarily, to be honest in our dealings with one another. But we also ought to acknowledge the freedom, dignity, and equality of all human beings under all circumstances at all times. Freedom, dignity, and equality are existential values, in his vocabulary. Existential values have to do with the stature of human beings; they are somewhat independent of but also orient the moral values. A division such as this will be helpful to the distinction between the good and the holy. Holiness, on my constructive reading, is the locus of exceptional value. It marks a status or stature that calls for special treatment and consideration. It is not reducible to moral value, but neither is it independent of it. The intuitions that we have of moral value are matched by intuitions of "existential value" or holiness. To secure the real content of the latter intuitions, we need to turn from pure naturalism toward transcendence. Symbolism will take us part of the way, but not far enough. Is a "theological realism" building upon a naturalistic, moral realism possible? I argue that it is unavoidable if we wish fully to warrant the extraordinary value that our core symbols capture. Full human flourishing points us toward a transcendent source for the authority of our norms.

Chapter 3 returns us to the theme of violence. So far, I have argued that God, the good, and the holy are allied. Moral conduct, in the Jewish tradition, has often been construed as acting in imitation of God (imitatio dei or, in the Hebrew, *v'halakhta b'drakhav*): "you shall walk in God's ways" (Deuteronomy 28:9). God's holiness should be a model for our own aspirations to holiness in conduct and character. The "canonical" version of this principle holds that Jews should emulate only such divine attributes as kindness and generosity.[22] God's anger, for example, should not be emulated. A safeguard such as this would seem to preclude direct imitation of divine violence, at least at the level of principle. Nonetheless, tensions between conduct that exemplifies love and respect for God's creatures and conduct that betrays harshness and hatred sometimes emerge. Some instances are embedded in the biblical text itself—notably, in the call to holy war against uniquely disfavored (Canaanite) others or in Pinḥas's zealous and lethal assault on a Midianite woman and her Israelite paramour (Number 25:1–9). Here, a concept of the holy seems directly to support a program or an act of violence. The ascribed impurity of others awakens disgust and condemnation. The pure people in the holy land should not tolerate incursions on their holiness. In subsequent Judaism, as mentioned, the idea that

Jews are a "holy seed," a people fundamentally distinguished by their holiness from other peoples, supports a range of attitudes from charitable paternalism to active contempt. Although such texts and attitudes did not lead straightforwardly to violent actions in the past, a critic could say that this was because of the relative political powerlessness of the Jews in their diasporic history. Jews may not have acted on their religiously inspired, violent inclinations because they did not have the means (or the numbers) to do so effectively. But now, the argument might run, given the reality of Jewish power in the State of Israel, the Jews are no longer an anomalous people; they have the means and, given the sorry situation of enduring hostility with much of the Arab world, the occasion to act violently. Unfortunately, there is something to this argument. Ugly views and occasionally ugly actions claiming the religious tradition as their warrant have emerged. Their targets can be both non-Jews and Jews, such as the late Prime Minister Yitzhak Rabin.

As mentioned at the outset, our focus is limited to violence motivated by ideas of holiness. But let us be more precise. To avoid reification, one should not say that holiness (or religion) *causes* violence. Rather, moral agents take beliefs about holiness as *reasons* for certain kinds of conduct. They attempt to justify their conduct by appealing to these religious reasons. It is likely, however, that in actual situations, such reasons, where they apply, are not the only reasons for the choices agents make. It may not be possible to disentangle them from other considerations. Take the conflict that consumed the former Yugoslavia in the early 1990s. It pitted Croatian Catholics against Serbian Orthodox against Bosnian Muslims and Kosovar (Muslim) Albanians. Religion was integral to the "tribal" identities of the parties to the conflict. The genocidal assault on Bosnian Muslims in Srebrenica by Serbs had elements of a holy war. "Ethnic cleansing"—a term translated from the original, deliberately euphemistic Serbo-Croatian—implies a religion-like concern with the alleged purity and impurity of territory and groups.[23] The propagandistic portrayal of the enemy in the run-up to the war drew on religious imagery and tropes— "vampires," "beasts in human form," "bearded animals on two legs," "bloodsuckers."[24] But none of this can be easily isolated from nationalistic motivations, *raison d'état*, remembered historical grievances, or the cynical manipulations of the leading politicians. Once such conflicts start, they take on a life of their own and trap their participants within them. New layers of rationale and motivation accumulate. Laying too much of this at the door of religion may just be lazy thinking.

Yet religion evidently plays a role in some contemporary acts of violence. The desire to achieve martyrdom mixes with anger at perceived historic or political humiliation in the hearts of would-be jihadists. They conceive of their actions as self-purification, achieving the greater jihad of self-struggle through the lesser jihad of struggle against the enemies of Allah. Elements of Islam (in tension with more pacific elements of Islam) give the jihadi a conceptual framework to motivate his action and fix its significance, both personally and socially. So too with other actors in contemporary conflicts or persecutions: Hindu Tamils and Buddhist Sinhalese; Muslim Rohingya and Buddhist Burmese. Religious concerns about identity and otherness, purity and impurity play their roles. But isolating just what roles religious ideas play requires careful, case by case analysis. That is probably a matter more of empirical psychology and anthropology than armchair philosophy.

In the Jewish instance, our only concern in this book, there is obviously ongoing violence between Israel and the Arabs (and other Muslims), both individuals and groups (such as Hamas and Hezbollah), although not, at present, nations (although the threat of Iran is never distant). The military actions that the Israel Defense Forces (IDF) have undertaken against Gaza, for example, lack any distinct religious component. These actions are ipso facto violent, but the political and military leadership believes that they are justifiable under both the international laws of war and Israeli military ethics. Internal Jewish religious thinking about "just war" has little directly to do with state policy.[25] Nonetheless, some troops may have religious ideas that shape their conduct, for good or ill, during an action. When ideas about holiness lead to degrading attitudes and morally (under the laws of war) unacceptable conduct toward the enemy, then the kind of violence that concerns us emerges. It emerges against a broader background of "secular" violence, but it has its own specific character.

In chapter 3, I consider biblical, medieval, and contemporary Jewish attempts to justify violence, both in wartime and in peacetime. I consider as well images of the non-Jewish other—in some of which human personhood and dignity are preserved; in others of which they are erased. I argue that the moral resources of the tradition are sufficient, especially when brought to light in a dialogue with general ethics, to correct the wrongheaded "justification" of violence. The holy does not displace the good. Advocates of violence in the name of the holy confabulate an alleged "higher ethics" that, they claim, overrides ordinary ethics. But their felt need to justify the override with a *moral* argument shows the weakness of their claim. Neither we nor they can escape the demands of ethics. Fabricating an exit from mere ethics while relying on normative argument shows how self-contradictory the effort is. The holy and the good, as chapter 2 argues, remain allies. The one intensifies and symbolizes the other.

Finally, where is God in all this? Far from the poetic symbolism of power, danger, and violence, I argue. That is a human discourse, drawn from our experience of nature. It takes our eyes off the real power and force of value. It misprizes holiness, which needs neither thunder nor lightning, neither sword nor gun. What holiness needs is attentiveness, stillness, receptivity to wonder and to beauty, and the ability to love and to cherish the goodness of being.

CHAPTER ONE

Holiness and Judaism

PHILOSOPHY ASKS peculiar questions, rubbing the obvious against its grain. Everyone in Socrates's world "knows" what courage or justice or friendship or piety is, but when pressed by him, they list examples rather than penetrate to something more genuinely explanatory. So too with holiness. Euthyphro became perplexed by it. We, on reflection, are bewildered as well. When we use the word, we wave at something religious. Mentioning a holy place or time or person is likely to pick out one connected with a religion. Why not then just use "religious"? What does "holy" add? We need to do what Socrates did and ask *ti esti* or "what it is" questions. We need to get beyond merely giving examples and try to find an underlying pattern. We want to know: Is holiness a *property* of places, times, objects, or persons? Is it a *status* conferred by an agent, perhaps by pronouncing a consecrating formula, or by God? Is the status a relation, such as possession, between a person (or God) and a thing? Is it a *value*, a way of designating worth? (And, if so, on what is that worth based?) Is it an artifact of a legal system, with no deeper significance than as a local convention of the way of life that the legal system helps to order? Is it a way of seeing things, of letting their ordinariness fall away and noticing something wonderful or awe-inducing in them? If so, is such "seeing-as" a psychological state or is there something in the world that guides our seeing?

We begin our inquiry with the Bible. The Bible, primarily in the writings attributed to the Priestly Source (P) and the related Holiness Code (H), described later, has much to say about holiness. The fact is, however, that Israel did not discover the sacred in a cultural vacuum.[1] The world was full of intuitions and cultural constructions of the sacred long before the Israelites came on the scene. Indeed, Israel's thinkers ranged their understanding of holiness against that of their ancient Near Eastern predecessors and contemporaries. More generally, cultures around the world have made distinctions between the sacred and the profane, identifying places, times, objects, and persons as having special significance.

Twentieth-century scholars like Emile Durkheim, Rudolf Otto, and Mircea Eliade regard the sacred/profane distinction as basic to all archaic cultures. For Durkheim, the idea of society as a mysterious collective composed of individuals yet transcending them in power and reality lay at the root of the distinction. Society is natural but is represented in our minds as a higher reality. What the members of a society take to be holy are unacknowledged symbols of the uncanny power of society itself. Most people, most of the time, lead mundane ("profane") lives, but at special times and in specially designated places they enter into an experience of the holy. This dimension of experience, although it presents itself as a link with a higher realm, is really an encounter with society in symbolic, transfigured form. The encounter builds social solidarity and enables society to endure. The sacred, in Durkheim's view, has nothing to do with genuine transcendence. It has to do with how societies represent themselves in the minds of their members and replicate themselves in patterns of action known as ritual. The "mystery" of the sacred is a mystification of the social.[2]

For Eliade, Durkheim's deflation of the sacred will not do. Archaic and ancient cultures divide the world into sacred and profane because there is a sui generis reality to the sacred, a genuine supernatural realm. This realm discloses itself in forms appropriate to the particular culture. The self-revelation of the sacred is a "hierophany."[3] Eliade does not say what the sacred is in itself, only, echoing Rudolf Otto, that it is "wholly other" (*ganz andere*) than the profane. He is concerned, rather, with how it becomes manifest and with what its effects are. Attentiveness to the disclosure of the sacred—and longing for it in the midst of quotidian life—is a pervasive trait of archaic humanity. This is something that modern men and women have, sadly, lost. Eliade is unapologetically romantic about the antique enchanted world. The sacred for him is both a mysterious thing-in-itself capable of disclosure in natural objects, artifacts, special places, times, and persons. It is also a "mode of being." Sacred and profane divide the world both ontologically and existentially. That is, the terms describe both the character of reality and how we live within it. Ordinary natural and social reality can be ripped open by a genuine hierophany. Whether we notice depends on whether we are dull, hapless creatures of disenchanted cultures or humans who by the luck of birth or by disciplined effort are attuned to the sacred.[4]

Durkheim rightly sees that sacred occasions have important, solidarity-building functions and that these are not limited to aboriginal cultures. In the United States, such secular celebrations as Super Bowl Sunday, Independence Day, and Memorial Day are in some ways functionally equivalent to religious holidays and their attendant rituals. No one who walked through Red Square in Soviet times and saw Lenin entombed in his mausoleum could fail to sense the religious role that his remains played in the secular, communist cult. (The significance of the embalmed and still visible Lenin in post-Soviet Moscow is harder to gauge.) Rousseau called this phenomenon "civil religion" and recommended that his ideal republic have a public cult where citizens could celebrate the polity and demonstrate their fidelity to it.[5] Durkheim recognized that sacred symbols—whether archaic totems or modern political sancta like flags, monuments, founding documents, and so on—have a numinous quality reflecting their importance in the life of those who cherish them. He rightly stressed the character of ritual. No society, if it is to be more than a mass of anonymous individuals, can do without public practices of self-representation and affirmation. Society must assert its claim to reality; it must articulate what it stands for.

Durkheim goes wrong in his positivism, however. For him, abstract and general ideas (including categories like sacred and profane) have society itself as both their origin and their content. In his view, we encounter only particulars. To reach the abstract and universal, the mind turns to the experience of human sociality. The sense that the group is more than a collection of individuals is for Durkheim the key to all the problems of epistemology. It is our first, formative step toward universality. There is a genetic fallacy here. Categories and concepts *do* have social functions and cultural histories. Human thoughts are the thoughts of social beings with an evolutionary history. But once emerged, thought has its own integrity. It cannot be reduced to its presumed origins. Furthermore, it is hard to see how human beings could communicate about matters on which early society depended, such as cooperation, curbing asocial behavior, dividing food, or assigning roles, without at least the rudiments of concepts antecedent to the social exchanges themselves. Durkheim goes overboard in making society the hidden content of *all* general ideas, especially those of the sacred and the profane.

Eliade was right to reject Durkheim's equation of the sacred with society. He took what his predecessor Rudolf Otto called the *mysterium tremendum et fascinans*, the mysterious, sublime, and fascinating power of the sacred as having reality in its own right.[6] Reductionists of Durkheim's bent still exist today. But they tend to see the veiled power of society, concealed by "discourse," as primarily exploitative rather than integrative. And they look to evolutionary theory or neuroscience for the real story of the holy. There is a cottage industry of debunkers who see attestations of religious (or mystical) experience as nothing but deviant brain activity. "In a more promising way," Pascal Boyer writes, "neuroscientists have found that particular micro-seizures, in which some part of the normal communication between cortical and other brain areas is impaired, do give people a subjective sensation very close to that described by mystics."[7] Eliade can be read to resist, once again, such genetic fallacies. Origin in the brain or in natural selection (or in the naturally selected brain) does not have a lock on destiny. The circumstances, environmental and genetic, that favored manual dexterity in humans did not foreordain that Beethoven compose—or that some lucky few prove able to play—the "Appassionata" sonata. There is a wealth of human creativity that reaches far beyond the underlying organic and dispositional capabilities that enable it. No evolutionary or neuroscientific account of religion, however explanatorily rich, will ever be rich enough. Eliade courts obscurity, but he does well to discern that the sacred is a category deserving of nonreductive exploration.

He overreaches, however. Worldwide attestations of sacred presences or powers cannot be taken to prove that people have veridical experience of supernatural entities or forces. One can resist neuroscientific reductionism—what William James called "medical materialism"—as a sufficient explanation of religious experience without accepting every supernatural claim.[8] One can believe that religion, like art or ethics, should be treated with respect as a unique human dimension of experience without rushing to debunk it. Eliade tried to keep religious phenomena from sliding into the purely psychological or sociological. But he unduly reified the sacred and overly generalized the sacred/profane dichotomy. It is not clear that all ancient cultures dichotomized the sacred and the profane in the way that he asserts. As Mary Midgley points out: "The stark division of life into sacred and profane often posited in the west has not been attempted in China."[9] Nor, we might say, was it attempted in ancient Israel and subsequent Judaism in so strictly dichotomous a manner. There *are* relevant distinctions between the holy and its contraries, but they do not precisely fit into Eliade's binary grid.[10] To get beyond the dichotomy, we need to explore biblical ideas of the holy more closely.

Biblical Holiness

Both Joseph Dan and Philip Jenson point out that the antonym to "holy" or "sacred" (*kodesh*) in biblical literature is generally not "profane" (*ḥol*) but "unclean" (*tamé*).[11] This seemingly small semantic distinction is significant.[12] Consider a parallel distinction between good and evil. For this distinction to be robust, one must believe that evil is substantive rather than privative. That is, one must believe that evil is something in and of itself, rather than an absence of good. If good is fundamental and evil is privative of or parasitic upon good, the distinction between good and evil needs to be understood in a subtler fashion than the surface grammar might suggest. This is also true of the sacred/profane dichotomy. On the surface, the two neatly divide the world. Whatever is not sacred is profane. And because the sacred is rare, most of what remains is a profane world. The profane has a comparable status to the sacred; it has its own durable reality. Thus, the majority of the world, which is nonsacred, is intrinsically isolated from the sanctum where holiness resides. (Indeed, our English "profane" derives etymologically from Latin *pro fanum*, before, thus outside, the gates of the sanctuary.) Given this framework, it is but a small step to the belief that the profane is broken, fallen, corrupt, contemptible, or worse. So our ordinary lives in the profane sphere are fundamentally flawed or wanting. Access to the sacred compensates for the truncated possibilities of life in the mundane. The world is *entzaubert*, disenchanted, but if we allow ourselves to achieve a special "mode of being," enchantment awaits. Ours is a misbegotten world from which we must be saved.

But if the antipode of the holy is the *unclean*, then there is no durable profane world that opposes it. Uncleanness, in biblical priestly thought, is a temporary condition. The natural world is ritually clean, but human action—ritual infractions or inadvertent or intentional moral sins—bring impurity. Uncleanness, however, is not evil; it entails temporary exclusion from cultic places or practices. It is as if one came in contact with a chemical or biological agent and needed to remain in quarantine until the agent became inert or was neutralized. Rather than one-half of a dichotomy, holiness is a spectrum or field. It maps onto stronger and weaker expressions over a range. The "holy of holies" in the Tabernacle is more sacred than the utensils on the altar outside it—which then grade off further into various stages of purity and impurity. God's presence in the Tabernacle or Temple establishes a hierarchy of sacred intensities, whose contrary is a range of impurities of increasing magnitude. There are distinctions to be made within the spectrum, but no fixed dichotomy carves up the universe.

The world, however, is God's Creation.[13] God created a good, indeed, a very good world in Genesis, chapter 1 (a text most scholars ascribe to P). That world is not profane. Nature is God's handiwork. Within this good order, divine holiness enters and engenders a set of sacred domains, spatial (Tabernacle, later Temple, Jerusalem, the Land of Israel), temporal (primarily the Sabbath, then festivals), and personal (priests, then Levites, then Israelites). Human beings through errors, ignorance, or recklessness negatively affect the sacred domains. *They do not, however, diminish the underlying goodness of Creation.* Nor do they irreparably harm the sacred domains. Human reparative action can banish the impurity and restore the world, so the holy, and its divine source, can continue to abide in their midst.

As a result, Judaism at its biblical foundation is not well described by the term "religion" in its familiar sense.[14] Religion implies a sacred way of life, set off against a profane world. The faithful "religionist" will be something of an alien in a strange land (I Peter 2:11–12). The hallowed life must take place at an alienated distance—if not a physical one, then a mental one. The Christians whom the author of the Epistle of I Peter addresses as aliens and strangers in a strange land are to live in inner exile. They must not let their souls be corrupted by the ambient opportunities for sin. They should hold up an image of holiness before a profane world. The biblical and rabbinic Jewish view is less categorical and sectarian (although analogues to this estrangement from the world can often be found). As bearers of a comprehensive divine way of life, the Jews seek to extend holiness from the sanctuary, so to speak, into the world. Religion is not a department of life, cleanly separated from the everyday. It has as much or more to do with how one conducts one's business as with the time, manner, and content of one's prayers. This suggests that the world is not to be rejected but perfected; it is something whose intrinsic worth must be realized in the sacred order. The holiness of the sacred domain can be spread into the world, elevating its inherent, primordial goodness and bringing it to its full potential. Holiness in Judaism is worldly.

Dan claims that Western scholars of religion inherited a fundamentally Christian conception of the sacred, which writers like Eliade unwittingly secularized and generalized. The early Church's dichotomous construal of holiness was based on Christian experience. Unlike Jews, born into a people in covenant with the divine, Christians came as individual converts from other, highly developed cultures. Ideally, they left these behind in a strongly committed way, entering a new and higher life discontinuous with their past. The new, higher life was holy; the earlier sinful and profane. Although their civil status remained unchanged, Christians now had a religion. The Church was to one degree or another set against the world.[15] The basic idea of holiness entering into and opposing a fallen, profane world was buttressed by the early missionaries. The Greco-Roman culture in which they worked was civilized and sophisticated but at best it needed either salvation or abandonment. Dan infers from this that the idea of holiness, conceived as a disclosure or an eruption of a special quality of being into quotidian life, which figures so strongly in the work of thinkers like William James, Rudolf Otto, and Mircea Eliade, bears traces of its Christian origins. Were we to start with a native Jewish idea of holiness, we would work from the hallowing of all aspects of human life, not just from extraordinary moments where the sacred/profane equilibrium is tipped in one direction.[16]

There are very valuable insights in Dan's view, but he somewhat overstates the case. What Dan characterizes as a Christian view of holiness originates in the Hebrew Bible, where disclosures or eruptions of divine presence occur, often violently. The diffusion of holiness across an entire normative way of life is more pertinent to rabbinic Judaism. A rabbinic Jew need not seek distance from the world—in a monastery, say—to pursue a pervasively holy life. The Torah and its commandments provide means to do that in the midst of a world of daily cares and concerns. Nor need God's overpowering presence be sought in extraordinary moments or places; deep, continuous immersion in the study and life of Torah fills the role of distinct human-divine encounters. Nonetheless, one should not diminish the force of a divine-presence explanation of holiness in the biblical world out of deference to subsequent Judaism. What we need is a view capacious enough to treat both the biblical and the rabbinic dimensions of holiness.

Returning to the idea of a spectrum will be helpful. A visual spectrum or aural scale consists of colors or tones that draw their value from comparison with other colors or tones along a range. No item stands alone, nor are any in contrast to just one other. A spectrum or scale signifies both a set of local differences and a composite whole. In Philip Jenson's view, holiness behaves in just this way in the priestly writings of the Bible.

To get a sense of this, consider the announcement in Exodus (a nonpriestly text) that God desires to dwell among human beings: "And let them make me a sanctuary [*mikdash*] that I may dwell among them. Exactly as I show you—the pattern of the Tabernacle [*mishkan*] and the pattern of all its furnishings—so shall you make it" (Exodus 25:8–9).[17] Who or what is this God that desires to dwell among men and women? God and human beings are ontologically unlike one another. The God of Israel, especially in the writings of the priests, is transcendent and mostly nonpersonal. Unlike the mythological gods of antiquity, this God is not just an imaginative exalted version of a heroic human being. God is, in Otto's phrase, "wholly other." The kind of dwelling that such a God would design and deign to frequent must be wholly unlike a human dwelling. God's energy will descend to the dwelling and radiate from it. God has appeared to Moses at the burning bush and to Israel at Mount Sinai. Those locations became temporarily holy, requiring special behaviors and restraints. But a permanent, if movable, sanctuary bids to make holiness an ongoing dimension of the world.

If God were at the center of a circle or sphere, everything along the radii toward the circumference would acquire some of God's holiness.[18] It is as if holiness were some kind of physical property spreading from a source and filling a space, or attaching to objects within the space. The farther from the central source, the less concentrated the property is. God expresses the desire to dwell among the Israelites; they are commanded to cooperate with the divine and build, to exact specifications, a spatial domain worthy of God's presence. If God did not wish to dwell in the world in a continuous way, holiness would have been a largely notional concept, like infinity. (Indeed, one meaning of holiness is "transcendence." Biblical Hebrew lacks a vocabulary for overt philosophical thought. The concept of "abstraction" is expressed by the noun *kodesh* and by the adjective *kadosh*.[19] Using these words to describe God is a way of diminishing anthropomorphism—of stressing the impersonal nature of the divine. Divine impersonality is a dominant feature of the priestly writings, which have a different theology from that of the other Pentateuchal sources, where a personal God of the Covenant is a principal character.[20])

The *mishkan* passage pivots from transcendence to divine immanence; to the presence of God within his Creation. That there is to be a "sphere of God's being or activity" in the world engenders the existence of holy things, places, and persons that belong in that sphere. Items along the radii are in a different state than they would have been were God not present at the center. A way of describing the special character of this sphere, its existence conditions, actuality, effects, and liabilities is now needed. The spectrum of holiness terms—"holy of holies" (*kodesh kodashim*), "holy" (*kodesh*), "pure" (*tahor*), and "impure" (*tamé*)—provides the conceptual vocabulary to construe this novel dimension of reality. Only because God has a presence, either static or dynamic, in the world does the language of holiness apply.[21]

The normal state of persons and things in the world is one of purity. (There are, however, some things designated as inherently impure or unclean, such as corpses, flows of blood or other fluids from a human body, outbreaks of skin disease or mold on houses, and so on.[22]) Normal, pure persons and things can be consecrated—brought along the spectrum from purity to holiness—by a divine or a human action. In Genesis 2:3, "God blessed the seventh day and declared it holy [*va-yikadesh oto*]." In Numbers 8:17, God tells Moses that he has consecrated (*hikdashti*) the firstborn of man and beast for himself (and that he will now replace them by the Levites). More typically, God and a human agent such as Moses cooperate to bring persons and things into the domain of the sacred. Thus, at the completion of the Tabernacle in which God will dwell among the People of Israel, the text makes visible both the graded nature of holiness and the divine-human interaction that brings it into the world:

> And the LORD spoke to Moses, saying: On the first day of
> the first month you shall set up the Tabernacle of the Tent
> of Meeting. Place there the Ark of the Pact, and screen off

the ark with the curtain. Bring in the table and lay out its due setting; bring in the lampstand and light its lamps; and place the gold altar of incense before the Ark of the Pact. Then put up the screen for the entrance of the Tabernacle. You shall place the altar of burnt offering before the entrance of the Tabernacle of the Tent of Meeting. Place the laver between the Tent of Meeting and the altar, and put water in it. Set up the enclosure round about, and put in place the screen for the gate of the enclosure.

You shall take the anointing oil and anoint the Tabernacle and all that is in it to consecrate it [*v'kidashta*] and all its furnishings so that it shall be holy [*kodesh*]. Then anoint the altar of burnt offering and all its utensils to consecrate the altar, so that the altar shall be most holy [*kodesh kodashim*]. And anoint the laver and its stand to consecrate it. You shall bring Aaron and his sons forward to the entrance of the Tent of Meeting and wash them with the water. Put the sacral vestments [*bigdei kodesh*] on Aaron, and anoint him, and consecrate him, that he may serve Me as priest. Then bring his sons forward, put tunics on them, and anoint them as you have anointed their father, that they may serve Me as priests. This their anointing shall serve them for everlasting priesthood throughout the ages (Exodus 40:1–15).

In this elaborate consecration ritual, the most holy (*kodesh kodashim*) things are set up first. The inner sanctum contains a cabinet with the Decalogue in it ("Ark of the Pact"). (Significantly, God's law engraved on the stone tablets somewhat displaces or stands in for the divine presence as such.) The cabinet is covered in pure gold, with golden figures ("cherubim") above it. This inner sanctum is partitioned by an elaborately woven curtain from the next domain ("the holy place"), in which the furnishings are also either covered in pure gold or made of it. Another, less elaborate curtain separates this domain from the next, the courtyard, where the sacrificial altar and laver are. The laver is made of bronze, a less valuable metal. This area, where sacrifice occurs, is again screened off from the outside. Surrounding the Tabernacle is the Israelite camp, where the tribes in order of importance are encamped about the sacred space. Conditions of purity must be maintained throughout, lest the holiness of the sanctum be compromised. Persons in a state of major impurity may have to be separated from the camp and put in the wilderness beyond until their impure status is resolved. On the Day of Atonement, when the sanctuary is thoroughly purged and ritually purified, a "scapegoat," which symbolically bears the impurities and sins of the sanctuary and people, is expelled to the wilderness beyond the camp (Leviticus, chapter 16). The inner and outer sanctums, courtyard, camp, and wilderness form a graded spectrum from most holy to most unclean.

Moses performs the actions. Consecration occurs by pouring specially formulated oil upon the items or persons. This oil may be used only for this purpose; an ordinary Israelite who blends this oil and uses it for a common purpose will be "cut off" from his kin (Exodus 30:33). That is a violation of its holy status. To be anointed is to be designated, set aside for divine service. The degree of holiness, here signifying closeness to God, is signaled by location, building materials, or dress. Aaron's garments are more elaborate and varied than those of his sons. In the developed priestly account of Leviticus, chapter 8, Aaron's consecration has more steps than that of his sons. All of the priests need to become holy to work in the sanctuary, but Aaron alone enters the inner sanctum. He must obtain the highest degree of holiness.

When Moses completes all of the requisite, divinely commanded actions, God fills the space. The consecration has taken effect and God's holy presence will now abide in the sanctuary. "When Moses had finished the work, the cloud covered the Tent of Meeting, and the Presence [*kavod*] of the LORD filled the Tabernacle" (Exodus 40: 33–34). The space and its furnishings are effectively brought into God's *possession*. The many restrictions surrounding the space and its contents indicate divine ownership, effective whether God is present or not. When God is present, there is danger associated with unauthorized entry or even with action inappropriate to the degree of holiness required by the location. Aaron's sons, Nadab and Abihu, having offered "alien fire," are consumed and obliterated by "fire that came forth from the LORD" (Leviticus 10:2). Jenson argues that the fire they used was taken not from the altar but from elsewhere. It thus lacked "the necessary holiness for the holy incense offering."[23] The order of the holy place and its procedures must be strenuously guarded and observed by the priests. If they fail, God will ensure the order and procedure. It is God's domain.

The idea of the sanctuary as a domain in God's possession implies an important comparison with the cosmos. Exegetes ancient and modern have observed that the construction and consecration of the Tabernacle mirrors that of the Creation of the world. The Tabernacle is a microcosm. Nahum Sarna points out that the instructions for building the Tabernacle (in Exodus 25:1–33:11) fall into six literary units beginning with "The LORD spoke/said to Moses." These mirror the "God said" clauses of the six days of Creation. The seventh unit deals with the Sabbath (Exodus 31:12–17), which parallels the sanctification of the Sabbath in Genesis 2:1–4. "When Moses had finished the work" (Exodus 40:33) parallels "God finished the work" (Genesis 2:2). The consecration of the Tabernacle mirrors God's blessing of Creation (Genesis 2:3).[24] Just as God created and possesses the world, God creates and possesses, now with human partners, a designated abode within the world. The order of Creation is initiated by God but sustained by human action, especially covenantal fidelity and righteousness. So too, the order and integrity of the holy place is maintained by human fidelity to God's instructions regarding holiness and purity. The goodness of Creation is complemented by the holiness of the Tabernacle and, ultimately, by its successors and surrogates, including the Jewish way of life in toto. The world is good, but holiness adds something. Holiness intensifies the good, making manifest the ultimate source of goodness.

In the text charting the graded holiness of the sanctum, "holy" functions as a term of *relation*, rather like "mine." God's possession of the domain and of the items within provides the logical condition for calling relevant things holy. The first tentative answer to our motivating *ti esti* (what is it?) question is that holiness is "a status acquired by relation." Holiness is not a property in a physical sense like "yellow" or "soft." "Holy" designates a relation of possession between the divine subject and humanly fashioned objects. Similarly, when a human being declares something—an animal designated for sacrifice or the Sabbath day—holy, this would mean that it is given to God or already God's.[25] Call this a "status analysis" of holiness.

A status is typically a social reality, a social or an institutional fact. To have the status of a sergeant or a five-dollar bill requires a background web of other social and institutional facts like a military hierarchy and a money economy. These conditions further require a cultural history, a political order, a capacity for symbolic thought, complex social relations, and, minimally, human consciousness and language use. Social facts are no less real than physical ones, but their existence conditions differ. The existence of snow and ice on Mount Everest is mind-independent. Although that existence is epistemically available to a properly situated observer, the existence of the snow and ice is not dependent on the observer. The existence of sergeants and five-dollar bills is not mind-independent in the same way. There must be a world of human subjects, of human minds, for this kind of fact to obtain. But they are no less objective and empirical for all that—they are real in a different way. Five-dollar bills are not mere fantasies. They are causally efficacious in the life of a group that designates a role for them. They are no longer mere pieces of paper. They are pieces of paper given a significance and function they would not otherwise have had.[26] We see them as devices that have value, that facilitate relations, that bear consequences. We engage in "seeing as" because there is something real, in context, to be seen.

Insofar as the status analysis of holiness is correct, holiness is a social or institutional fact, not a natural or brute one. It comes into being by "consecration." (This analysis, as we will see, is followed by Maimonides.) Once holiness obtains, it is consequential in much the way that law is perhaps the premier social or institutional fact of human cultures. To say "nothing will happen to me if I break the law; after all, it's only subjective" is to lose one's mind and will likely lead to the loss of one's liberty as well.

There are merits in the status analysis but weaknesses as well. Let us consider the merits before turning to the weaknesses. Consecration clearly plays a decisive role in biblical holiness, as we have seen with the dedication of the Tabernacle and the initiation of its priests. Persons and things do not come into the world as holy; they acquire that status. This goes some way toward illuminating the uses of *ḥol* and its verbal forms found in Scripture. I claimed (following Dan and Jenson) that the sacred/profane dichotomy stipulated by scholars of religion was not suitable to biblical Israel or later Judaism. The proper contraries were holy (or sacred) and unclean. But Scripture does use the term "profane" (or "common" as Jacob Milgrom prefers to translate *ḥol*). The profane has to do with acting in a way that *desecrates*, that attempts to remove holy status from an object or person. It is not precisely to render an object unclean but to undo its acquired exceptional status and to treat it as ordinary or common. Thus,

> When you sacrifice an offering of well-being to the LORD, sacrifice it so that it may be accepted on your behalf. It shall be eaten on the day that you sacrifice it, or on the day following, but what is left by the third day must be consumed in fire. If it should be eaten on the third day, it is an offensive thing, it will not be acceptable. And he who eats of it shall bear his guilt, for he has profaned [*ḥillail*] what is sacred [*kodesh*] to the LORD; that person shall be cut off from his kin (Leviticus 19:5–8).

The sacrifice is a gift given to God. In this case, it is a gift that the priests and donors can eat in God's presence. They share a meal with God, so to speak, the fat especially being God's portion (Leviticus 3:16). If it is not consumed by the third day, it must be burned. To treat it in a common way, as if it were not God's possession, is to profane it. Even more emphatically, Leviticus 19:12 stipulates: "You shall not swear falsely by My name, profaning [*ḥillalta*] the name of your God: I am the LORD." (Compare the third commandment of the Decalogue, Exodus 20:7.) God's name is his effective presence and repute in the world. Nothing is possessed as intimately by God as his name (*shem*) and his presence (*kavod*).[27] To lie deliberately under an oath invoking God as witness is to desecrate the name. In neither case is ritual impurity at stake. *The profane has to do with desacralizing what is holy, undoing what God or humans have consecrated.*[28] A crucial role for the priests is to instruct Israel about the holy things so they do not treat them in a sacrilegious way (Leviticus 10:10–11; Ezekiel 44:23). There is nothing inherently wrong with the common. What is wrong is to downgrade sacred things.

A signal instance of desecration or profanation relates to the Sabbath, which God declared holy as *his own* day of rest (Genesis 2:3; the first use of the term "holy" in Scripture). The human imperative is not to consecrate the Sabbath de novo— God has already done that—but to remember its status. "Remember the sabbath day and keep it holy . . ." (Exodus 20:8–11), and to observe it through relevant performances and prohibitions (Deuteronomy 5:12). We must not render it common by acting on it as we do on all other days. God keeps the Sabbath.[29] Humans honor God by doing so as well. To profane the Sabbath is to dishonor God, treating something dear to God as if it were inconsequential. Here the logic of the profane, as opposed to the unclean, is obvious: time, being nonphysical, cannot become ritually unclean. The profane then has to do with diminishing what has been made holy.

Thinking about holiness as a status is helpful, but an explanatory gap remains. If someone were to say "the landscape painting belongs to Reuven," the hearer would learn a social or an institutional fact about the painting. Reuven acquired it in some effective way, perhaps through a legal purchase. The painting has the status of belonging to Reuven. That may be, however, the least interesting thing one could say about the painting. We would likely want to know many things about the painting that have nothing to do with its ownership status. Perhaps other matters of status would interest us: who painted it, when in the painter's career it was painted, whether it can be associated with some familiar style or school, whether it is an oil painting or a watercolor, and so on. All these concerns are unintelligible apart from social realities, so they all concern status. But if we were to ask about qualities internal to the painting—for example, its use of perspective, of the contrast of light and shade, of geometric shapes and their relations, of the color palette, or of the relation between the image and the external landscape—we would be asking a different sort of question. We would want to know not about how the painting relates to other paintings or other things, but about the painting itself. What are its qualities and characteristics? Perhaps our questions would lead to deeper and more general ones about the nature of art. What makes this a painting in the first place? What properties are criterial for designating something as a painting and how does this painting exemplify those properties? To an extent, we are also after social realities here; paintings don't occur in nature.[30] Nonetheless, we seek to get at something more intrinsic to the painting than facts about its external relations.

This is true of holiness as well. The holiness of an item cannot be exhaustively explained by saying that "we call it holy because it belongs to God (or the Tabernacle, or the Temple, or the priests)." Aren't there properties intrinsic to the item that count as well? Why, for example, should the objects in the inner sanctum be made of gold while the ones in the outer courtyard are made of bronze? What is it about gold that makes it more valuable than bronze, such that items made from it are holier than those made from bronze?[31] Is that just a matter of proximity to the divine (and hence of status), or are there internal properties of these metals that are pertinent— that provide the reason for choosing one over the other to be most proximate to God? Why should one kind of incense or fabric be holier than another? The question of an internal criterion for holiness comes up most strikingly in the case of God: God is often called holy by himself or others. In Leviticus 19:2, God says: "You shall be holy, for I, the LORD your God, am holy." God names holiness as his own characteristic. He is not saying that he possesses himself. The holiness of God does imply God's ontic *separateness* from the created world (and thus a status), but that is insufficient to account for divine holiness. We should follow Jenson's principle that separation is an effect of holiness, not its essential meaning.[32] Holiness seems to be a positive property of God, not just an artifact of his relationship with his Creation. In Psalms 89:36, for example, God swears by his own holiness. He elsewhere swears by his life, his faithfulness, and his power.[33] In Psalm 99, the repeated affirmation "He is holy!" follows descriptions of God's king-like attributes (among which are greatness, awesomeness, justice, and equity). Holiness is either comparable to these attributes or is warranted by them. There is something intrinsically powerful about God that licenses, indeed, demands, calling him holy.

Call this a "property analysis" of holiness. In this view, what warrants the description "holy" is some characteristic or set of characteristics that are internal to the holy object, person, time, or place. They need not be original characteristics. They might have been conferred or acquired through an act of consecration or through contact with other holy things. But once consecrated, what makes such things or persons holy is the acquisition of a seemingly occult property. There is an ontological dimension here—holy things are (or have become) essentially, not just situationally, different from nonholy things. It is not just a matter of occupying a status; it is a matter of being inherently different. Holiness is a reified trait. There are echoes of this view in subsequent Judaism, as we shall see. The Land of Israel is thought to have different properties from other lands. The Jewish people are thought to have a different kind of soul from other peoples. These alleged properties are highly reified in the mystical tradition. Jews become a higher order of humanity. These are dangerous, perhaps morally irresponsible views. What is their pedigree? To what extent does holiness qua property have traction in Scripture?

One way of answering this question is to look at the contrary of holiness, impurity or uncleanness (*tumah*). Impurity lends itself to a property analysis. To be ritually impure in Mesopotamian societies was to be the victim of demonic activity, invasion, or possession. Fearsome occult creatures conveyed a dangerous, "material" impurity. One of the great innovations of the Bible is the elimination of demonic forces. As Jacob Milgrom puts it:

> The Priestly theology negates these premises. It posits the existence of the supreme God who contends neither with a higher realm nor with competing peers. The world of demons is abolished; there is no struggle with autonomous foes, because there are none. With the demise of the demons, only one creature remains with "demonic" power— the human being. Endowed with free will, human power is greater than any attributed to humans by pagan society. Not only can one defy God but, in Priestly imagery, one can drive God out of his sanctuary. In this respect, humans have replaced demons.[34]

In the Bible, therefore, impurity may still have a property-like quality, but it does not flow from some alleged occult realm. Impurity follows organically or mechanically from certain contingent events, such as scale diseases of the skin, as well as in fabrics or on the walls of houses (Leviticus, chapters 13–14), chronic genital flows (Leviticus, chapter 15), or touching a corpse. Persons or places that have these disorders must be separated until the impurity-producing condition passes (and appropriate sacrifices are brought), lest the disorders prevent God from abiding within the sanctum. Impurity, no longer demonic, "merely" prevents entrance into the holy place, first the Tabernacle and later the Temple, for those subject to it.

The physical aspect of impurity suggests a symbolic dimension. In Milgrom's view, impure substances symbolically imply death. Impurity constitutes the antithesis of the life-giving force of divine holiness. Impurity entails that the force of life (semen, blood), which is dissipated in genital discharge, or the healthy intactness of the body, which is violated by wasting disease at its boundaries (scales, earlier erroneously translated as "leprosy"), is being vanquished by the pull of death. The restoration of sufferers from these conditions reenacts a Creation-like victory of life over chaos, disorder, and death. "No wonder," Milgrom writes, "that reddish substances, the surrogates of blood, are among the ingredients of the purificatory rites for scale-diseased and corpse-contaminated persons (Leviticus 14:4; Numbers 19:6). They symbolize the victory of the forces of life over death."[35]

Does holiness have as physical an aspect as impurity seems to have? Consider Exodus 30:29. After prescribing the ingredients for the anointing oil and the procedures for its future use, God commands: "Thus you shall consecrate them [the altar and other appurtenances of the Tent of Meeting] so that they may be most holy; *whoever* [kol] *touches them shall be consecrated.*" Similarly, Exodus 29:37: "Seven days you shall perform purification for the altar to consecrate it, and the altar shall become most holy; *whatever* [kol] *touches the altar shall become consecrated.*" The plain reading of the text seems to be that persons or things that come in contact with the altar absorb its holiness.[36] From Leviticus 6:11, we learn that the meal offering of unleavened cakes, which God has designated as a portion for the priests to eat, is such that "anything that touches these shall become holy." In Ezekiel 44:19, the priests are instructed to take off their holy robes when they enter the outer courtyard where laypersons are, "lest they make the people consecrated by contact with their vestments." The subject of the sentence is the priests but the process by which the people could become holy is automatic and inadvertent. If the priests allow the people to touch their robes, holiness becomes contagious. The priests must prevent this from happening, insulating the vestments in special sacred compartments. The idea that holiness is *contagious* strongly implies its physicality. Holiness has been reified into a communicable property spread by contact. Baruch Schwartz writes that "direct contact with any of the most holy food-gifts of the LORD communicates holiness, conceived of as a contagious, dynamic effervescence of the deity's Presence which renders whatever comes into contact with it holy."[37]

That is the way impurity works. Touching a ritually unclean item (*davar tamé*), which sometimes correlates with naturally repugnant things such as organic remains, conveys ritual impurity (Leviticus 5:2–3; 11:24–40). But it is odd to think of holiness working in an analogous way. For the most part, Jewish tradition narrowed or rejected this idea. Holiness is not supposed to be some kind of *mana*. Medieval exegetes read these texts as warnings to prevent ordinary items from coming into contact with holy ones, *lest the holy items lose their status*.[38] Baruch Levine, a contemporary interpreter, endorses this approach. For Leviticus 6:10, the standard translation of which is "anything that touches these [that is, the LORD's offerings] shall become holy," he substitutes: "Anyone who is to touch these must be in a holy state."[39] Levine argues that an incident recorded in the prophecy of Haggai tells against the idea of contagious holiness.

Thus said the LORD of Hosts: Seek a ruling from the priests as follows: If a man is carrying sacrificial flesh in a fold of his garment, and with that fold touches bread, stew, wine, oil, or any other food, will the latter become holy? In reply, the priests said "No." Haggai went on, "If someone defiled by a corpse touches any of these, will it be defiled?" And the priests responded, "Yes" (Haggai 2:11–13).

Here impurity is conveyed by physical contact. If a man in a state of ritual impurity due to contact with a corpse touches any of these foodstuffs, the foodstuffs become ritually impure. But if a holy object, meat from a sacrifice, comes in contact with common foods, they do not thereby become holy. Levine adds that "substances do not become holy merely through contact with sacred materials. *An act of consecration is required.*"[40] He distances the text from any hint of magical thinking. Holiness depends on intentional acts of consecration, not alleged quasi-physical processes.

Milgrom emphatically rejects Levine's reading and affirms that the priestly literature upholds "sancta contagion"—"contact with a most sacred object brings absorption of its holiness."[41] He discerns different traditions as to the sources and recipients of communicable holiness, as well as a historical process of narrowing the range of the phenomenon. The earliest stage was likely one where both persons and things that came in contact with the most holy objects absorbed a lethal contagion, even when human contact was respectful. The holy was conceived as "high voltage" power, an energetic property with fatal consequences. A retainer of King David, Uzzah, touches the Ark when it was about to fall off the ox cart on which it was being transported and "the LORD was incensed at Uzzah. And God struck him down on the spot . . . and he died there beside the Ark of God" (II Samuel 6:6–7).[42] Similarly, the men of Beth Shemesh "looked into the Ark of the LORD" and God struck down either seventy or fifty thousand (the text is unclear) of them (I Samuel 6:19)! Although both texts ascribe anger to God and present the victims as having paid the price of provoking him, the process could just as well have been automatic and impersonal, like falling onto the third rail of a subway track. In the Exodus story of the Sinai theophany, God repeatedly warns the Israelites not to touch the base of the mountain or try to ascend it. Whoever infringes on its (transient) holiness must be put to death. But the execution must be from a distance, by stoning or spearing, not by physical contact, lest the trespassed holiness of the mountain by communicated to the executioner (Exodus 19:12–13). When God descends on the mountain, he tells Moses to "go down, warn the people not to break through to the LORD to gaze, lest many of them perish. The priests also who come near the LORD, must stay pure, lest the LORD break out against them" (Exodus 19:20–22). It is as if God himself cannot control his holiness; he must warn Moses that the consequences of contact or viewing are out of his hands. His holiness will break out against trespassers and destroy them.[43]

The property analysis has direct application to our interest in holiness and violence. Holiness qua property is akin to energy, whether of an explosive or of a radiated kind. The Tabernacle is a vessel for channeling and domesticating divine power. The acute concern for hierarchy and purity keeps the source of holiness in situ. Impurity would drive God from the midst of his dwelling and hence drain power and blessing from the midst of Israel.[44] The Israelite camp might become a less dangerous place if God's potentially lethal holiness were to depart, but the outside world, ever full of danger, would then impinge unchecked. Deprived of divine power and protection, Israel would be exposed to the depredations of its enemies.

Milgrom argues that compared to other sources, P reduces the range and power of the sancta that communicate holiness. Eventually, the altar and vessels (but not garments) can communicate holiness, but only to foodstuffs, not persons. For Haggai and then for the rabbis, only those foods that have already been on the altar (and that therefore have been designated as holy) absorb the altar's holiness. Furthermore, when a holy object and an unclean one come in contact, "impurity always wins." The holy object requires purification; it can never purify the impure.[45] Thus, for Milgrom, the idea of holiness as a physical property diminishes in importance. This trend continues in rabbinic Judaism.[46] There is truth in this observation, but it also overstates the case. Holiness as physical property will continue to have a long life in Jewish thought. (In the next chapter, I will argue that something like a property analysis is needed for a constructive theory of holiness today.)

The status and property analyses reveal some constitutive dimensions of holiness in the Bible. But they ignore another dimension: holiness as a project. In our inherited, conventional use of the term, holiness involves striving toward an ideal of conduct and character. It implies a value-oriented project of self- and communal transformation. These ideas are also rooted in the Bible. This suggests, in addition to the status and property analyses, a "value analysis" of holiness: holiness as a superlative value that should orient and govern individual and communal life. The locus classicus of holiness as value is Leviticus, chapter 19. God commands Moses: "Speak to the whole Israelite community and say to them: You shall be holy, for I, the LORD your God, am holy" (Leviticus 19:2). As Knohl points out, holiness is no longer monopolized by God alone and by those persons and things closest to him in the cultic realm. Now, the entire people are called to participate, imitatively, in divine holiness. The chapter enumerates a complex list of commandments, joining those that from a modern point of view are ethical with those that are ritualistic. Living according to these commandments "will raise whoever observes them to holiness, thus becoming like the holy God."[47]

Before we turn to the text, a few observations about its literary setting and putative provenance are in order. Since the nineteenth century, academic biblical scholars have distinguished Leviticus, chapters 17–26, from the rest of the book of Leviticus. These chapters, typically referred to as the Holiness Code (H), have unique features. As mentioned, they blend (for lack of better terms) "ethical" with "ritual" commandments. The Priestly Source (P) is not overtly concerned with nonritual conduct. It may assume the normative background of Genesis and Exodus, but it does not treat ethical matters in a fully explicit way. H, by contrast, introduces moral laws. It does so in the context of holiness; every commandment that ostensibly treats conduct among human beings actually treats relations between humans and God. God is the source and goal of a morality that is ordered to holiness; morality is not a domain sufficient unto itself.

Another feature of H is that it addresses not just Moses and the priests but also the Israelite people as a whole. The God of the Holiness Code is once again personal, unlike the impersonal God of the rest of Leviticus and other P-derived texts. He is a God who can be imitated. Holiness is a divine attribute, akin to power, justice, and life. Knohl argues that the Holiness Teaching, as he calls H, is a response by priestly circles to the same social, political, and religious distress that was the focus of the prophetic movement. Knohl dates the composition of the Holiness Code to the second half of the eighth century BCE, during the reign of King Hezekiah. H thus reflects many of the concerns of such prophets as Isaiah and Micah.[48] Matters of social justice and moral rectitude now become integral to the concept of holiness. "Purity" takes on an ethical overtone. Henceforth, ritual and moral impurity, cultus and ethos, are forever interwoven.

The Holiness Code introduces a positive element into the priestly conception of holiness. In P, the main concern is negative: how to prevent the departure of God's presence from the sanctum and the camp; how to control and expunge impurity so that God can continue to dwell in the holy place. With H, the concern shifts: how can the entire people become holy so that God will dwell among them? The entire people are to practice the commandments (*mitzvot*), both ritual and moral, so as to imitate God in holiness, separating themselves from all that is unworthy.[49] Unlike P, where priests are often the addressees of the divine command, the practice of mitzvot applies to all, including foreigners who are resident in the land (Leviticus 24:22). The whole land, not just the sanctuary, is to be a fit habitation for the divine.[50]

Leviticus, chapter 19, begins, as we have seen, with an injunction to *all* the Israelites to be holy, for God is holy. Immediately, a crucial "ritual" observance, the Sabbath, is linked to a "moral" one, revering father and mother (19:3). Injunctions as to the proper conduct of sacrifice (19:5–8) are juxtaposed with procedures for harvesting one's field so that produce remains for the benefit of "the poor and the stranger" (19:9–10). (These norms, amplified by prophetic teaching, become foundational for the later, extensive Jewish concern with the welfare of marginal classes.) Stealing, deceptive commercial practices, fraud, retention of a worker's wages, mocking, taking advantage of, or treating cruelly the deaf or the blind are all violative of the holiness of God. To deal falsely with human beings is equivalent to swearing falsely by God's name, "profaning the name of your God" (19:12). The text is regularly punctuated with the reminder "I am the LORD" to underscore how much is at stake.

God becomes an affected party in every human interaction. There is no conduct purely *inter homines.* Whether the implications of divine holiness are recognizably moral in modern terms ("Love your fellow as yourself: I am the LORD"; 19:18) or rather alien to modern sensibilities ("You shall not make gashes in your flesh for the dead, or incise any marks on yourselves: I am the LORD"; 19:27), correct action enables and protects God's presence in the world. Unholy action diminishes or banishes it.[51]

H develops a teaching about moral impurity that parallels the standing priestly concern with ritual impurity. As Klawans puts it:

> Moral impurity results from committing certain acts so heinous that they are considered defiling. Such behaviors include sexual sins (e.g., Lev 18:24–30), idolatry (e.g., 19:31; 201–3), and bloodshed (e.g., Num 35:33–34). These "abominations" (*toevot*) bring about an impurity that morally—but not ritually—defiles the sinner (Lev 18:24), the land of Israel (Lev 18:25; Ezek 36:17), and the sanctuary of God (Lev 20:3; Ezek 5:11). This defilement, in turn, leads to the expulsion of the people from the land of Israel (Lev 18:25; Ezek 36:19).[52]

Moral impurity is both like and unlike ritual impurity. Ritual impurity disables one temporarily from entering the sanctum, but moral impurity can lead to the long-term degradation of the sinner and the land. The one who is ritually impure has not sinned; he has just had contact with an impure object. Moral impurity is a result of grave sin, however. Nor is there any ritual of ablution to banish it; a murderer or an idolater cannot bathe his sin away. (Nor need one who touches such a morally impure person bathe. Moral defilement is not communicable by contact.[53]) Ritual impurity requires cleansing; moral impurity requires atonement, a more complex process involving intention and expiation.

It is tempting to see some kind of moral evolution here, as if the primitive were absorbed and transformed by the ethical. But we should not overlay our own predilections on the material. Clearly, both ritual and moral dimensions are significant for the text, as for the prophets as well. (The portrayal of the prophets as opposing ritual, primarily sacrifice, wholesale is an imported prejudice. What they oppose is the presumed sufficiency of ritual.) The incorporation of identifiably moral elements into the concepts of holiness and purity seems like a gain for both. Holiness expands beyond the cultic sphere, which modern readers perceive to be archaic and alien. Morality is heightened by its association with the holy; holiness lends morality ultimacy.

A concise depiction of this coalescence of the cultic and the ethical can be found in Psalm 15:

> LORD, who may sojourn in Your tent,
>> who may dwell on Your holy mountain?
> He who lives without blame,
>> who does what is right,
>> and in his heart acknowledges the truth;
>> whose tongue is not given to evil;
>> who has never done harm to his fellow,
>> or borne reproach for [his acts toward] his neighbor;
>> for whom a contemptible man is abhorrent,
>> but who honors those who fear the LORD;
>> who stands by his oath even to his hurt;
>> who has never lent money at interest,
>> or who accepted a bribe against the innocent.
> The man who acts thus shall never be shaken.

The opening question of the psalm should be taken literally: who is fit to ascend Mount Zion and enter the holy precincts; who has the requisite purity to do so? Scholars suggest that the opening lines indicate a ritualized dialogue between a priest and a worshipper, an "entrance liturgy."[54] Entrance into the outer sanctum requires ritual purity to be sure, but here purity is delineated in strongly moral terms. Ethics does not in any sense replace or displace the ritual purity norms. Ethics has a bearing as an element in an integrated, holy way of life. Ethics is part of the ritual and moral purity/impurity system. Mary Douglas has shown how pollution and purity rules often back up moral ones, especially when the latter are in danger of failing. They constitute another set of sanctions that marshal social disapproval, thus augmenting or supplementing moral disapproval.[55] This can strengthen the moral life of the group and contribute to its survival.

It can incur a philosophical cost, however. By integrating or even incorporating morality into purity, the ethical into the holy, the ethical is at risk of being subordinated to seemingly higher considerations. Mere ethics cannot compete with an ethics of holiness, anchored in the will of God. Extending the writ of holiness might mean that there is no mere ethics; the divine plan for holiness acquires a normative monopoly, introducing a tension between the divine will and the good. The Bible itself signals the tension in Abraham's challenge to God over the fate of the people of Sodom and Gomorrah: "Shall not the Judge of all the earth deal justly?" (Genesis 18:25). Abraham implies that there are standards of just dealing to which God, too, is answerable. Moral norms—however they came into being—are no less normative for God than for humans. This imputes some degree of independence to ethics. Had Abraham thought that his sole option was to imitate or obey God, he could not have challenged him. Holiness as a value-driven project has promise but entrains normative problems as well. Holiness must be integrated into a broad normative context where its potential, positive and negative, can be tapped *and* checked.

The relevance of these three frameworks reveals the complexity of the idea of holiness in the Bible. It has elements of relation and status, yet it is also presented as a quasi-physical property, and as a norm or source of norms. It is associated strongly with ritual criteria for purity and impurity, themselves related to physical substances. It also relies on deliberate acts of designation (consecration). It applies to a class of persons, the priests, and in the Holiness Code, to laypersons as well. It applies to the nation as a whole, who are to become a "kingdom of priests and a holy nation." Holiness was restricted originally to the highly ordered sanctum, but H envisions that the entire promised land will be holy. We have seen as well a kind of democratization of what it means for holiness to be realized in the world. At first, it is solely a matter of divine presence and initiative. Human beings must ensure only that the domain they control is ritually clean and fit for God to enter. In the Holiness Code, however, the practice of moral and ritual commandments—of walking in God's ways—enables human initiative. Holiness becomes a project of self-transformation, a task of God's servants. Yet, the other frameworks remain. Holiness continues to be understood either discretely or as a coalescence of property, status, and/or value in postbiblical Jewish literature.

Holiness in Ancient and Medieval Rabbinic Judaism

The group known as the rabbis or the sages was one of the streams of Second Temple Judaism. After the Roman destruction of the Temple in 70 CE, they gradually became the dominant force in Jewish life, both in the Land of Israel and in

Babylonia. They were preceded by the Pharisees, although scholars no longer view them as the direct descendants of that movement. They shared with the Pharisees a concern to broaden the application of the purity laws to ordinary Israelites, allowing them to participate more fully in holiness. Laypersons should strive to conduct their "secular" activities, especially eating, in a state of Levitical purity, as if they were eating of a sacrifice in the Temple precincts.[56] In keeping with biblical ideas, the holiness of the Temple should radiate to the entire land and people. God's holy presence, residing in the Temple, would make itself felt throughout the land.

Rabbinic Judaism, although it preceded the destruction of the Temple, fully developed in the postdestruction era. Its key texts, the Mishnah, the legal and nonlegal interpretations of the Pentateuch (Midrash), the great commentaries on the Mishnah known as the Talmud Yerushalmi and the Talmud Bavli, and other works come from the second to the seventh centuries CE. Rabbinic Judaism, for the most part, does not know the Temple as a living reality; it remembers the First and Second Temples of the past and projects an idealized one in the future or in a higher world. The system of sacrifices, the vastly ramified laws of purity and impurity, and ideas of spatially located, tangible, property-like holiness continue to be cultivated. These topics occupy two of the six main textual divisions ("orders") of the Mishnah. But they are also displaced. The synagogue and school, the prayer and study halls that arose during the Babylonian exile and in Second Temple times, played an ever larger role after the destruction of the Temple. Bereft of the Temple, rabbinic Jews sought God's presence in the synagogue, which the rabbis called a "miniature Temple" (*mikdash ma'at*, after Ezekiel 11:16), in study of the Torah, and in performing the commandments.[57] Torah in a way displaced active, divinely generated holiness as the structuring principle of rabbinic Jewish life.[58] Yet holiness remained both a property and a status for the rabbis as well as a value, marking out an idealized way of life.

God chose the Jews and the Land of Israel, so Israel must continually consecrate itself, make itself worthy of God's choice.[59] God has given it the means—Torah and commandments—to do so. Without the Temple and after the dispersal and humiliation of the Jewish people, observance of God's commandments becomes the main manifestation of holiness. "Since the day the Temple was destroyed, there is left to the Holy One, blessed be He, in His Universe the four cubits of Halakah alone" (b Berakhot 8a). The rabbis' God is highly personal, passionate, even vulnerable—less a barely containable, often dangerous "consuming fire" (Exodus 24:17) than a fellow sufferer exiled with Israel (b Megillah 29a). The anger, once so prominent in God's biblical character, is now suppressed by divine restraint. God's awesome power, still able to destroy the nations that have subjugated Israel, shows itself in patient waiting (b Yoma 69b). The consuming fire has become an ardent if patient teacher of Torah, a healer of broken hearts, including his own. God wields a pen, rather than a sword. Divine holiness becomes intimate.

Rabbinic Judaism further develops the themes of Israel as a holy land and of the Jews as a holy people. Rabbinic Judaism continues the structure of graded holiness in the spatial sense that we have observed with regard to the Tabernacle. A mishnah (Kelim 1:6) states:

There are ten degrees of holiness. The Land of Israel is holier [mikudeshet] than any other land. Wherein lies its holiness? In that from it they may bring the Omer, the First fruits, and the Two Loaves, which they may not bring from any other land.[60]

The Torah commands that Israel bring the first sheaves (*'omer*) of barley from the spring harvest to the priest (Leviticus 23:10). This commandment was to begin when Israel entered its land. Likewise, the first fruits (*bikhorim*; Deuteronomy 26:2) and the commandment to bring two loaves of bread made from the grain of the second harvest, fifty days after the *'omer* (Leviticus 23:17). That these offerings of gratitude to God can be brought only from the soil of the Land of Israel marks the unique sanctity of the land. Only its products are fit as gifts for God. It is not clear here whether the land has *kedushah* in a property-like way or whether its holiness is an artifact of the special actions that can be performed only there, a status or relational sense.

The Mishnah details more exclusive and intense domains of spatial holiness, always linking their holiness to the performances and prohibitions the places require. The rising gradient includes the walled cities of the Land of Israel, the area within the city walls of Jerusalem, the Temple Mount, the surrounding rampart of the Temple, the Court of the Women, the Court of the Male Israelites, the Court of the Priests. The holiest areas, as in the Pentateuch, are the most internal sections of the sanctuary:

> Between the Porch and the Altar is still more holy, for none that has a blemish or whose hair is unloosed may enter there. The Sanctuary [*heikhal*] is still more holy, for none may enter therein with hands and feet unwashed. The Holy of Holies is still more holy, for none may enter therein save only the High Priest on the Day of Atonement at the time of the [Temple] service (Kelim 1:9).

The substantive, holiness-as-property view here is hard to find among the legal stipulations. So Tzvi Novick argues that Torah, especially in its legal dimensions, has become the ordering category (rather than holiness per se) for rabbinic Judaism. Holiness has become a forensic category. But that is not the whole story: explicit indications of the reified holiness of the Land of Israel may be found in the midrash, the imaginative rabbinic interpretation and commentary on biblical texts.

The holiness of the land takes on a property sense in *Bereshit Rabbah*, the great collection of midrashic commentaries on Genesis from the fourth to fifth centuries CE. Israel appears as an enchanted land with qualities unknown in any other. Jacob, in the Bible, asks Joseph to bury him "with his fathers" in the cave of Machpelah (Genesis 49:29). The midrash puts Jacob's request more sharply, in the negative: "Bury me not in Egypt!" It explains that Jacob yearns to be buried in Israel because of the extraordinary nature of the land. In the view of the midrash, Israel is a "land of the living" (Psalms 116:9); the dead who are buried in Israel will be resurrected in the days of the Messiah and will enjoy his reign. Those not buried there die two deaths: a physical one and a second "spiritual" one. Their souls will not be reunited with their bodies. God will not reinvigorate them in the messianic age with his spirit. Jacob was anxious lest this postmortem fate befall him—hence "bury me not in Egypt!" A Rabbi Simon questions the justice of this. Surely righteous Jews buried outside the land cannot conceivably fail to be resurrected in messianic times? God, Simon avers, will make tunnels in the earth leading to Israel. The righteous will trundle through them and emerge resurrected from graves in the land of Israel (as suggested to R. Simon by the famous dry bones prophecy of Ezekiel 37:11–14).[61]

A special quality in the air of the Land of Israel makes people wise (b Baba Batra 158b). Before Israel was chosen by God, other lands were fit for prophecy and revelation. But after God chose Israel, he would communicate to his prophets only there. Before the Temple was chosen, God would speak to prophets throughout Jerusalem. After the Temple was chosen, he would communicate only in the Temple. Indeed, God's presence (*shekhinah*) does not reveal itself outside land. Thus, Jonah's flight from Israel was a flight from God's command.[62] These midrashic claims about divine disclosure being limited to the Land of Israel run into the obvious objection that prophecy occurred in Egypt, in Babylonia, and elsewhere. The midrash wrestles with this and asserts that prophecy on foreign soil was due only to the merits of the prophets' ancestors, who lived in Israel, or because it was for the sake of the land, or because it occurred by rivers, which made the foreign land sufficiently pure. Yehuda Halevi, who advances a strong theory of the uniqueness of the land based on prophecy occurring only there, faces the same objections.

One of Eliade's criteria for a sacred place is that it links worlds—a sacred space joins an upper realm to the human sphere. The Land of Israel has such a function. The rock that Talmud and midrash locate in the Holy of Holies of the First Temple was called the "foundation stone" ('*even shtiyah*). It was the foundation of the world, the first spot of land to emerge from primeval chaos. The Ark stood on this stone; the foundation of moral and spiritual life resting on the foundation of the physical world.[63] The Temple Mount was also identified as Mount Moriah, where Abraham sought to sacrifice Isaac, the highest example of obedience to the divine will imaginable. As Jacob fled the land of Israel, he experienced (in a dream) angels ascending and descending (Genesis 28:12). The midrash interprets this epiphany as a foreshadowing of the future Temple, to be built on the spot. The ascent of the angels alludes to the upward path of the smoke of burnt offerings (Bereshit Rabbah 68:12). The land is an *axis mundi*, linking heaven and earth.

Rabbinic teachings about the special relationship of the divine presence to the Land of Israel, its supernatural qualities, and the merit of living there could be enumerated indefinitely. The sources still show the ambivalence to which we alluded earlier. At times, the holiness of the land is substantive, an ontological matter. It is the seat of God's throne (b Ketubot 110b–112b). It holiness is an objective property. At other times, the holy deeds, the mitzvot, that can be performed there make it holy. The very performance of the mitzvot in the land consecrates it. The relationship between reified and performative holiness, between holiness as property and holiness as status, remains an open question, a rich site for theological reflection.[64] Let this brief overview suffice to support the view that the Land of Israel is considered ontologically holy in some strands of rabbinic thought.

We now consider the situation of the Jewish people. Rabbinic biblical interpretations stress the closeness and mutuality of Israel and God. Israel is often compared to a wife whom God has espoused. Invoking the injunction of Leviticus 19:2, "you shall be holy because I am holy," a sage has God say: "I have attached you unto me, as it is said 'For as the loincloth clings close to the loins of a man, so I brought close to me the whole house of Israel' (Jeremiah 13:11). Another explained: 'The matter is to be compared to a king who sanctified a woman (by wedlock) unto him, and said to her: Since you are my wife, what is my glory is thy glory, 'be therefore holy even as I am holy.'"[65] In this midrash, it is as if Israel absorbs God's holiness by tangible contact; God has wed her and cleaves to her; thus, she participates in his holiness. Similarly, in the halakhic midrash on Exodus, Israel and God are lovers who praise one another with biblical verses. Israel sings "Hear O Israel, the LORD is our God; the LORD is One ['eḥad]" (Deuteronomy 6:4). The Holy Spirit replies "Who is like your people

Israel, a unique [*'eḥad*] people in all the earth" (I Chronicles 17:20).[66] The same exchange of verses is found in the imagery of God wearing phylacteries (*tefillin*). Israel's tefillin contain a passage affirming the holiness and uniqueness of God; God's tefillin proclaim the uniqueness of Israel (b Berakhot 6a).[67]

Yet the holiness of Israel as God's beloved people is not automatic. Israel must keep the mitzvot to remain holy. "*You will be holy*—at the time that you fulfill my commandments you are made holy [*m'kudashim*] and the fear of you is imposed upon the idolaters. If you separate from the commandments, however, you become profane [*m'ḥollelim*]" (Bemidbar Rabbah 17:6). (Indeed, in this midrash, the mitzvot are more than a matter of sacred and profane; they are a matter of life and death. They are like a rope thrown by a captain to a man at sea. If he holds on to the rope, he will remain alive; if he lets it go, he will die—thus the sense of the biblical verse "you who held fast to the LORD your God are all alive today" [Deuteronomy 4:4].) Israel's charge to keep its holiness intact requires separation from the nations, acts that imitate divine action, ritual and moral purity, circumcision, and the constant study and practice of the commandments. A midrash commenting on the verse "You shall be holy for I the LORD your God am holy" (Leviticus 19:2) claims that holiness requires separation from the ways of the nations. *Kedoshim tihyu* (you shall be holy) means *perushim tihyu* (you shall be separate). Separateness rises to holiness. Israel's project of differentiation requires a self-consecration or, more radically, the *making holy* of God himself:

> If you sanctify yourselves, I will consider it as if you had sanctified Me, and if you do not sanctify yourselves, I will consider it as if you had not sanctified Me. But perhaps the meaning is: If you sanctify Me, I am holy [*mekudash*], and

if not I am not holy [*'ayni mekudash*]. It is, therefore, written "for holy am I"—I remain in My holiness whether or not I am sanctified (by men). Abba Shaul says: What is the duty of the King's retinue? To follow in the footsteps of the King (and to be holy).[68]

This midrash has come down to us with two textual variants for the verb translated as "sanctify." One (in the *hiphil*) means to make holy (*makdishim*), the other (in the *piel*) to declare holy (*m'kadshim*). Is God holy only when Israel makes him so? The midrash raises but then dismisses the idea, taking the repeated refrain in Leviticus, chapter 19, "for holy am I" (*ki kadosh 'ani*) to imply God's intrinsic, inviolable holiness, regardless of human action or inaction.[69]

Moving from claims about the interdependence/independence of divine and human holiness, the midrash seeks the ground of the duty to be holy, implicitly likening God to a king and Israel to his retainers (*familia*). The *familia* of the king should imitate him. (But why they should remains an open question.) The king's retainers do not automatically absorb his glory. They must strive to do so; they are not like a loin cloth—holiness must be their project. All three analyses of holiness are in play in these texts.

The Talmud envisions a collaboration between God and Israel in the pursuit of holiness. "If a person sanctifies himself a little, they (in heaven) sanctify him much; if a person sanctifies himself below (on earth), they bestow upon him (more) holiness from above" (b Yoma 39a).[70] But just what is this holiness? It seems odd to think that it is only separateness or even heightened closeness to or possession by God. Perhaps holiness is a virtuous circle; the experience of a special way of life strengthens one's commitment to the goods constitutive of that way of life. If so, holiness is the engagement in Jewish religious life as such. Yet holiness continues to function as a property. If so, to be sanctified from above means to receive (and even experience) an extra measure of power, blessing, purity, or honor. The Talmud (b Avodah Zarah 20b) implies such a reified, experiential character to holiness in a teaching about the acquisition of moral and religious virtues.

> Rabbi Phineas b. Jair said: study leads to precision, precision leads to zeal, zeal leads to cleanliness, cleanliness leads to restraint, restraint leads to purity, purity leads to holiness, holiness leads to meekness, meekness leads to fear of sin, fear of sin leads to saintliness, saintliness leads to [the possession of] the holy spirit, the holy spirit leads to life eternal.[71]

The context for this saying is a discussion about the impermissibility of gazing at beautiful women (or their undergarments drying outdoors) or at copulating animals. One must keep oneself from indulging in lewd thoughts during the day lest one fall into ritual impurity, which presumably means a nocturnal seminal emission. There is also the danger of moral impurity. The basic claim is that Torah study brings one to a keen awareness (*zehirut*) of the Torah's warnings and prohibitions. This leads to zeal (*zerizut*) in the avoidance of sin and impurity. One strives to be in a state of hygienic cleanness (*nekiut*; a precondition for ritual purity). That demands separation (*perishut*) from all that is unclean. (The just cited translation gives this word a moral connotation—restraint. That is the sense given by medieval exegetes like Rashi and Naḥmanides. It indicates a further ethicization of the trope.) Separation enables one to live in ritual and moral purity (*taharah*), which, as in the Bible, is a necessary condition for holiness (*kedushah*).

Holiness is not the final destination on Rabbi Phineas ben Jair's ladder of virtues. Holiness facilitates the moral/religious virtues of humility, fear of sin, and saintliness (*ḥasidut*). Saintliness seems here higher than holiness.[72] It may be more overtly ethical, entailing an ideal of character and conduct. A still higher stage, fitness to receive the holy spirit (*ruaḥ ha-kodesh*), is a kind of prophetic ability caused by the divine presence. This finally prepares one for the resurrection of the dead (*teḥiyat ha-metim*), the restoration of soul to body and renewed life in a messianic kingdom.

This teaching conflates elements of holiness as a status, a value, and a property. The individual and the nation must strive toward ever higher levels of virtue. There is a clear path to the well-lived life. Such a life is not only inherently excellent; it is instrumentally so. It is ordered to the goals of prophecy and resurrection in a world to come. The very nature of one who achieves holiness, saintliness, and the holy spirit is materially changed. He or she becomes a kind of Jewish *Übermensch*, a superman. The medieval Jewish philosopher, Yehuda Halevi, builds on this theme and makes Israel out to be a higher, indeed, the highest version of humanity.[73]

Halevi's classic, *Kuzari: The Book of Refutation and Proof on Behalf of the Most Despised Religion* (ca. 1140), is a philosophical dialogue between a rabbi and the pagan king of the Khazars. The king has dreamed that a mysterious voice tells him that God is pleased with his intentions but not his actions. In search of a way of life that will guide him toward right action, he consults a philosopher, a Christian, and a Muslim. All of these views contain flaws, which the king recognizes. Dissatisfied, he finally calls in a representative of the "despised" religion. To his astonishment, the Jew has the most compelling story. Halevi's rabbi (*ḥaver*) argues from the historical and philosophical particularity of the relationship of Israel to God. He eschews natural theology; the Exodus, not the Creation of the world, is his starting point.[74] Veridical tradition

outweighs cosmological speculation.⁷⁵ The biblical tradition
of the Jewish people, which the other theists must acknowledge as basic, is truthful. Even its antagonists must grant that.
Thus, the tradition of the Jews as a people anchors Halevi's
argument.

In Halevi's modified Neoplatonic world picture, God ema-
nates his "influence" to receptive minds. These minds are
shaped by physical conditions insofar as these affect the bodies, character, and upbringing of persons and nations. Climate,
food, soil, temperature, and geography—factors first theorized
by Hippocrates—have a decisive role in forming those physical
conditions. The ancient Greeks thought that Hellas was located in the center of the world and had the most advanta-
geous climate for producing ideal human beings. This view
was appropriated by Muslim thinkers, who shifted the ideal
land to Iraq.⁷⁶ Halevi adopted this framework and applied it
to Israel; Israel is at the center of the best (temperate) zone of
the earth. It is thus the land of prophecy; both the land and its
Israelite inhabitants are worthy of the divine influence (*inyan
elohi*).⁷⁷

Halevi offers an origin story for the superiority of the Jews
(*gedulat ha-am ha-zeh*).⁷⁸ God created Adam as a being perfect in body and attributes. He was created as an adult, not
dependent on the physical conditions of nutrition, climate,
water, or soil. He was blessed with every perfection—intellect
of the highest grade, complete vitality of soul, and a divine capacity (*koaḥ ha-elohi*) to grasp great truths without interme-
diation or instruction. Adam could achieve a connection with
the divine realm, a cleaving of the human knower to the transcendent objects of knowledge. Adam was a son of God (*ben
Elohim*), and whoever among his seed was like him is also a
son of God. Halevi then argues for a kind of "recessive trait"
theory of holiness: Not all sons of Adam are true Adamites,

true human beings. Abel resembled Adam in his perfection; Cain did not (hence Cain's jealousy and murderous act). The line was restored with Seth, the "purest" or "choicest part of Adam"—"the flower or the heart of him."[79] (Ibn Tibbon translates Halevi's Arabic *safwatuhu* as *segulah*, a word in biblical Hebrew conveying the sense of a treasured possession. For the Bible reader, segulah is strongly associated with Israel. God takes the People of Israel to be his treasured possession [Exodus 19:5]. In Deuteronomy 7:6, Israel is a "holy people" [*'am kadosh*] and a "treasured people" [*'am segulah*], unlike all the other nations.) Seth's purity was passed on to Enosh and then to Noah and Eber. God's influence has an episodic manifestation down through the ages, reappearing in Abraham and Isaac. With Jacob—the sole segulah of Isaac—God's influence becomes the property of an entire people. Jacob/Israel as a whole (*b'nai Ya'akov kulam segulah*) inherits the capacity for connection with the divine in part because they occupy the land at the center of the world. Abraham banished Ishmael from Canaan; Esau also left. The unique connection between the "genetically" perfect people and the climatologically perfect land insures that a flow of holy, divine influence will be expressed by them. Using the language of fruit, Halevi claims that Adam's true descendants are his kernel or seed (*gareeno*); all others are shells, rinds, or husks (*klipot*). This latter term will have a role to play in kabbalistic thought about Israel and other peoples.

One consequence of Halevi's racial or biological construal of Jewish difference is that the Khazar king, the fictional interlocutor in Halevi's dialogue, although he can (and does) convert to Judaism, cannot truly be equal to a Jew.[80] There is a "biological" dimension to Jewish superiority that non-Israelites cannot attain. The purity of soul, inherited from Adam and strengthened by climate and the virtuous life of Torah, enables the Jew uniquely to attain the rank of a prophet; to come into contact with the holy spirit. Prophecy is not possible for non-Israelites, nor is it possible outside the Land of Israel. As we've noted, the Talmud too makes this claim, but it does not accord with the biblical narrative. Halevi argues that although prophetic activity occurred in Egypt (Moses) or Babylonia (Jeremiah, Ezekiel), it was only for the sake of the Land of Israel or because the prophets had earlier lived there and came from a pure lineage.[81] Unsatisfying as these patched-up claims are, they attest to the tight linkage of land, people, and holiness—in a reified, property-like way—in Halevi's thought. Religious deeds are not merely expressive but also efficacious. Halevi likens fulfillment of God's commandments to natural processes (*ha-mitzvot domot l'ma'asim teviim*).[82] They have causal efficacy within the natural world. The religious deeds of the Jews accomplish what alchemists wish for but, lacking a true tradition, cannot achieve.

On Halevi's account, Israel is "radically discontinuous with the rest of humanity."[83] The roots of the discontinuity thesis, as described by James Kugel, are found in the postexilic portions of the Bible. The Book of Ezra gives us a hint. Deuteronomy (7:3–6) bans intermarriage with the Canaanite peoples because such marriages would turn Israelite children away from God to serve other gods. Israel would threaten its holy status by acts of disloyalty. Ezra 9:2, by contrast, bans intermarriage because the "holy seed" (*zera ha-kodesh*) that is Israel would become "mingled" with the peoples of the land. Israel is holy by nature, at the level of its "seed."[84] It offends its own intrinsic, substantive holiness through biological mingling with nonholy peoples. Noncanonical Second Temple texts like the Book of Jubilees assimilate Israel to the angels. Israel's metahuman status is shown by the fact that only she and the angels observe the Sabbath, as God did at the very beginning.[85]

A breach is opened in humanity; Israel is an angelomorphic, even theomorphic race.

Halevi's view will inform the medieval mystical tradition of Kabbalah. He was opposed robustly by Maimonides. For Maimonides, holiness is purely an artifact of the law. It has no substantive nature. Neither the Jews nor the Land of Israel are distinct in any essential way from other peoples and lands. The Jews are descendants of Abraham and so share an ethnicity. But Jews, as it were, convert to Judaism when they accept the Torah. So do all others who literally convert. Israel is a community of believers, bound by rational truths and a revealed law that can, in turn, be affirmed on rational grounds. The community of believers has an ethnos at its core, but there is nothing whatsoever intrinsically holy about the ethnos. The community is holy by having a law that distinguishes it from other peoples. Holiness signifies Israel's "sound knowledge concerning God," a *status* it may share with all those capable of attaining and demonstrating the relevant metaphysical truths.[86]

For Maimonides, holiness is a status, an intellectual achievement built upon a normative way of life under law. The law facilitates moral and intellectual virtue allowing the highest good—intellectual love for and communion with God. The law designates some items as holy because of their importance. But such facts are historical and contingent. Summing up Maimonides's stance on holiness, Kellner writes:

> According to his view holiness cannot be characterized as ontological or essentialist, since holy places, persons, nations, times, and objects are in no objective way distinct from profane persons, nations, times, and objects; holiness is a status, not a quality or property. It is a challenge, not a given; normative, not descriptive. It is institutional (in the sense of being part of a system of laws and determined by

those laws) and hence contingent. This sort of holiness does not reflect objective reality, it helps constitute social reality. According to this view, holy places, persons, times, and objects are indubitably holy, and must be treated with all due respect, but they are, in and of themselves, like all other places, persons, times, and objects. What is different about them is the way in which the Torah commands that they be treated. Holy places, persons, nations, times, and objects derive their sanctity from the roles they play, the uses to which they are put.[87]

On Maimonides's account, holiness is a normative artifact, an institutional reality rather than a "natural" one. (Recall the distinction earlier between social and institutional facts and physical or natural ones.) This view, shorn of its Neoplatonic and Aristotelian metaphysics will gain traction in modernity.

Halevi and Maimonides set the parameters of the debate about the holiness of people and land for centuries to come. Views like Halevi's surface powerfully in the kabbalistic literature of the thirteenth century and beyond. Maimonides's views await the Enlightenment to be fully welcomed. For the Zohar, Israel is a "holy seed" (*zar'a qaddisha*) that has emerged from the ten emanations/manifestations/powers (*sefirot*) of the divine. The other nations derive from "the demonic 'other side' (*sitra ahra*), the realm of ten impure potencies on the left that correspond to ten holy *sefirot* on the right."[88] The impure powers are husks (klipot), with no part in holiness.[89] They form their own sefirot-like system of impurity and evil. The physical and spiritual being of the Jew derives "from the stuff of the world of divine emanations."[90] The other nations count for nothing in God's sight. They are the products of Eve's illicit union with the serpent. Only Jews are the descendants of Adam, who was originally a theomorphic being. The nations remain tainted with an original sin-like deformity. Indeed, Adam, in kabbalistic thought, *is* Jewish. His true descendants have the Torah, which purges any residual taint. The nations, impure in their origin and lacking the Torah, are incapable of holiness. As Moses de Leon, one of the presumed authors of the Zohar puts it:

> You know that all of the Gentiles (*goyim*) and all of their matters are in the category of the impure.... You must know and discern that the Gentiles come from the side of impurity, for the souls of the Gentiles derive from the side of impurity.... [S]ince their cause is impure their bodies will perish and their souls will burn; their root and their source is impure.[91]

Similarly, the Kabbalist Joseph of Hamadan writes:

> Foreign peoples have no sanctity in them whatsoever, and they have no flame in their souls that consumes the impurity; rather, they draw it to themselves, and thus they eat impure foods in order to draw the impurity to themselves.... Happy are we and fortunate is our lot that God, may he be blessed, desires us and gave us his Torah and granted us impurity and purity, for it is the perfection of the world.[92]

Both holiness and impurity are reified here as constitutive in Jewish and gentile souls. Purity and impurity are given a substantive character. Impurity is like a toxin that corrupts and degrades the body; purity purges and transfigures bodies, a redemptive process possible only for Jews, who have the means, through Torah, of distinguishing pure from impure. Jewish and gentile souls are occult entities with definable characteristics. The nations have a bestial soul (*nefesh behemit*); only the Jews are capable of having a human one (*nefesh adam*).[93]

The view that Jews have holy souls and gentiles have bestial ones was popularized in the eighteenth-century spiritual classic of Ḥabad Hasidism, known as the *Tanya* (or *Likkutei Amarim*).[94] Shneur Zalman of Lyadi (d. 1812), the author and founder of the Ḥabad Hasidic dynasty, claims that Jews, who share a baseline physical nature with other forms of life, have, like gentiles, a vital, animal soul. But the animal soul of the Jew comes from the fourth husk (*klipat nogah*), while the animal soul of the non-Jew comes from the three lower impure husks (*klipot tumaot*).[95] The fourth klipah mediates between the divine sefirot and the base, evil world of the sitra aḥra. Klipat nogah thus has within it elements of good; the other klipot are undiluted evil. The soul of the Jew, when it prompts the body to engage in mundane activities, can yet redeem those activities, restoring materiality to spirituality. The soul of the gentile, however, hits a spiritual dead end. Nothing gentiles do can be elevated to holiness; their souls, acts, thoughts, wisdom, and lives remain trapped in the lower, unholy world of the impure klipot.[96]

When Jews act to satisfy their physical, biological needs, they must direct their intention to heaven. If they act out of unmediated natural necessity, their souls will be animalistic. Their actions then flow from the sitra aḥra, through the mediation of the fourth klipah. If an act is not directed to God (*l'shem shemayim*), it has a demonic, negative quality. But even the demonic side of the Jew's soul is different from that of a gentile. A Jew might eat meat and drink wine to satisfy his hunger and thirst—a purely animal act—but the food and drink might help bring him to a mood suitable for true joy on Shabbat or festivals, expanding his consciousness of God and of his Torah. The same is true of sexual intercourse. If there is sexual intercourse out of lust, the seed will be unholy. This could be decisive for the character of any children thereby conceived.[97]

If one allowed the food in one's belly to serve only one's appetite, one's body would be reduced to impurity. Only turning meat and wine into proper worship and joy frees one from the impurity of the three lower klipot, although one might still require suffering in the afterlife to purge fully the taint of the lower klipot.

The reification of holiness and impurity implies an objective difference between forbidden and permitted food. Permitted (kosher) food can be raised to holiness in the chemistry of one's body and by the intention of one's mind. Forbidden food is unredeemable and damaging. Gentiles, being ignorant of the forbidden and permitted, are unaware of these risks and possibilities. Non-Jews, who lack the Torah, are bereft of knowledge of the divine and ignorant of the praxis to redeem bodily activities for the sake of heaven. They are condemned to a degraded life. Their souls are mired in the miasma of the profane.

Into Jewish Modernity

The foregoing discussion makes clear the extent to which premodern Jews could construe holiness as an occult property. Entities like the Jewish people, the Land of Israel, and the Jewish soul became bearers of a presumed property. This line of thought became increasingly difficult to sustain for modern men and women. Holiness as an occult property requires a metaphysics like that of the Zohar and the *Tanya*, wholly at odds with a modern scientifically informed worldview. It assumes a world of supersensible entities and nonphysical causes, of spiritual potencies that can be known only through the acceptance of an esoteric religious teaching. There is no room in the explanatory, causal accounts that modern philosophy or science tells for "holy seed" and "impure seed" as, for example, determinants of character, worth, or destiny. To the extent that modern science accepts determinism (say, in the way that genes determine hair or eye color), it can specify the causal mechanisms behind the physical outcome. The anonymous author of the medieval *Iggeret ha-Kodesh* (*Letter on Holiness*), a treatise on sexual relations and the conditions most propitious for conceiving righteous offspring, also thought that he could specify relevant causal mechanisms. But the latter putative causes correspond to nothing observable, measurable, or testable. There is no credible physical or biological theory in which they count as causes. Whatever role they may play in a symbolic economy, they can play no role in an empirical one. There is neither need nor space in a modern epistemic project for such a version of holiness; it cannot be a property in the way that medieval Jews imagined. Arch-traditionalists continued to write of holiness in the old ways. They still do. But for many Jews, those old ways were (and are) no longer rational or compelling.[98]

Holiness for modernity must be conceived on the lines that Maimonides proposed as a morally and spiritually distinctive way of life that achieves an intellectual comprehension of the highest truths. For many, those truths are construed, as in Kant, as *purely* ethical ones. If holiness no longer has to do with speculative metaphysics, then it will have to do with a metaphysics of morals. Holiness will describe an integrated project of life under norms, not a supposed feature of the world on a par with its material properties. In modern Jewish thought, holiness will figure as value, a view that is partially available, as we have seen, in the Holiness Code.

Equally difficult for modern Jews to believe are those ancient and medieval views that assert a strong, ontological difference between Jews and gentiles. In a world where Jews were ridiculed, held in contempt, hemmed in by laws, ghetto walls, invidious theological portrayals, or violent persecution, sharply negative religious views of the non-Jewish other were intelligible.[99] In a world that began to accept Jews as citizens if not yet social or cultural equals, sustaining Jewish-gentile differences on a metaphysical plane made ever less sense. With the lowering of legal and social barriers between Jews and Christians and the spread of Enlightenment intellectual norms, Jewish thinkers increasingly construed holiness as an ethical ideal discovered by ancient Israel and taught to the nations through prophecy and by example. Holiness was no longer a mysterious proprium of Israel alone, but the moral goal of all.

This change is visible in the work of a contemporary of Kant's, Moses Mendelssohn (d. 1786). Mendelssohn and his circle were active in promoting acculturation to German Enlightenment views and norms among Jews. They hoped to persuade the Prussian state to emancipate Jews from their disenfranchised status. Mendelssohn and his associates translated the Hebrew Scriptures into German, printed in Hebrew characters, and appended a Hebrew commentary, known as the *Biur* ("elucidation"). Commenting on Exodus 19:6, "you shall be to Me a kingdom of priests and a holy nation," he wrote: "All the nations are like one people (*ke-'am*) and you are like their priests, united for the service of God to bring understanding and to instruct the entire human race (*min ha-enosh*) to call God's name together."[100] Here, Mendelssohn affirms the particularity of the Jewish people and their holy, priestly role in the world. Yet that role is for the sake of humanity, for a universal purpose: instructing human beings in what God truly desires—which turns out essentially to be brotherly love.

Commenting on Leviticus 19:2, "You shall be holy for I the LORD your God am holy," traditional, medieval exegetes, like Rashi and Naḥmanides, stressed the moral sense of "be holy!" For Rashi, one should abstain from forbidden things, especially the illicit sexual acts enumerated in Leviticus, chapter 18. To renounce desire and sin in that sense is to be holy. For Naḥmanides, to be holy means abjuring undue indulgence and minimizing the desire even for *permitted* things, like sexual relations within marriage, kosher wine and meat, and so on. One should not be a scoundrel with the permission of the Torah. Mendelssohn endorses these views but goes further, counseling distance from all moral deficiencies (*peḥitiyot*). Everyone, according to his ability, should walk in God's ways, pursuing holiness both in the terms the Torah commands and more generally. Holiness is imitation of God's ways. Just as God is above moral deficiency, so should human beings strive for an ideal beyond mere compliance with the Torah's prohibitions. God created the world and accomplished miracles for Israel. Israel should strive for the miraculous by transcending its own fleshy nature "and sanctify itself in thought and deed against the natural propensities of the heart."[101] Mendelssohn is saying nothing that a medieval commentator could not say. But his stress is on the universal. He shuns kabbalistic references. There is no talk of upper and lower worlds, flows of divine influence, or reified purity and impurity. Holiness is framed entirely in terms of ethics.[102]

Kant, too, who exercises a vast influence on modern Jewish thought, refers to holiness several times in his ethical writings; the concept plays an important role in his moral philosophy.[103] Without entering into the details of the elaborate Kantian theory, holiness is a moral ideal, unattainable in this life, to achieve "perfect purity of disposition."[104] We are beset by radical evil, a perversity of will native to human beings, which we must constantly struggle to surmount and extirpate. The struggle against our inborn propensity for self-regard and the satisfaction of instinct constitutes virtue. More precisely, virtue is the disciplined self-command and courage to live freely and cheerfully according to the moral law. Unlike the ever beyond-reach end goal of holiness, virtue *is* attainable. Virtue is, in part, the courage to persist in devotion to the unattainable idea. Why should holiness be unattainable? Holiness is the "complete fitness of intentions to the moral law" and thus "a perfection of which no rational being in the world of sense is at any time capable."[105] Only one rational being, God, can be completely holy. Kant proposes, however, that from God's point of view, there might be holiness in human life. God, in viewing our lives as a protracted virtuous struggle, may find a "whole conformable to moral law."[106] That whole, which only God can glimpse, might be reckoned holy. Holiness for Kant, therefore, describes a moral ideal (of paradoxical character: we must strive for it but cannot, in this life at least, attain it), as well as the moral law per se, as well as God's will. The divine will is holy because it alone has a complete fit of intention to the moral law. Given these various deployments of holiness, it might seem as if "holy" functions as a property to describe metaphysical entities, such as the moral law and God, but this is to misunderstand Kant. Within Kant's constraints on specu-lative metaphysics, the concept of holiness functions in a moral register (as a concept of "practical reason"); religious discourse maps largely onto ethics. Kant keeps the old theological words but radically reconstructs their content. Jewish thinkers often followed Kant's lead, but with a difference. To one degree or another, most try to claim some residual religious sense for holiness above and beyond the predominantly ethical one that they otherwise endorse.

The most rigorously Kantian Jewish philosopher of the late nineteenth and early twentieth centuries was Hermann Cohen (d. 1918). For Cohen, like Kant, holiness is an infinite task: the task of morality. "The holiness of man consists in self-sanctification, which, however, can have no termination, therefore cannot be a permanent rest, but only infinite striving and becoming."[107] "Self-sanctification" is Cohen's gloss on Leviticus 19:2, "You shall be holy." He sees human self-sanctification, the infinite striving to live an ever-renewed moral life, as humanity's way of hallowing God. God wants humanity to sanctify the divine: "You shall not profane My holy name *that I may be sanctified* in the midst of the Israelite people" (Leviticus 22:32). God and humanity are related by holiness. It is crucial to Cohen's thought that the relationship between God and Israel be understood as a "correlation." Correlation in Cohen's philosophy indicates conceptual codependency. (Think hot and cold, sweet and sour, hard and soft, and so on.) One can't properly think about God without thinking about humanity and vice versa. The concepts are mutually implicated. Humanity is ultimately defined by its striving for moral purity; the divine is ultimately concerned with the moral redemption of humanity. "God accomplishes his holiness in man," and "men fulfill their striving for holiness in the acceptance of the archetypal holiness of God, in imitation of which they sanctify themselves."[108] More provocatively: "Holiness unifies God and man. And this unified holiness unambiguously defines itself as morality."[109] The concepts "God" and "man" are correlated by holiness.

The poetic way in which the religious tradition depicts this correlation is through the biblical term "holy spirit." The holy spirit for Cohen is not a mediator or a supernatural force; it is not reified in any way. Rather, holiness and the holy spirit are conceptual ways to frame the theoretical and practical challenges of moral life; they are not theological-metaphysical entities or properties. "The holy spirit is the spirit of moral action, and as such the spirit of man."[110]

Holiness, as the spirit of moral action, becomes human; indeed, it is the constitutive spirit of humanity. Tracking Kant's shift from theoretical (or "pure") reason to practical reason, all of the traditional theological problems concerning the divine should properly be seen as problems for ethics. God and man are unified, as it were, in the correlation that is holiness/ethics. Holiness loses the sparkle of the metaphysical. "Holiness is an elevated state neither of knowledge nor of action, but is only the task and ideal of action. You desire to strive for holiness: prove it by your humble self-restraint to do your purely human action."[111] Yet, given the correlation of humanity and divinity, the humble moral task is the most elevated imaginable. Ancient dreams of holiness and the holy spirit as the presence of the living God or visitation by prophetic power were illusory; misleading reifications of an ethical ideal. Cohen writes long after the age of miracles has passed. His work is premised on a thoroughly disenchanted world, yet a world illumined by human rationality and dignity. Holiness is a name for the ideal of endless human striving in just such a world. It is a *religious* ideal, not solely a moral one insofar as it speaks to the individual in his or her sin, loneliness, despair, and hope. It speaks in more than the austere Kantian language of universal moral duty. Morality as such (in Cohen's mature view) cannot know individuals; religion must. That is Cohen's claim for the residual "religious" character of holiness.

Jewish thinkers after Cohen, at least those attuned to modernity and writing in European languages, largely accept a moral reading of holiness—but try to resist a complete equation of the holy to the good. For Martin Buber, holiness describes a way of life characterized by genuine encounter, meeting, or relation with others (whether human, divine, animal, plant or artifact). "All actual life is encounter," Buber wrote.[112] Holiness goes to the mundane yet extraordinary dimension of such moments and a life attuned to transformative-redemptive ("I-Thou") encounter. One hears in Buber an echo of Kant's categorical imperative to treat the other always as an end and not as a means, and of Cohen's adaptation of that teaching wherein the "one next to me" becomes "my fellowman." This is essentially a normative, moral relation. Buber adapts and deepens this framework, unfolding its implications for psychology, sociology, and epistemology.

Later thinkers, like Abraham Joshua Heschel, also stress the experiential aspect of holiness. For Heschel, ethics is not the highest goal; holiness is the ideal that orders ethics, disclosing of the significance of our being in the world. The disclosure is attended by a sense of awe and wonder, praise and gratitude. It is from the significance of our being that ethics acquires its imperative voice. Heschel wants a holiness beyond "the good" but certainly not one that violates the good.[113] His vision is fundamentally ethical, interwoven with a romantic's attraction to the sublime and a mystic's yearning for the Infinite. For both Buber and Heschel, Cohen cedes too much territory to an abstract, highly conceptual ethics. Holiness must pick out a distinctive dimension of experience. For Buber, that dimension is found in "actual life" and genuine "encounter." For Heschel, it is found especially in the experience of the Sabbath, "holiness in time."[114]

Another thinker who reacts to Cohen's reduction of holiness to ethics is Joseph B. Soloveitchik. Educated in the German philosophical tradition (although writing in Hebrew), Soloveitchik criticizes the "liberal Judaism" of Cohen and of his predecessor Moritz Lazarus for introducing an artificial distinction between ethical holiness and ritual holiness, to the detriment of the latter.[115] Indeed, such a distinction stems from Christian theology and is alien to Judaism. The Torah knows no such distinction. For Soloveitchik, following Maimonides, holiness is an artifact of halakhah, Jewish law. It is not a property of times, places, persons, or things. It is a locus of normative conduct mandated by law. Holiness may originate in the mystery of God's descent to give the Torah, but once given the halakhah has a monopoly on holiness:

> Holiness does not wink at us from "beyond" like some mysterious star that sparkles in the distant heavens, but appears in our actual, very real lives.... The beginnings of holiness are rooted in the highest heavens, and its end is embedded in the eschatological vision of the "end of days"— holy forever and to all eternity. But the link that joins together these two perspectives is the halakhic conception of holiness: holy upon the earth, the work of His might—the holiness of the concrete.... Holiness consists of a life ordered and fixed in accordance with Halakhah and finds its fulfillment in the observance of the laws regulating human biological existence, such as the laws concerning forbidden sexual relations, forbidden foods, and similar precepts.... Holiness is created by man, by flesh and blood.[116]

Soloveitchik strongly endorses Maimonides's anti-ontological view. Holiness describes conduct, performative utterance, prescribed behavior. It has nothing to do with mysterious eruptions of power or presence. Holiness is about the commandments, not about the *mysterium tremendum*. The one who would lead a holy life is "halakhic man," not the transcendence-seeking *homo religiosus*, sought by Buber or Heschel. Soloveitchik deflates the experiential dimension and, in a Cohen-like move, develops a cognitive and normative account of holiness. His commitment to revelation and the authority of the Torah marks his difference from Cohen. Yet, like Cohen's, his view of holiness is chiefly normative, albeit legal rather than moral. Given the normative supremacy, indeed, monopoly for Jews, of halakhah, a conflict between ethics and halakhah might seem possible. However, for Soloveitchik, genuine ethical norms and correct halakhah overlap. Halakhah would be shielded, on his account, from the possibility of grave ethical violation. So holiness gives no offense to ethics, properly conceived.[117]

Rather like Soloveitchik, Franz Rosenzweig argues for a holiness that sets Jews apart from all other peoples. For Soloveitchik, Jews have access to holiness only insofar as they are cognitively and practically engaged in halakhic life. Presumably, there is nothing ethnic or racial in this. A convert to Judaism who is Torah-observant would have the same status as a born Jew for Soloveitchik, given his Maimonidean predilections. For Rosenzweig, however, the Jewish people are essentially distinct from others. There are marked Halevian tendencies in Rosenzweig. The first is his emphasis on "Jewish blood," a phrase that was perhaps less grating on Jewish ears before the Holocaust, when Rosenzweig wrote, than after. Other nations build their endurance in time through life in a territory, through an adaptable language, and through a set of laws and customs that change with circumstance and regime. Their temporal duration is a matter of evolutionary adaptation, so to speak. Rosenzweig, following Halevi, argues for an *essential* Jewish difference. Jews are timeless. To be an *'am olam*, an eternal people, is to live beyond time. Jewish eternity is carried in the blood. Other nations endure by political exertion; Jews inherit eternity biologically. They have a "natural propagation of the holy."[118]

Rosenzweig's account of holiness rests on a set of essential distinctions between Jews and other nations. He contrasts "the" gentile relation to land, language, and law with "the" Jewish one. No Zionist (indeed, an anti-Zionist), Rosenzweig identifies what is holy in the "holy land" as the *impossibility* of Jewish life there. The land is holy because it is a land of longing. When Jews actually lived there and became comfortable there, they forgot what was essential to their peoplehood, their status as perpetual immigrants and strangers. The holy land is eternal because Jews forever long for it. So too the Hebrew language; it is not spoken so it is not subject to the incessant adaptation of historical exigency and to the very flux of time and change. As an eternal language, it is outside of time. It cannot be brought to daily use. The languages Jews have spoken over the millennia and have made their own (Judeo-Arabic, Ladino, Yiddish, and so on) are never fully their own, never eternal. Hebrew, the unspoken holy ideal language used for the eternally repetitive cycle of prayer, always stands in judgment of these temporal languages, never allowing the Jew to be at home in them. Likewise, the pattern repeats with custom and law. Rosenzweig contrasts gentile customs and laws, subject to the cultural selection pressures of historical circumstance with eternal Torah law. "[E]verything in which the existence of peoples takes root, has long ago been taken from us; land language custom and law long ago departed from the sphere of the living and for us is *raised from the living to the holy*; but we, we are still living and live eternally."[119]

Rosenzweig has set up a stark dichotomy—holiness as atemporal existence; the profane as historical, changing existence—but, as a student of Hegel, he can't quite leave it at that. There must be a synthesis between the thesis of worldliness and the antithesis of holiness. The Jews, it turns out, live between "a worldly and a holy life," never fully at home in either.[120] They take atemporal holiness and bring it into the life that they, as flesh and blood historical people, actually live. Holiness does enter into time, into the flux of life. Worldliness is transmuted into the *lived* holiness of the Jewish world. Jews go about their ordinary human business but enact holiness within it. They say a blessing (over food, for example) that "seizes all the ordinary and lets nothing remain ordinary any longer; but keeps everything holy." This Jewish importation of holiness into time has the effect of letting the nations participate in the blessing that is the people Israel, "so likewise suddenly the pious and wise men of the nations partake of the life of the world to come, which just now still seemed reserved for Israel alone and those blessed themselves become a blessing."[121] Unlike Halevi, Rosenzweig envisions an eschatological consummation in which Jews and gentiles, Judaism and Christianity, have an equal share, neither of which tracks God's full truth. Jews and Christians are "workers on the same task," yet, in this world, there is "an enmity set for all time."[122] The binding together of Jew and Christian "in narrowest reciprocity" mitigates or at least contextualizes the racially tinged doctrine of "Jewish blood."

With its borrowings from Halevi and its kabbalistic theurgy, Rosenzweig's *Star of Redemption* offers a more traditional, less reductive treatment of holiness than that of his teacher, Hermann Cohen. Holiness is returned to a theologoumenon. It is not just a rhetoric appended to a predominantly ethical discourse. Rosenzweig's theological construction of the status of non-Jews moves beyond the ethnocentrism of Halevi and Kabbalah, but his vision of near permanent enmity may also be sclerotic. The return of Jews, in political sovereignty, to the Land of Israel and the renewal of Hebrew as a spoken, all-too-human language raises serious, perhaps fatal problems for his ahistorical idealizations. Locating holiness as the status of being outside of time puts a metaphysical gloss on the old trope of holiness as separation. Returning holiness to the midst of the temporal, everyday world by the consecrating power of performative utterance is more promising, perhaps because Rosenzweig, more than other modern Jewish thinkers, fuses the elements of property, status, and value in his account of holiness.

The preceding discussion has displayed the complexity of the concept of holiness in Jewish thought. None of the three frameworks of analysis, in isolation, captures the range, meaning, or reference of *kedushah*. Perhaps holiness should be thought of as a "family resemblance term," Wittgenstein's term of art for complex concepts such as that of a game. There is no one essence that pulls together solitaire and soccer, tic-tac-toe and ring-around-the-rosie. Rather, there is a variety of items with overlaps as well as dissimilarities—just as in an extended family.[123] Holiness comprises elements of property, status, and value, but all of these elements need not be present simultaneously or in equal proportions. Some thinkers, like Maimonides, emphasize status and value; other texts privilege property. These resonances and weightings can change with historical context and intellectual world-picture. The failure to recognize that holiness is a family resemblance term and not a uniform concept with a single "essence" or definition can skew scholarly discussion and lend undue obscurity to the term.

A fair amount of philosophical perspective has informed our analysis so far, but I want to shift now to a more explicitly philosophical register. We have been engaged in a phenomenological project; we have tried to let the texts that speak of holiness generate and guide the categories we have used to interpret them. It is now time to begin to analyze, synthesize, and criticize the categories themselves. The three analyses that we have used—property, status, and value—are methodological devices. They frame what people in the tradition have said or thought about holiness. But they do not settle what holiness really *is*. They describe and interpret a phenomenon across a range of Jewish cultures. But they don't take us far enough in answering the *ti esti* question, unless we are willing to take the texts at face value. If we were willing to submit to the authority of the most canonical of them (the Pentateuchal and rabbinic ones), that might settle what holiness is. But that would arrest the intellectual adventure, as Michael Oakeshott put it. It would be a surrender of the critical stance, the "pathos of distance" that modernity has bequeathed to us. Yet insofar as modernity has greatly disenchanted the world and desecrated much that was long thought holy, we must be critical of it too. There's a fine line to walk between respect for modern norms of critical, philosophical inquiry and respect for Jewish tradition, with its deep convictions about the goodness and sacredness of life.

Based on our inquiry so far, the following questions arise. Is holiness a reality *de re*, not only *de dicto*? That is, does holiness exist in the world in such a way that traditional talk about it has an object to which language *responds*? That holiness is a way of institutional, culturally salient speaking (on the status analysis) or a demanding religious-moral project (on the value analysis) does not seem controversial. Holiness as a social or institutional fact or as a value can simply be what the mass of the religious tradition over time says it is. (Thus, holiness has existence *de dicto*.) But this, in my view, does not go far enough. It does not shield the ascription of holiness from charges of arbitrariness or conventionality. There are no reasons for it, no rational justification to be given, aside from the stipulation of a divine will. In more secular terms, if holiness is simply the cash value of the symbols central to a society or a culture, if it is constituted entirely in a functional way, then it is merely conventional. The Aztec culture's valorization of human sacrifice is holy for it. The Nazi sacralization of the supposed Aryan race is holy for it, and so on. Conventionalism bleeds into moral relativism. It divorces the holy from moral evaluation and renders it irrational. Without moral brakes, irrational holiness can abet and underwrite violence.

Even on logical grounds, for holiness to be cogent at a social, institutional, or legal level, it must be differentiable from other concepts of status or of value. Holiness cannot just mean "separate" or "possessed." If so, it would add nothing to those ordinary concepts. It would be a mere verbal flourish. Although *kedushah* certainly has important work to do in the symbolic economy of Jewish life at the *de dicto* level, we need to explore whether it might also have *de re* existence—whether talk of holiness picks out a dimension of how things are, prior to how we think and speak of them. Prior—not independent. Holiness is not independent of our thinking and speaking in the sense that it has a fully extra-mental existence *simpliciter*. I will argue, rather, that holiness is a quality of things that emerges in our relations with them. It is something that we notice and respond to because we are constituted to have the necessary awareness. There needn't be anything queer about this; it is similar to dispositional properties like color. What emerges as color perception requires the prior existence of light—but then much neural (and cognitive) work goes into seeing a frequency as red.[124]

The tradition began with locating holiness in the world as a real property, imbued in things by the divine presence. This is a hard, possibly dangerous view to reclaim. The misuse of holiness for violent purposes has a taproot in divine commands that supposedly override ethics, as in the genocidal conduct of holy war. The ideas of holy people and holy land may have invidious implications for nonholy others. An attenuated, socially constructed view of holiness à la Durkheim would unmask such morally suspect pretensions and allow for the critique of claims to holiness. The diminution of holiness to a means of institutional maintenance, or even of moral aspiration would, similarly, defang the most problematic implications of the concept. But they would also leave us with a forlorn, deflated view of the world in which nothing has value other than what we decide to desire, prescribe, or impute. We ourselves would lose value in such a world. If we divest the holy of its legitimate content, legitimacy itself is weakened. Holiness orients us to transcendence; it draws us to what makes human beings wonder and feel gratitude for the strange fact that they exist. Holiness provides a language in which such thoughts and attitudes can be expressed. There is a dimension of holiness that outstrips its obvious social and institutional uses. I don't think we can do without it and continue to lead recognizably human lives.

Difficult though it is to retrieve, I want to return to the idea of holiness as a property, a real aspect of things. I will argue that holiness is an intrinsically valuable property; call it a "value-property." Here the analyses of status, property, and value come together in a theory of holiness. That theory uses the stance in philosophical ethics known as moral realism. The aim is to anchor value in the world and to break the hold of a world-picture in which facts and values are entirely separate from one another. Holiness is found in the entanglement of fact and value. If we have the proper awareness and receptivity (or the grace), the world reveals itself as suffused with value, both as a whole and in its most revealing parts. Holiness and goodness lie at the root of that natural revelation. There are aspects of the world properly conceived as sacred. Correlatively, there are ways of acting in the world that should be thought of as unholy, as desecrations. A realism about holiness should bring these existential and moral facts to light. Although it will not map entirely onto the historical phenomenology of holiness in Judaism, the "natural history of holiness" that I will propose is compatible with Jewish understandings. It will also afford critical resources for restraining those teachings that violate moral norms in pursuit of holiness.

CHAPTER TWO

Holiness and Ethics

IF HOLINESS IS a value-property, on what is the value based? How does it come into the world? How does holiness relate to other values, preeminently to moral ones? Are holiness and ethics separable, or identical, or mutually dependent? Is holiness prior to ethics; is it more primordial or primitive? Should ethics constrain or order holiness? A theory of holiness in Judaism must take these questions seriously. A concern for how holiness may factor into violence makes the questions imperative.

To motivate our inquiry into the relation between holiness and ethics, consider two texts: the first from the Book of Leviticus; the second from the modern Jewish thinker, Abraham Joshua Heschel.

> When the daughter of a priest desecrates herself by harlotry, it is her father whom she desecrates; she shall be burned by fire (Leviticus 21:9).[1]

We have seen that holy persons, in the Israelite case, priests, must take special care to avoid impurity, both ritual and moral. In this text, a priest's daughter—who is in some way implicated in the holiness of the priesthood as such—has some kind of unapproved sexual relations (z'nut), possibly premarital sex, which profanes (teḥel) her. More importantly, she desecrates or profanes (miḥallelet) her father's holy status.[2] The judgment is summary: she is to be burned alive. The Talmud (b Sanhedrin 50a–52a) does not soften the punishment, but it does try to contextualize and thereby justify it. The woman is assumed to be married, although the applicable stage of the rabbinic marriage process, betrothal or full marriage, is a matter of controversy. Thus, on the rabbinic reading her crime is *adultery*, which is also a capital crime, although its biblical punishment is not burning but stoning. In addition, for the Talmud, she diminishes her father's reputation.

Rabbinic interpretation moves away from the blunt, if rather vague emphasis on holiness in the source text, framing her guilt in the more familiar, moral-legal category of marital infidelity. Even in that context, however, this is a terrifying text. It strikes us with the same horror as the "honor killings" we read about in Afghanistan and elsewhere. If her crime or sin is not adultery and the consequent shaming of her father, as the rabbis would have it, but a symbolic violation of her and her father's holy status, our sense of moral outrage at her punishment is even greater. How could conduct, within the framework of a cultural-religious symbolic system, be considered grave enough to warrant a gruesome, torturous execution by burning? Who was hurt? How can her father's reputation or his "holiness" justify such treatment of his daughter? It is hard to read such a text without feeling that it gravely offends our morality. The rabbinic reworking of it does not lessen the offense. Here is a case of holiness in tension with ethics—at least with contemporary Western ethics with its emphasis on rights, freedom, and individuality. One can argue, of course, that importing modern ethical norms into the biblical world is methodologically irresponsible or perhaps culturally parochial on our part—fair criticisms to an extent. But Jews and Christians like to think that biblical ethics is a (or *the*) font of our own best morality—that there are universal truths about goodness and rightness expressed by the Bible. The problematic relation between a view of holiness and its moral implications cannot be avoided if we want to make the latter affirmation.

The second text is a reminiscence of the spiritual struggles of Abraham Joshua Heschel during his student days in the early 1930s at the University of Berlin. Heschel writes: "The problem to my professors was how to be good. In my ears the question rang: how to be holy." He continues:

> To the philosophers the idea of the good was the most exalted idea, the ultimate idea. To Judaism the idea of the good is penultimate. It cannot exist without the holy. The good is the base; the holy is the summit. Man cannot be good unless he strives to be holy.[3]

Heschel is alluding to the Platonic idea of the good as the form of forms. The good functions for Plato rather like the Holy One of Israel functions for Jews. Heschel wants to order the good to the holy, a move that the philosophers do not make. His professors want to be followers of the good; they do not grasp the possibility of something even higher.

Heschel does not for a moment imagine that holiness and goodness are in tension. The holy completes and orients the good. For him, to be good is ultimately to be *like* God, not "merely" to do what he commands; "not to obey what He wills but to *do* what He *is*." To be good wells up from and flows into holiness. "We live by the conviction," he writes, "that acts of goodness reflect the hidden light of His holiness. His light is above our minds but not beyond our will. It is within our power to mirror His unending love in deeds of kindness, like brooks that hold the sky."[4] Holiness is the consummation of goodness, never its contradiction. He would disagree that true holiness and goodness can pull in opposite directions. The human striving for justice and generosity is of concern to God. The ethical question is: What ought I to do? But the religious question, the question of holiness, is: How can I act in the world in such a way that I do not abuse the power my Creator has vested in me? How can I act so as not to desecrate God? The answer must be provided by human beings, but God waits and hopes for the answer. Holiness provides what Heschel calls a "meta-ethical approach," an ultimate framing of human decision and action.[5]

Heschel's construal of holiness can be inspiring, but is it philosophically cogent? Does goodness need holiness? What precisely would holiness add? And what should be done when holiness overrides, as it arguably does in the case of the priest's daughter, ordinary judgments of morality? Doesn't Heschel beg the question by mapping holiness onto moral goodness (mirroring unending love, deeds of kindness, and so on) in the first place? What of those many places in the Bible where God does not dispense "unending love" or manifest "deeds of kindness?" Does Heschel not scant an uncanny, potentially dangerous God who can show himself to be "essentially discontinuous with human norms?"[6]

Morality and Primordiality

The case that I want to make here is that holiness and morality are equally primordial, equally original to the human condition. They are entangled with one another, contributing to an integrated view both of the world and of our place in it. Morality governs and guides our conduct, as well as shapes our expectations for what a flourishing, meaningful, and good life ought to be.[7] Holiness alerts us to the loci of extraordinary value in the world, in reference to which our moral conduct acquires its point. Further, reflection on the holy orients our conduct and expectations toward the source of value, which for Jews is the Highest One. Holiness informs the deepest and most comprehensive context in which we take the measure of our lives and chart, to the extent that we can, their courses. But although holiness and morality are conceptually correlated and, in an ideal sense, contribute to an integrated view of the world and of our place and role within it, we can experience them as pulling against one another. We need to do the work of integration—to earn that deep and comprehensive framework within which a good and holy life can be lived. Heschel's faith in the mutual dependence of the holy and the good is well placed, but more work needs to be done to give that faith a rational warrant. I will try to make that case here. The first step of the argument is to establish the coevality of the holy and the good.

Both holiness and morality make claims to primordiality. (As we consider holiness, let us bracket, for now, the question of whether the holy comes from on high, so to speak, or is simply an emergent feature of our life-world, a dispositional property. I shall assume the latter provisionally but advocate for a more theological view as the argument develops.) The division of the world into domains of pure and impure, sacred and profane exemplified by Leviticus occurs in many archaic cultures. Indeed, dualistic thought and "the human propensity ... to attach moral, religious, or ritual significance to dualisms" is a human universal.[8] Although, as we have seen, a binary grid of sacred/profane is too crude to capture the dynamics of Israelite priestly thought, Israel shared with other ancient cultures the cognitive disposition to find or assign extraordinary meaning and value to persons, places, times, and objects. That disposition is rooted in basic capabilities of the human mind—in particular, the capacity to symbolize.

Sacred things come fully into view with symbolic thought. Thought as such is impossible without symbolism.[9] For Langer, sentient beings use signs, but symbols, the building blocks of thought, are different from signs. Animals are alert to signs and respond to them within their environmental niches. They also produce them, using plumage or sounds or other displays and presentations to influence conspecifics, predators, or prey. The antelope takes movement and rustling in the distant grass to be a sign of a lion and then takes flight. Human beings might well do the same. But human beings also take a lion to be a *symbol* of strength and majesty, ferocity and danger. The lion is *qua symbol* a compact idea for abstract concepts. That is not an operation in an antelope's cognitive repertoire. A symbol operates at a higher level of conceptuality than does a sign. Arguably, the ability to symbolize—to turn signs into ideas that can play a potentially unlimited range of roles in linguistically articulated thought—separates human beings from other, even highly intelligent creatures.[10] Symbolization and *Homo sapiens* arise together. Without the capacity to symbolize, primitive intuitions of holiness would have remained formless and incommunicable.

Creating a meaningful world appropriate to human life relies on symbolization. All cultures treat familiar objects, such as water, fire, blood, mountains, certain plants, various animals, righthandedness, the sun and moon and stars, and so on, as having symbolic purport. Most cultures develop myths in which symbols are expressive of "natural conflicts, of human desire frustrated by non-human powers, hostile oppression, or contrary desires." Universal human experiences are symbolized and given narrative form by mythic stories of "the birth, passion, and defeat by death, which is man's common fate."[11]

Symbolizing and myth-making are human universals.[12] Perhaps the most "natural" or universal symbol is the human body. Mary Douglas, following Durkheim and Mauss, categorically asserts that "the human body is always treated as an image of society and there can be no natural way of considering the body that does not involve at the same time a social dimension."[13] The integrity of the skin, the control of the bowels, the inflow and outflow of bodily fluids—all concerns of the biblical purity laws—are symbolic markers of social boundaries, of social entrances and exits. "We cannot possibly interpret rituals concerning excreta, saliva, breast milk and the rest unless we are prepared to see in the body a symbol of society, and to see the powers and dangers credited to social structure reproduced in small on the human body."[14] For Douglas, the constitutive, universal human experience of sociality is symbolized by the body. Human beings are thus primordially symbol-making, meaning-seeking creatures. The general principle is that the symbols that are most central and important to a culture, most revelatory of the meaning and value of its social life, are its sacra. They are repositories of holiness.

Both of these ideas—that symbolization is fundamental to human language use and thus to human cognition, and that there are universal "natural" symbols that express our fundamental sociality—seem correct. But the second (Durkheim-Douglas) claim is not deep enough. It is not fully shielded from challenges of arbitrariness and conventionality. Are there substantive, not just functional, bases for ascribing or discovering holiness? Are some things sacred in themselves before social beings symbolize them as such? For Durkheim and Douglas, because society is primordial, the sacred (as its symbolic expression) is primordial. Without prying human beings away from the social and cultural contexts in which they are always embedded, I want to ask whether holiness is grounded in something deeper than our contingent social-cultural location. Is there a ground for the primordiality of holiness deeper than the symbolic expression of the core values of a society or of society as such?

Morality—or at least its building blocks—is also primordial. Human beings are evaluative animals. Moral sense or sentiments, as Adam Smith called them, are native to our lineage.[15] Kindness, even altruism, as well as selfishness, sharing, and the ability to shame or approve, forgive or condemn, are found among our evolutionary cousins, the chimpanzees and bonobos.[16] Infants at eight months are able to express judgments of good and bad. They not only prefer puppets who, in the little skits developmental psychologists design, are kind or helpful, they want to *punish* puppets who are mean. By one year, they have a grasp of the value of sharing and the blameworthiness of selfishness. They are strongly biased toward equality of distribution and show surprise when that norm is violated.[17] Our moral capacities and reflexes are part of our evolutionary heritage. As a social species, we are disposed toward morality. We go in for morality as we go in for language, with brains adapted to the production of both. Morality and language are native capabilities, which familial and social life help to develop and determine.

Whether the evolutionary origin of our native moral capabilities determines the *normative content* of an ethics is another matter. (Advocates for that view work at developing so-called evolutionary ethics.) Explaining the normative at the level of theory (giving a scientific account of morality) and making a move in a normative framework (judging, praising, arguing for a value, claiming a right, and so on) are different matters.[18] Explanation in a scientific sense is analytically distinct from justification in a moral sense. There are good reasons to believe that morality, once emerged in human culture

and consciousness, has some independence from the evolutionary and psychological conditions that enable it. Morality
has its own logic.[19] Nonetheless, the "ethical project" cannot
be held entirely aloof from the evolutionary history of modern
humans. Morality is in part the story of our survival as a species.[20] The old, central, Platonic and Aristotelian ethical question of what constitutes a good, flourishing, or happy (*eudae-
mon*) life cannot be divorced from biological questions about
what creatures such as ourselves need to thrive. The logic of
a developed morality cannot be entirely severed from claims
about human nature. Even as anti-naturalistic a moral philosopher as Kant was constrained to consider the role of the latter in his theorizing about ethics.[21] Explanation and justification are related.

To return to the main point, why is it important to claim
that the capacities to discern, attribute, or experience the sacred and to live in a normative register are equally primordial?
On the one side, there is the view that religion comes late to
the moral party. In Kitcher's account, our hominid ancestors
struggled to work out the social arrangements that allowed
them to survive and thrive. As groups grew in size beyond the
extended family, the problems of trust and of non-kin (recip-
rocal) altruism became acute. How to motivate early humans to
care about others beyond their immediate kinship circle? How
to punish failures of the altruism that allowed cooperation,
trust, and solidarity? Religion enters the picture, in this story,
with its useful fiction of an "unseen enforcer." Belief in the in-
visible presence of a moral, judgmental god evolved as a technique of normative control. "Prevalent in human cultures—
in the successful surviving experiments—is an appeal to un-
observable entities that respond to breaches of ethical codes.
Western monotheisms use the device: there is an omniscient
deity who observes all, who judges, and who punishes lapses

from commandments."[22] The presumed universality of religious beliefs in unseen enforcers conveyed survival advantages
on the groups that held them. Religion "permeates human history because groups that did not invent some form of unseen
enforcer were less able to reap the benefits (Darwinian and
cultural) of socially embedded normative guidance; with lower
levels of cooperation and social harmony, they were losers in
cultural competition."[23] Religion (and thus all thought, myth,
and ritual dealing with the sacred) is an attempt to solve the
problems of trust and cooperation, the problem of "altruism
failure" in primitive societies. The holy, such as it is, is an evolutionary footnote to morality. The explanation for it debunks.
It disposes of the *explicandum* once the latter's function is, by
Kitcher's lights, understood.

On the other side, there is a tendency to denigrate the primordiality of morality in favor of an allegedly more primitive,
authentic experience of the cosmic power and vitality of the
holy. Although he doesn't talk about holiness as such, Nietz-
sche's *The Birth of Tragedy*, with its stark opposition between
the Dionysian and the Apollonian, and its celebration of the
former and denigration of the latter, is a ready example of
privileging an allegedly pre-ethical primitive condition. The
most influential study of holiness in the last century, Rudolf
Otto's *The Idea of the Holy* (1917), has been read to argue that
holiness (*das Heilige*) is more primordial, more fundamental
to human experience than ethics. Ethics does come to overlay
the holy, especially in the Bible, but the "numinous" is primary—
mysterious, tremendous, and gripping. The "wholly other"
(*ganz andere*) God is uncanny and inconceivable. Encounter
with the numinous is a basic, orienting experience of primitive
humanity. Ethics is an attempt to contain and constrain the
experience (and the god so experienced).

Although many have read him this way, Otto himself resisted this rather Nietzschean interpretation of his work.[24] In the view that our encounter with the holy is what is most fundamental, morality becomes a kind of veneer layered over a supposedly more original, wild human nature.[25] The holy would better capture our inner primitive, our savage experience of the world, than our morality. As such, the holy might make a higher or at least more original claim on us than morality. It might be thought more authentic or ultimate than the civilized restraints that seek, in this view, to contain and control it. If the holy has primacy over morality, then it needn't pay morality any respect. The call of the holy, regardless of its moral consequences or violations, could have the strongest voice.

Getting Otto right, seeing the balance in his account, is important to my coevality claim. But Otto will not, in the end, give sufficient support to the integrated view of holiness and ethics that I want to advance. Let's see why. Otto's view is that holiness has rational and irrational dimensions. Modern Christianity has overly emphasized the rational, by which he means ethical, elements. A more authentic religiosity, which gives full vent to both feeling and belief, needs to restore the irrational elements to their proper place. "Holiness" in modern languages has a distilled, ethicized meaning; it signifies, as in Kant, "complete goodness." But this is an attenuation. Holiness is a "category of interpretation and valuation peculiar to the sphere of religion." Its transference to ethics is secondary. Within the sphere of primordial religion, "if the ethical element was present at all, at any rate it was not original and never constituted the whole meaning of the word."[26] Otto agrees that the mature use of "holy" in the Hebrew Bible (*kadosh*) and in Greek and Latin sources (*hagios* and *sanctus* or *sacer*) contains moral elements; at the "highest stage of development," holiness has, as

part of its meaning, "good, absolute goodness."[27] But this reflects a long cultural and intellectual development. The most
fundamental part of the holy is the feeling of the "numinous,"
a term of art that he devises from the Latin *numen* (divine
majesty, divinity, deity). The numinous inspires awe; it over-
powers; it is full of energy, even of wrath. It is incomprehen-
sible, yet magnetic and entrancing. Otto famously describes
the numinous by three Latin terms: *mysterium tremendum et
fascinans.*

In the following quote, which describes the feeling of the
numinous as "mysterium tremendum," one can see how the
Nietzschean reading gets a foothold:

> The feeling of it may at times come sweeping like a gentle
> tide, pervading the mind with a tranquil mood of deepest
> worship. It may pass over into a more set and lasting atti-
> tude of the soul, continuing, as it were, thrillingly vibrant
> and resonant until at last it dies away and the soul resumes
> its "profane," non-religious mood of everyday experience.
> *It may burst in sudden eruption up from the depths of the
> soul with spasms and convulsions, or lead to the strangest
> excitements, to intoxicated frenzy, to transport, and to ec-
> stasy. It has its wild and demonic forms and can sink to
> an almost grisly horror and shuddering.* It has its crude,
> barbaric antecedents and early manifestations, and again
> it may be developed into something beautiful and pure and
> glorious.[28]

The feeling is polymorphous. It can shape diverse conceptions
of deity. The terrifying and barbaric is not necessarily more
primal than the tranquil and blissful, but it is easy to take that
view especially given that all of these emotional states are *distinct from* morality. As, in some measure, a Kantian, Otto takes
morality to have a strong rational basis. The turbulent world

of emotions, particularly of the feeling of the numinous, is pre-ethical. If one is inclined to see human beings as basically cruel and barbaric, the numinous can figure against that ground. The irrationality of the holy can be given a dark depiction and a broad scope.

As much as Otto wanted to describe and analyze the primitive feeling of the numinous, he also wanted to balance irrationality with rationality in his full account of the holy. The numinous is an *element* of holiness; it is not the entirety of the holy.[29] "Rationality, purpose, personality, morality" come completely to permeate the holy; the "daemonic dread" of primitive religious consciousness is "rationalized and moralized, that is, filled with rational and ethical meaning."[30] Ultimately, for Otto, holiness exists in *fact*—it is an ontological feature of the world (that is, a property) perceived through an inherent (a priori) capacity for numinous feeling—and it has *value*. It is not enough to equate holiness with transcendence, for that only marks its ontic separateness (that is, holiness as a status). We must also acknowledge its supreme value (*augustus*). In its presence, we feel our own smallness, our profane nature, not because of anything we have done morally but because of what we *are*. (The purest case of this for Otto is Job's confession in Job 42:6, where he recants and relents his challenge to God insofar as he now realizes he is mere "dust and ashes.") The only right response is praise and recognition that the holy has a supreme right "to make the highest claim to service, [it] receives praise because it is in an absolute sense worthy to be praised." The term that Otto uses to designate the holy as the highest value against which we feel our own nullity and in light of which we want to serve and praise is *augustus*, the august or "illustrious" quality of the holy.[31]

In the rounded view of Otto's work, we can see how the ethical moment of holiness and the premoral or amoral experience of the numinous are synthesized. He does not come to praise or celebrate the irrational. Nonetheless, I find the sequence troubling. Why should the numinous be temporally prior to the moral? What does that say about the status of morality? About our moral psychology? About God, to whom the numinous refers? The priority of an amoral *mysterium tremendum* can make sense, at an interpretive level, of the sometimes impassioned God, jealous of his holiness and alert to incursions on his sacred space, who appears in Scripture. But it cannot make much sense philosophically. If that is what holiness is and that is who God is, then we would be left in a position not of gratitude and love toward the Highest One but cowering in fear and needing to propitiate a tyrant. That would undermine the ethical value of Judaism. To move the thesis of the coeval primordiality of the holy and the good, we need better intellectual resources than Otto provides. Turning to the evolutionary development of our species will give us some clues.

Toward a Natural History of Goodness and Holiness

Although the idea of a "natural history" of religion goes back to antiquity, David Hume gave the project its modern impetus.[32] Hume sees religion emerging (as many contemporary atheists do) as a failed quest for explanation. The quest has an intellectual/conceptual motivation, but only to a small degree. It has mostly to do with human passion: "the anxious concern for happiness, the dread of future misery, the terror of death, the search for revenge." Ordinary "affections of human life" drive confused, meaning-seeking primitives to populate heaven and earth with beings imagined to be like themselves. Religion basically begins in "diffidence, terror, and melancholy."[33] Otto is more generous toward religion than Hume, but he follows the same arc. Our savage ancestors experienced a savage god. In the beginning is something dark, terrible, and irrational. Civilization—and its more rational, moral portrayal of God—comes much later. Freud adds his own touches to this portrait, but we needn't linger on them here.

I want to propose a different natural history. This history focuses on our evolved capacities to cooperate, empathize, care, and ultimately to love as integral to the survival of our lineage. It roots both our sense of the holy and our moral dispositions in those capacities. Such a history sees our moral emotions, values, and basic repertoire of social behaviors against the deep temporal dimension of mammalian evolution. It sees striking continuities as well as crucial discontinuities between humans and "other apes."[34] Both are important. We should not repudiate, as so much self-aggrandizement, our own deep sense of distinction from the natural world, but neither should we scant our objective participation in its evolutionary record. Indeed, human distinctiveness becomes all the more poignant against the background of a shared mammalian nature. I want to try to contextualize holiness against this background.[35]

Holiness and morality are coeval, entangled in the evolutionary origins of modern humans. How so? Begin with morality. Morality requires that there be others in the world who make claims on me; that we ought to treat one another in certain ways, given the kind of creatures that we are. Morality, in an evolutionary context, depends on the phenomenon of "shared intentionality," or "theory of mind" as it is sometimes called. Shared intentionality refers to the sense that others are like me—they are beings with minds like mine. They can engage with me in common endeavors with respect to common norms. I can attribute goals to them that are comparable to my goals. We can share ends such as hunting, foraging, playing, fighting, or celebrating.

Our evolutionary cousins, the chimps and bonobos, are also capable of shared intentionality. Highly intelligent chimpanzees (as opposed to slow or average ones) understand that their own experiences can be shared by others. They grasp that their human handlers can also experience the difficulties that they have. In one experiment, a human keeper led chimps to a locked bin of food, took a key from around his neck, and opened the bin. As the experiment progressed, the keeper was blindfolded. The chimps led the human to the food but then didn't know what to do when the human couldn't open the bin. Sometimes the chimps just reached for the key themselves, bypassing the inactive keeper and getting their own food. But one smart chimp figured out that when she removed the blindfold, the human could then see the bin and open the lock. She understood the difficulties the human was having and acted appropriately to help him and bring about a good outcome for her. Henceforth, the chimp consistently helped the human to see and act appropriately. Summarizing the results, the Premacks write "seeing is only one of the several mental states that chimpanzees attribute to the 'other one.' Chimpanzees also attribute goal-directedness and intention, mental states that human infants attribute as early as the tenth or the eleventh month."[36] If at least some chimpanzees are capable of taking a human's point of view, how much the more so are they able to do this when the other is a chimp. The ability to take the other's point of view, to consider the other as like oneself and, crucially, as "deserving" of comparable treatment is basic to morality. The capacities to do this, among higher primates, likely go back to the experience of maternal care.

Unlike monkeys, apes console one another and their young. An ape mother cuddles and comforts an upset youngster, much as a human mother does. She is attuned to her infant's needs and moods. The capacity to read the infant's mind, to know what it needs, is correlated with self-awareness. Chimpanzees and other great apes are highly *self-aware*. Alone in the animal kingdom, they recognize their images in mirrors and act in ways that the mirror image facilitates, such as removing things from their fur that they otherwise could not have seen. Human infants acquire this ability between eighteen and twenty-four months—the very same time that they "develop helping geared to the needs of others."[37] Self-awareness and other-regarding behavior are linked. Young children begin to grasp that the other is both different from them *and* like them; the other has needs, feelings, and intentions comparable to their own but not their own. To get to morality, one has to separate one's own needs from the others' and to recognize their (comparably) compelling status. To have such a view of the other requires having a distinctive, bounded view of oneself. The mirror image is me, but it is also not me. It represents (or symbolizes) me, but I am distinct from it. I am not the whole world. The other, who is independent but also like me, shares the world with me. He or she deserves to be treated as I would want to be treated. This is, to be sure, an overly rational formulation of a capacity felt in an intuitive way.

This genealogy of "theory of mind," awareness of the needs of others, and the moral dispositions of young children raises an immediate philosophical objection. As a deduction of an "ought" from an "is," followers of Hume will be displeased by the seamless transition from the factual claim that the other is like me to the normative one that the other therefore "deserves to be treated" in the way that I would want to be treated. That criticism gets to the deductive rigor of the argument, but it does not change the fact (if it is, as I believe, a fact) that our moral capacities came into being through our capacity for shared intentionality and empathy. Nonetheless, one who upholds the fact/value dichotomy would say that all of this is a matter of psychology and it cannot carry us over to morality. We cannot *justify* on the basis of the facts of our evolutionary psychology that, for example sympathy is better than hostility or cooperation is better than aggression, all things being equal. But surely the factual basis of morality is relevant to ethics. If nothing else, we can take the facts on board and use them as reasons in a distinctly ethical argument.

Empathy is part of the story. It begins with the lineage of placental mammals, which goes back 220 million years. "This is when babies began to be born so helpless that mothers needed to be attuned to the smell, sounds, and slightest perturbations in the conditions of vulnerable young that had to be kept warm and fed."[38] The offspring of mothers who were attentive to their young survived better than those of disengaged mothers. The genes of attentive mothers were passed along, fixing the mammalian pattern of maternal care. With motherly care came an increase in the size of brain regions associated with empathy and thus with increasing sociability, intelligence, and theory of mind. "Empathy is part of a heritage as ancient as the mammalian line. Empathy engages brain areas more than a hundred million years old. The capacity arose long ago with motor mimicry and emotional contagion, after which evolution added layer on layer, until our ancestors not only felt, but understood what others might want or need."[39] Mammalian empathy, intelligence, and sociability, like shared intentionality, are existence conditions for human morality.

Our remarkable ability to understand the thoughts, intentions, feelings, moods—the minds and hearts—of our fellow human beings is a necessary but, I hasten to add, not sufficient condition for human morality. It builds upon the development of empathy in mammals generally, in other primates, and in our extinct hominid ancestors. In apes and in humans, however, empathy can rise to *sympathy*—kindness or compassion toward others manifested in acts of helping.[40] Although conventional language blurs the line between empathy and sympathy, a proper distinction exists. Empathy includes, for example, the ability to sense and imagine another's pain. But one might respond to that by distancing oneself from the other, as people who lived near Nazi concentration camps were able to do. The sympathetic or compassionate ape or human, however, tries to alleviate the distress.[41] Sympathy although also natural relies more on will and choice than empathy does. Sympathy or compassion has the characteristics of a virtue; it is discerned, chosen, cultivated, and inculcated.

Affirming sympathy as a value and cultivating it through attention and action brings us to human morality, or at least to one of its main features. Are nonhuman animals capable of something like this? Observing empathy, sympathy, and "targeted helping" among apes, as well as dolphins and elephants, de Waal concludes "they may not know the golden rule, but they surely seem to follow it."[42] I hesitate to say that this makes apes moral or practitioners of a simian morality that is isomorphic, taking species differences into account, with ours. Nonetheless, we can see the precursors of our own moralities here. We who know the golden rule sometimes make it our maxim and sometimes (immorally) do not. That is our choice, not a foreordained implication of our phylogeny. But had our species not evolved, under natural selection, to be preternaturally aware of the mental states of others, to be eager to connect, share, help, and cooperate with them, human morality would not exist. Natural selection working on the primate lineage put the elements in place that constitute the necessary, albeit not sufficient conditions for human morality.

Mothers of many species nurture and protect their young. But only among apes and humans can we find the behavior that the pioneering Austrian ethologist Eibl-Eibesfeldt calls "cherishing."[43] The origins of love and friendship are found in the mother's care for her young. Her behavior toward them responds to the signs or signals that they present. Their signs of need are met with care. As Eibl-Eibesfeldt puts it, "The cherishing behavior patterns of parental care have their natural counterpart in the signals that release them, which have been taken over into the repertoire of contact-making and aggression-inhibiting behavior patterns as 'infantile appeals.'"[44] Infants call forth our sympathy. (Thus, older children or adults, deliberately or spontaneously, sometimes act in infantile ways to elicit sympathy.) The mother senses acutely the momentary needs of her young by the signs they present. She suckles, comforts, grooms, protects, encourages, and eventually teaches and disciplines them. Her "cherishing" them in response to their needs reveals her perception or, for human beings, her conception of their intrinsic worth. The object of motherly care has extraordinary value, to which a fit or healthy mother responds with great, self-sacrificial investment. Its value stands out from its environment as figure to ground, guiding the mother's behavior and emotion.

Cherishing, I want to argue, is not only the basis for love, *it is also the natural basis for holiness*. Goodness and holiness are revealed together. The extraordinary worth of the cherished young is a (or the?) natural model of inherent value. Response to this value is intuitive. It can be frustrated or derailed, shaped or warped by culture. But in the typical case, immense positive value differentiates the infant from all other persons and things. A gloomy adult may question the worth of life, applying Moore's "open question method" to a newborn. "Is it really good to bring a baby into the world?" he might ask. But a loving mother, who bonds with her child, could not ask such a question. It is "one thought too many." If anything is good, this child is; this mother-child bond is. The child is good not because of what he or she will become or produce but simply because of what he or she is. It is true that some animals, as well as some apes and humans, practice infanticide. A dominant male that displaces a prior alpha in a chimpanzee group may kill the latter's young in order to populate the group with his own.[45] Some human cultures expose infants because males rather than females are thought more desirable. Conquerors throughout history have slaughtered men and children but enslaved women, using them to propagate their own progeny. Our deep revulsion at such practices, in the first instance at the human ones but, by extension (empathy!) to the apes, attests to our intuitive sense of the sacredness of new, vulnerable, irreplaceable life.

By seeing holiness as coordinate with cherishing, the otherwise difficult notion of holiness as a dispositional property becomes intelligible. There is at least one "item" in the world that has an extraordinary status and guides our response to it on the basis of its sheer being. We do not *ascribe* value beyond price, as Kant puts it, to our newborns; given the kind of creature we are, we *discover* it. If anything should be called sacred, an innocent newborn should be so called. It does not have worth or dignity because of its potential; it has a special status on account of what it presently is. The fact/value dichotomy collapses in the face of the newborn.[46] The finite fact of its being opens a world of infinite value. Holy things are like this. They have an aura of ontic power (*mysterium tremendum*) that quickens our fascination. We are moved to care for and protect them, to guard their distinction from the rest of the world. They are sacred over and against the common or profane.

A skeptic might, at this point, claim that it is gratuitous to call infants sacred. Valued, yes; sacred, no. Steven Pinker argued that the term "human dignity," for example, is gratuitous.[47] It seems to add a mysterious, religion-infected characteristic to human beings that obfuscates more than it clarifies. To say that human beings have rights or are worthy of respect should suffice; "dignity" adds nothing but a misleading rhetoric that, Pinker opines, gives moral and religious conservatives an unearned advantage. Analogously, couldn't we just say that human beings are important, worth caring about, valuable, and so on without the rhetoric of holiness? I have claimed that "if anything should be called sacred, an innocent newborn should be so called." But perhaps nothing should be so called. Is the sacredness of human life something about which we could be skeptical?[48]

We might decide to shed the language of holiness or sacredness, but I doubt that we could coherently reject the thought behind it.[49] Every attempt to do so in a strong sense would boomerang. A strenuous argument, if such were available, that human beings are not of surpassing worth would founder. Why bother to justify our supposed negligible value, if we don't matter? Why try to know the truth about us if we are not beings who have the unique distinction of being able to know? Human projects pursue goods, integrating our disparate aims into the high good of a flourishing life. But if it is a matter of indifference whether human flourishing matters, then it is hard to see why one should inquire, raise skeptical doubts, frame arguments, seek rationally to persuade others, or engage in any other activity premised on the pursuit of a good. Our very engagement with the search for knowledge, with trying to get to the truth about things, attests to an implicit concern for human flourishing. The skeptical stance cannot escape being implicated in ethics: the project of leading a flourishing life. It cannot be *external* to that project, as if one could evaluate the worth of human life from the point of view of a Martian. A skeptical dismissal of the worth of human life remains "within" ethics. Seeking to persuade oneself or others that none of us has value is not meta-ethical; it is unethical. We may choose to express that fundamental orienting value by a term other than "sacred," but the concept will continue to function in the same way. There is a pressure of reason, a "must be thought" quality to the concept of the holy as it applies to the extraordinary value of human beings.

External skepticism toward the value of human life will not work. Arguably, however, to say that human life is sacred is not an all or nothing-at-all judgment. A skeptic could claim that the right contrast to the claim that human life is sacred is not "human life doesn't matter" but "human life, like other forms of life, has value but its value does not exceed the value of nonhuman life." One can be an *internal* skeptic, not rejecting value claims about humanity but moderating or limiting them, disputing the absoluteness and basicality implied by the term "sacred." One might take the view that the use of the term "sacred" is important, even essential, but that its proper substantive is not "the human infant," for example, but "the planet," or "the biosphere," or "all sentient life." One could spread holiness about as a way of marking the extraordinary value of a range of things, disdaining to elevate humanity above the rest or even to mark its strong distinction. Although some contemporary ethicists want to claim that animals are persons and equal to humans in this regard, I find it difficult to believe that anyone can actually live by this claim. If you faced a choice between saving your daughter or saving your dog, both of whom you love, could you really believe that one is as "choice worthy" as the other? If you saved your dog and let your daughter drown, could your theoretical view that animals are persons function as a justification for your action? We can certainly raise skeptical challenges to our intuitive sense that human beings occupy an extraordinary status, have irreplaceable worth, and radiate a special ontic character, especially through their faces and eyes, but we can't quite cash out those doubts without the taint of immorality. Internal skepticism is also a move within morality. Despite skeptical challenges, which can never be fully diffused, we have good grounds to make strong claims about human value and to describe that value within the register of holiness.

I have been arguing that the natural roots of morality and of discovering and attributing sacredness are entangled. Neither is more primordial than the other. Ethics and holiness arise together with humanity's sense of a normative dimension within experience. Let us begin to consider how this experience takes on cultural and discursive form. For human beings, babies are more than sign-generating creatures to which we should respond in nurturing ways. They are also symbols, the basic language of culture. Keeping in mind the distinction between sign and symbol urged by Langer, we can say that newborns represent innocence, vulnerability, possibility, futurity, renewal, continuity, newness, and hope. Their tiny frames bear a heavy symbolic load. They represent the value of life itself and of our wonderment at the strange fact that we exist. Even after our deaths, something of us will live on. These are properly "numinous" or, as William James would say, "oceanic" attitudes and emotions. They are central to our intuition of the goodness of the gift of life. Holiness strikes root in this soil. Hannah Arendt takes the symbol of the infant to a high pitch, contrasting the concept of "natality" with inevitable human mortality.

> The miracle that saves the world, the realm of human affairs, from its normal "natural" ruin is ultimately the fact of natality.... It is, in other words, the birth of new men and the new beginning, the action they are capable of by virtue of being born. Only the full experience of this capacity can bestow upon human affairs faith and hope.... It is this

faith in and hope for the world that found perhaps its most glorious and most succinct expression in the few words with which the Gospels announced their "glad tidings": "A child has been born unto us."[50]

A more authentically Jewish example of this symbolism can readily be found. In Solomon's Temple, the innermost sanctum, the Holy of Holies, where God was thought to dwell, contained an image of angelic creatures with human faces, the so-called cherubim. Although these creatures were variously imagined in the Bible, a rabbinic source (b Sukkah 5b), pictures the cherub as a child. This is the likely basis for the Renaissance depiction of cherubim as infants. Another rabbinic source (b Yoma 54a) pictures them as intertwined with one another, as if they were a man and a woman in loving embrace. The point is that rabbinic Judaism uses the human face, the loving embrace, and the image of the young child as symbolic expressions of the highest degree of holiness. The Talmud weaves together the founding of the world—through reference to the foundation stone (*even shetiyah*) from which dry land spread—the Ark containing the Decalogue that stood upon it, and the cherubim atop the Ark, on which God was enthroned. On festivals, the priests would part the curtains of the inner sanctum. The worshippers, who were barred from entering the Holy of Holies, would see the faces of the cherubim in the inner chamber. An image of an innocent human face mediated the presence of God in the holiest space of the Temple to the human world.[51]

The symbols of holiness in the Bible—the Tent of Meeting, the Ark, the cherubim, the priests, the Land of Israel and so on—are, of course, a long way from actual babies. I am not suggesting that we can draw a straight line between the cherishing behavior of humans and other mammals and the *specific* symbols of holiness designated by a highly developed culture such as that of ancient Israel. I am suggesting that the natural experience of care for an object of extraordinary inherent value provides the basis and model for further experiences and instantiations of the holy. In the face of the infant, we meet the mystery of vitality in an otherwise nonliving universe, the goodness of being, and the holy incarnate. Cherishing the infant is the matrix for the basic intercourse of humans with value. This is an intimate experience, scaled to the particular persons involved. It is also, for human beings, a very public one. Having found a basis in personal experience for holiness, we can rejoin Durkheim and Douglas in seeking a social one.[52]

Unlike apes, human mothers cherish their young *in public*, so to speak. Ape mothers are highly protective of their infants and do not want other mothers or younger females to touch them. An ape mother will seclude herself and not let her infant out of her grasp (literally) for at least three months. Although her conspecifics are eager to touch her baby and to help, she will not let them.[53] Strikingly, human mothers share the care of their young with others. Among hunter-gatherers, babies are never left alone; others in the group are always holding, suckling, and caring for them. Human mothers are as hypervigilant as ape mothers but they are not as hyperpossessive.[54] With human thought comes the ability to understand "how beneficial it is for a baby to be introduced to a community of others. By sharing her baby, the mother sends a clear signal that both she and her offspring will be counting on help from the clan. By exposing [others] to the sight, sound, and smell of her alluring little charge, the mother lays the groundwork for emotional ties binding her baby to potential caretakers and vice versa."[55] They trust the good intentions of those around them, overcoming the hypervigilance of their primate ancestors. Indeed, the evolutionary anthropologist Sarah Hrdy traces the emergence of modern humans to this very split in modes of parenting. Our heightened capacity for empathy; sympathy; intersubjective "mind reading" of other's moods, feelings, needs, and thoughts; and the neural architecture that makes them possible may well have been born in sharing the experience of care. The arrival of a newborn into a human group was (and is) an occasion for celebration, for a shared experience of sacred value, of mystery and renewal. Thus, we come to the role of ritual in stabilizing and expressing the holy in culturally salient ways.

If sacred symbols, born in the experience of cherishing, are the *terms* of communication about what is ultimately valuable in the world, ritual is their *syntax*, their orderly, public expression. Ritual involves common action, purpose, and moods—all enabled by shared intentionality. In concert with sacred symbols, rituals express the imagined order of the cosmos, mark its changes and transformations, and locate the place of human beings within it. Symbols map and model the salient features of the ordered world and ground human moral and social behavior. Rituals formalize, dramatize, preserve, as well as innovate the beliefs, if that is not too cognitive a term, of the group that practices them. Rites take place in public, making manifest the implications of what a group cherishes and avows. For Clifford Geertz, religious symbols "dramatized in rituals or related in myths, are felt somehow to sum up . . . the way the world is, the quality of the emotional life it supports, and the way one ought to behave while in it."[56] Ritual fuses feeling, thought, and action; "the moods and motivations which sacred symbols induce in men and the general conceptions of the order of existence which they formulate for men meet and reinforce one another."[57]

The symbols of holiness, such as priests, Temple, Land of Israel, and so on, model a sacred cosmos, as well as give Israel a roadmap for how to navigate such a world. In biblical Israelite thought, holiness enters the world with the divine presence, symbolizing the relation of this world to a higher one. By careful ritualized attention to holiness, God can exist in our world, joining all of his creation-cosmos into an ideal whole. Ritual keeps the world intact; keeps the force of the divine, of pure ontological holiness, in its midst. Rituals, such as sacrifice in the Temple, are ways of acting that "promote the authority of forces deemed to derive from beyond the immediate situation."[58] Biblical ritual channels the force of divine holiness, proclaiming its power, authority, and manifestation in the midst of Israel.

Whence might ritual emerge? From the point of view of a natural history, the shared experience of ritual has prehuman antecedents. One of its sources may well be mammalian play. Play, among both animals and humans, is an activity that no doubt has adaptive value but also seems to function as a good in itself. The purpose of play is the practice of play. The space of play is different from the space of other encounters; it has its own integrity, rules, liberty from hierarchy. Animals, such as dogs, initiate play with a gesture, the "play bow." The dog crouches on its front legs while its back legs remain erect, inviting a partner to play. Play fighting is different from real fighting. Often the play bow will be repeated to signal that "I still want to play" and thus preclude real fighting. Chimpanzees raise an arm to initiate play and may yelp or nip to signal to a partner that play is getting too rough. If the partner doesn't return to the behavior appropriate to play, violating the implicit rules of the game, then play is abandoned and a real fight might break out.[59] Play occurs in its own space and time.

Robert Bellah constitutes play out of shared intention, shared attention, shared norms, and inherent value. Shared intention, as mentioned, manifests in cooperation to play, as opposed to ignoring one another. Shared attention refers to the mutual noticing of the movements and behavior of one's playmate so that one can respond appropriately. Furthermore, play occurs in the presence of norms, both for animals—as when ritualized combat prescinds from lethality and when the engagement ends by a gesture of submission—and for humans. Children make up rules of the game spontaneously. The rules hold only while the game is on, but they are crucial to the conduct of play. Finally, according to Bellah, the main good of play is internal to its practice; it sets up an alternative reality to the everyday.[60] These are characteristic of ritual, as well. Ritual often breaks with ordinary life, occurring in its own (literal or metaphorical) space. Ritual time is also experienced or presented as a break. Special gestures or words initiate ritual action. Formal, traditional patterns govern its procedures. Shared intention, attention, and consent to norms are pervasive. Some of this applies as well to animals. For humans, however, the presence of symbols signifies a break from animal precedents. Ritual, however much it relies on performance, is also a cognitive activity.

Nonetheless, ritual, like play, involves a good deal of "make-believe." Although ritual invites us to think about the meaning of the symbols it employs, to consider the cosmos it models, its cognitive content is not principally propositional. Taking utterances out of ritual modes and exposing them to the harsh light of conceptual analysis might make them wither. Ritual seems part of what Nelson Goodman referred to as "world making." It is akin to, and often employs, art and music. It produces an alternative reality. If ritual, like play, is a good in itself, then one wouldn't criticize it for failing to achieve other goods, such as presenting a scientifically defensible account of the world. The picture of the cosmos that rituals, in their symbolic idiom, express is good enough. This view has some merit. My worry, however, is that unmooring ritual and the symbols it employs from extrinsic standards of accountability makes the holy arbitrary or conventional—a case of pure make-believe. It might also put candidate symbols of holiness beyond the reach of moral assessment. If the justification of a sacred symbol, object, practice, and so on appeals simply to the role it plays in a self-sufficient ritual/game, there will be no room for ethical critique. Ethical critique (as in "No! Child sacrifice is always wrong!") would be foreign to the game at hand and thus a kind of category mistake. If we can't criticize the "science" of ritual, one could argue, why should it be different with its "morality?"

Arguing that ritual produces its own reality and inherent normativity, Catherine Bell comments on "ritual-like" activities such as cherishing and caring for the American flag. Bell claims that "while ritual-like action is thought to be that type of action that best *responds* to the sacred nature of things, in actuality, ritual-like action effectively *creates* the sacred by differentiating such a realm from a profane one." Ritual creates its own world and populates it with its own creatures. Bell admits to circularity here, implying that were a real source of the sacred, in the divine, to exist, then symbol and ritual would have a ground. But she brackets that possibility. Sacredness just comes down to "a quality of specialness, not the same as other things, standing for something important and possessing an extra meaningfulness and the ability to form emotion-filled images and experiences."[61] Sacred symbols, as artifacts of ritual experience, may fill us with emotion and provide heightened experience—but hallucinatory drugs do that, too. Is the alternative reality of play or ritual anything more than escapism? If holiness equates to our cognitive and performative engagement with some set of symbols that are meaningful only in a ritual context and the ritual context is a merely virtual world, then holiness has little to do with the actual world. It is a matter of fantasy or make-believe, a distracting shadow on the wall of Plato's cave. By contrast, we have attempted to relate holiness to *an objective reality of value*—to construe holiness as something to which we *respond* rather than *create* out of whole ontological cloth.[62] The natural history of holiness has given us a genealogy of the birth of the sacred—and its twin, the good. If that reconstruction is plausible, then holiness is rooted in a value to which ritual responds. Ritual does not create that value; it makes it explicit and gives it a cultural, symbolic language. Ritual heightens holiness; it does not originate it.

The argument I have been making requires that at least some value is discovered, rather than invented; found, not made. That human beings create value that did not previously exist, by making works of art, for example, cannot be doubted. But that *all* value is added to the world by human beings and that *none* is discovered by them is, ancient roots in Sophist conventionalism notwithstanding, a modern conviction. It rests on the belief that the world is a matter of brute, insignificant fact and that such significance, or value, as facts have is added to them by human desires and attitudes. There is a bright line between fact and value, so the story goes. The former is a matter of stone-cold truths; the latter is a vaporous cloud of subjectivity.[63] Overcoming this picture will help to support the idea that holiness, in a limited but real sense, is a property that abides in some of the good things of the world.

Holiness, Goodness, and Realism

Premodern Jews had no problem affirming with the Bible that the world, as God's creation, was "very good" (Genesis 1:31). The brute factuality of the world—its objective givenness—was suffused with value. True, existence holds vast reserves of misery, but there was nonetheless something fundamentally good about life. Existence contains suffering, even great tragedy. But life as such is not a tragedy. It is a cause for gratitude and thanksgiving. The goodness of Creation, of human existence, and of God were joined. Moses asks to see God's face and is told that "no man can see my face and live." He is shown God's "goodness" (*tuvi*) instead. God's goodness is as close as humanity can get to God's holiness, God's essential being (Exodus 33:18–19). The Bible knows only one word (*tov*) for the goodness of God and the goodness of Creation. The word is not used equivocally. The Psalmist exhorts us to "taste and see how good [*ki-tov*] the Lord is" (Psalms 34:9), as if goodness were a sensible property. The same formulation—*ki-tov*—is used six times in the Genesis, chapter 1, account to evaluate the stages of Creation. In the end, the entire ordered whole is "very good" (*tov meod*); the "very" (*meod*) is taken by the rabbis to include even death (*mavet*). We shall return to the claim that existence is good, with some help from Maimonides, at the end of this chapter.

That the world in its sheer being is good does not entail that every natural or factual situation is good; indeed, much in the status quo, particularly the human status quo, is not good. But the underlying structure is good. If the biblical scholar Jon Levenson is correct, the majestic declaration of the goodness of Creation that is Genesis, chapter 1, comes after a long existential and literary experience with unstable, less-than-good imaginations of Creation. Other biblical texts reflect the common ancient Near Eastern myth of a theomachy, of warfare among the gods. The winning gods build the cosmos out of the corpses of the vanquished ones. The threat of a return to chaos, of the un-forming of the world, always looms. The calm, unopposed unfolding of Creation in Genesis, chapter 1, represents ancient Israel's overcoming of the terror of chaos. Nonetheless, the lordly sovereign Creator of the priestly story needs human help. The fundamentally good world brought into being in Genesis, chapter 1, needs the work of the cult and Temple to remain fully stable. Underlying goodness needs holy cult and, eventually, holy life for goodness to stabilize, endure, and flourish.[64] (Perhaps Heschel had in mind a version of this biblical motif in his assertion that the Good needs the Holy.)

Seeing the world as fundamentally good because of its dependence on a fundamentally good God sheltered Israelite and Jewish worldviews from corrosive skepticism, conventionalism, and nihilism. This taken-for-granted shelter is denied us, at least those of us who are influenced by modern scientific naturalism. I would argue that it is not ultimately denied us; we can attain a fair approximation of it with sufficient philosophical vision and work. But it is denied us in a taken-for-granted sense. As Christine Korsgaard puts it: "Plato and Aristotle came to believe that value was more real than experienced fact. Indeed, the real world was, in a way, value itself.... [For us] the real is no longer the good. For us, reality is something *hard*, something which resists reason and value, something which is recalcitrant to form."[65] Reality is matter, not form; reality is an impersonal, if lawful, play of objects and forces. There are no divine intentions infusing or guiding the world. Explanation for how it operates must be drawn from within its material and energetic constitution. No great chain of being and value binds the lowest—the inanimate—with the highest—the personal and the divine. Indeed, there is no "lowest" and "highest." In the biosphere, there are only entities, selected by environmental and genetic factors, more or less well adapted to their niches. Ultimately, there is nothing but matter, energy, emergent order and disorder, and (strangely) laws. Value, such as it is, is not found but imposed. Reality is "hard." Human imposition of value on a hard, material world makes human life possible. But that has nothing to do with the world as it is; it has everything to do with a human life-world we create for ourselves within it.

One might live with such a view but at an enormous cognitive cost to the biblical outlook sketched earlier and to subsequent Judaism. Holiness could endure as a make-believe, imaginary order of symbols and rituals that facilitate a common religious life, but that life would be based on nothing other than the conative, prerational survival imperative of a human group—here, the Jews. (Here, once again, is a cause for concern about the idea of ritual and its related symbols as goods that terminate in themselves. That ritual practices have inherent value is correct, but pressed too far, this claim can be an evasion. If sacred rituals and symbols are ultimately about nothing but themselves, about nothing really grounded in the world, then they make no claim on our rational belief.) There is no good reason to believe in holiness or, for that matter, in goodness. Yes, they help human beings to survive. But human survival, premised on (fast retreating) human value, loses its ground. "Why survive?" becomes a live question. For Camus, it was the only serious philosophical question.

Figuring out how to live with the disconnection of value from the natural world, of value from fact, has motivated much modern moral philosophy. Some modern moral philosophers have taken the route of noncognitivism. Value concepts both thin ("good," "right," "virtue," and so on) and thick ("chaste," "gracious," "disdainful," "holy," and so on) hook on to the world only at the level of our attitudes and emotions. They are merely ways of expressing approval and disapproval, the verbal equivalent of shrugs, grunts, or claps and equally irrelevant to matters of truth and falsity. Few ethicists take so reductive and dismissive a view any longer, although the idea that there is a stark dichotomy between factual statements and "value judgments" retains traction. Supposed "value judgments" are then faulted for their subjectivity (as against the presumed objectivity of factual, scientific judgment) or their culture-boundedness. Some ethicists, such as Bernard Williams, do find that a culture's judgments about ethics and values can be true or false, but only *within* the culture or only by observers who could imagine taking on the culture's way of life. From an "absolute" point of view, achievable by a "final physics," statements of value would not belong to the real world. Values are not primary qualities of the universe as it is in itself.[66]

Some of the attempts to push back against this picture of value as imposed by human subjectivity upon a value-free natural world cluster under the philosophical label of "realism." For this family of views, it is wrong to carve up the world into facts, which are allegedly value-neutral, and values, which allegedly express a mind-dependent judgment about the significance, moral and otherwise, of those facts. That tidy picture, for some realists, distorts our epistemic situation, as well as how the world is. In a realist picture, there is at best a porous borderline between fact and value, explanation and evaluation. It is a *distinction* (not a dichotomy) worth making with regard to certain cognitive activities and one worth dropping with respect to others.

The idea that there is a strong dichotomy between facts and values was formulated by Hume. In Hume's view, one can have an idea of an apple, as well as an idea of virtue (or vice). The former idea corresponds to something in the world; the latter is a confection of attitude or "sentiment" that does not correspond to anything definite in the world. Facts are anchored in the world; values are attitudinal glosses on facts. The world is about what "is." What we "ought" to do or be is unrelated to and certainly not justified by what is. That one should not base an inference as to what one ought to do on a fact-situation, on the way the world is, has been called "Hume's law." No "ought" from "is." The fact that smoking causes lung cancer does not, by itself, allow you to infer "don't smoke." You would need other nonfactual premises such as "you ought to do whatever you can to stay healthy," "you ought to preserve your own life," and so on to close the gap between "is" and "ought." These various ought-statements, which Hume believed were covertly smuggled into typical moral arguments and wrongly claimed to possess the firm ground of fact, are not factual at all. They are not warranted or justified by fact, by the way the world is independently of what we want it to be or of how we want it to go. What then warrants them? For Hume, the answer is sentiment, a set of attitudes that all right-thinking (eighteenth-century) people have. There is nothing in the universe as such that dictates "murder is wrong" or "cruelty is evil." Those judgments rest on attitudes specific to our upbringing; moral sentiments have been inculcated in us and, indeed, have a huge role to play in making life tolerable and livable. But there is no absolute ground for the sentiments. Neither divine law or will nor natural law—alleged entities that claim a fact-like status in the universe—underwrite our morality. Sentiment and passion do. As there are no moral facts to be known (such as "cruelty is evil"), there is no moral truth nor is morality in any way other than an instrumental one a rational matter. (That is, reason is and should be subservient to passion and sentiment. Desire fixes on an object; reason figures out the means of satisfying desire.)

Part of what is wrong with Hume's picture, Hilary Putnam points out, is its naïve confidence in the notion of fact. Hume lived in a world where "it was not unreasonable to maintain that there were no scientifically indispensable predicates that refer to entities not observable with the human senses. . . . Indeed, the Humean notion of a 'fact' is simply something of which there can be a sensible 'impression.'"[67] The idea that a fact is a "sensible impression" is no longer tenable in contemporary science. Putnam argues that, at its most penetrating, scientific theory is shaped by value considerations—in this case, by the pressures of "epistemic values" such as coherence, simplicity, preservation of past doctrine, "the beauty of a hypothesis.... Theory selection always presupposes values."[68] We can't get to facts without a framework of theory within which facts acquire their determinative status, nor can we get to theory without value considerations. Furthermore, theories have to be judged on the whole. There is no decisive one on one correspondence between factual statements and the world-as-it-is-in-itself. Theory allows for a whole range of phenomena to be understood, explained, predicted, rationally mapped. But competing theories might do as good a job as a favored one. Deciding among them entails necessary appeals to epistemic values. Nor do we get to choose those values arbitrarily. Our thought already presupposes value dimensions. Fact and value are *entangled* in science, in the very heartland where empiricists thought a cold, hard factual view could prevail.[69]

Epistemic values are both different from and related to moral values. Both guide choice and action. Both seem to well up from we know not where and to be grasped in an intuitive way. Moral values, whether abstract and "thin" or culturally particular and "thick," range over interpersonal conduct in a way that epistemic (or aesthetic) values do not. In Putnam's view, it is mistaken to believe, as Williams does, that there is some absolute conception of the world, to be attained by a final physics that shows the world to be value-free. But it is *also* mistaken to think that there is a metaphysical or an absolute ground for the moral values that are integral to a way of life (for example, the value that equality of persons before the law has for democratic life). "The very idea of explaining how ethical knowledge is possible in "absolute" terms seems to me ridiculous," Putnam writes.[70] So if we want to root the reality of sacred value in an "absolute conception of the world," Putnam will disappoint. There is no absolute conception available; none of us has a God's-eye point of view. What he does illumine for us, however, is the phenomenon of the *unavoidable* entanglement of fact and value. If Putnam's kind of moral realism holds, it is less mysterious how the sheer being of an infant and its simultaneous possession of intrinsic value are possible. Designating that value as "sacred" or "holy" would likely, by Putnam's lights, be expressive of the central role the value plays in a form of life. But the form of life as such has no a priori justifying ground. Nor should it. For him, justification for a way of life does not come in advance. It develops, if at all, through the course of argument on its behalf. And the argument will always be with people who, with respect to their own forms of life, are always in the same boat. There is nowhere else to be. The alternative, to continue the maritime metaphor, is to drown. This is a very chaste view—and by no means unattractive.

An alternative proposal, by Philippa Foot, takes a more sanguine view of the facts served up by nature. She sees those facts as accompanied by "natural normativity."[71] Foot's move is to give "goodness" a naturalistic content. Broadly following Aristotle, she wants to construe the goodness of plants and animals as success in fulfilling the conditions of flourishing particular to the species in question. Talk about good rhododendrons or barn swallows takes into account specific facts about their life cycle, self-maintenance, and reproduction. Judgments about the goodness or defectiveness of individuals are not artifacts of human subjectivity. The species themselves set the terms for success and failure; the norms are natural, "independent of human desires or interests."[72] To *describe* an individual of a species correctly, relative to its species-specific functions, is to *evaluate* it. Or rather (as in Putnam), there is no hard dichotomy between descriptive/explanatory and evaluative language; between fact and value.

Foot's next move is to argue that "good" in the natural context of particular species does not take on new and discontinuous meaning in the human context. How to do that without slipping into the crudity of social Darwinism? Foot does not want to make human goodness coterminous with the simple criteria that define flourishing for subrational creatures. But in keeping with her insistence that goodness is relative to what a particular species needs, human beings need things that other species do not. This makes the human good sui generis, but it does not change the underlying conceptual structure.[73] The crucial move is this: humans "need virtues as bees need stings"—the virtues are as integral to our species and its conditions of flourishing as fleetness is to deer.

> Men and women need to be industrious and tenacious of purpose not only so as to be able to house, clothe, and feed themselves, but also to pursue human ends having to do with love and friendship. They need the ability to form family ties, friendships and special relations with neighbours. They also need codes of conduct. And how could they have all of these things without virtues such as loyalty, fairness, kindness, and in certain circumstances obedience?[74]

There is a thoroughgoing naturalization at work here. We share basic needs with many other animal species, but we have unique needs that we pursue in unique ways. Nothing here need change the basic claim to natural normativity.

What is naturally good is what benefits a species in its specific mode of life. "Good" describes as well an individual animal or plant's success in maintaining and propagating that mode. For human beings, good has added complexity because humans are capable of choice. Goodness relates to the will. A mare that cannot conceive and give birth is a defective horse and in that sense, not good. But a woman might choose not to conceive and bear children even if she is capable biologically of doing so. There is nothing defective about her choice if her will is good. Her choice fits into a plan or project of life in which values are weighed, balanced, and emphasized. Values other than motherhood had weight for her. Her life can be quite good in Foot's naturalistic account. What would make her life bad is if she willed in a bad or vicious way. It is one thing to choose not to have children for some suitable set of reasons; it is another to choose out of spite for one's own parents or spouse. Foot wants to distinguish reasons that are compatible with virtues from reasons that exemplify vices. Because there are natural norms, virtues and vices are not arbitrary or conventional.

I take Putnam and Foot's efforts to show how fact and value are entangled to give some plausible (not, of course, conclusive) philosophical support to a realist understanding of holiness and goodness. Claiming as I do that certain "items" in the world, such as infants and, more generally, human persons, radiate sacred value and call for a fitting response to that value does not require positing queer entities. Nor does it assume some special moral property detector or ethical sixth sense. It requires freeing ourselves from a picture—overcoming an exclusive, binary opposition between fact and value. That picture or binary was bequeathed by positivism. It failed to make sense of our intuitions of value in the world. Let us now focus on those intuitions themselves.

Intuitions of the Good, the Right, and the Holy

Intuitionism, as a modern moral philosophy, is associated with two early twentieth-century British philosophers, G. E. Moore and W. D. Ross.[75] A word about Moore in order to put Ross, who is more important for our purposes, in context: Moore thought that goodness is a simple, unanalyzable, nonnatural property of which we have immediate (intuitive) awareness. The fact that we can question whether any natural candidate for good, such as pleasure, is truly good indicates that no natural good can be identified with goodness straight off.[76] If the good and the pleasant were identical, then saying "pleasure is good" would mean the same as "pleasure is pleasant." Insofar as it does not, Moore argues that goodness is not equivalent to any natural property or state of affairs. The question of what goodness is vis-à-vis natural properties will always remain open. For Moore, goodness is an intrinsic value not to be identified with any natural fact. It exists as a nonnatural fact, so to speak. It is not a Platonic form, subsisting independently in a metaphysical realm and then instantiating in objects or states of affairs. Moore eschews such a metaphysics. Goodness is a real property of things, much as texture is a property of material surfaces.[77] Goodness has its own integrity, simplicity, and irreducibility. Moore is of help to realism but, obviously, not to a naturalistic realism. Nonetheless, the stress on intuition is illuminating.

Moore thought that we had intuitive, noninferential access to the good. He did not, however, think that we have such immediate awareness of the right—of what actions are duties or obligations. Goodness was more basic. Ross disagreed. For Ross, we know what our duties are, at least prima facie, in the same way that we know the axioms of arithmetic or geometry. The intuitive rightness of "promises are to be kept" or "one ought to have gratitude toward benefactors" is "just as much part of the fundamental nature of the universe (and, we may add, of any possible universe in which there were moral agents at all) as is the spatial or numerical structure expressed in the axioms of geometry or arithmetic."[78] For Moore, moral knowledge rests on intuitions of what is good and, for Ross, of what is right and wrong. These intuitions need to be developed in reflection, in careful assessment of our given moral situation or problem, and in judgment; they don't ensure infallibility in any given case. (Indeed, duties often conflict. Competing obligations must be sorted out. We intuit basic moral principles, not individual moral judgments.[79]) To say, as Ross does, that basic duties are self-evident does not mean that they are obvious or indefeasible. It means that there is no more basic justification for a duty such as keeping one's promises than the force of the duty itself. If one were a utilitarian, one would say that promise-keeping contributes more utility to the world than promise-breaking. We keep promises to maximize overall utility. Ross inveighs constantly against such a view. *Genuine duties commend themselves as inherently right—there is no further way of proving them.* The basic claim of intuitionism is that there is no further justification for our moral knowledge than our moral intuitions. Justification stops there.[80]

What are the prima facie duties that Ross takes to be the objects of our moral intuition? There are six rubrics. The first he calls "duties [that] rest on previous acts of my own." There are positive and negative subcategories here. The positive one is "duties of fidelity," such as having made a promise to someone. If one has done so, one has a positive duty to keep one's promise. They also include a negative version. If one has harmed another, one has a duty to make that person whole again. These are called "duties of reparation." The second category is duties that rest on the previous acts of other men. These are called "duties of gratitude." The third and fourth categories have to do with the distribution of benefits to persons based on their deserts (or lack of desert). Ross constructs the first category negatively. Distributing benefits to those who do not deserve them would be an injustice. Preventing an unjust distribution constitutes "duties of justice." The fourth category is positive: benefiting "the other beings in the world whose condition we can make better in terms of virtue or intelligence or of pleasure." These are called "duties of beneficence." Fifth is improving ourselves with respect to virtue and intelligence: "duties of self-improvement." Sixth is the "duty of non-maleficence," the duty not to harm others.[81]

Philosophers argue, rightly, over whether these duties are self-evident, as Ross claims. Self-evident means, roughly, that when one grasps the duty, one grasps its normative force and accepts it as a sufficient reason to perform it. No further argument on its behalf is necessary. Even if this were true, what would this pluralistic set of duties amount to? John Rawls criticizes Ross for giving us "an unconnected heap of duties with no underlying rationale."[82] Intuition doesn't give us any criterion for ranking or weighting them when they conflict. How can appeal to them justify moral conduct if what is really needed is a method for adjudicating between them? A higher-level synthesis would be what has justificatory force rather than an appeal to duty x itself. For this reason, contemporary philosophers who want to salvage the truth in Ross's account try to synthesize his insight into the self-evidence of basic moral principles ("duties") into an ordered whole. What would justify our conduct is not the sheer existence of duty x, as intuited, but the rightness of what we do with it: incorporate it as a reason into our agency, make it a part of our normative project of personhood, test it against the categorical imperative, and so on. The problem, from a realist point of view, is that such moves qualify or even undermine moral realism, shifting the burden of justification from a value-laden fact about the world (duties exist and we apprehend them) to a reflective, constructive process of decision, choice, and action.

Such criticisms have a point, but they should not be allowed to undermine the resources that Ross exposes. The duties that he asserts are fundamental and (with qualifications) self-evident as products of our evolutionary history. When we intuit them and their apparent rightness, we get in touch with traits that nature has imbued in us—with dispositions that have allowed us to survive as a lineage of social primates who depend on and must cooperate with one another. Ross's duties reflect ancient habits of cooperation and coordination already evident in preverbal human toddlers. Moral intuitions are not just primitives posited by armchair philosophers to do justificatory work in meta-ethics, they are signs of our basic human nature as shaped by natural selection and stabilized by culture. We cannot flourish in defiance of them. If we want to flourish in distinctly human ways, we have to consider them and give them proper weight in the rational design of our lives.

In experiments with six- to ten-month-old infants, babies were shown a scenario with geometrically shaped puppets. A puppet was trying to go up an incline. Another puppet came from behind and helped the first puppet to ascend. In another scene, another puppet came from above and hindered the puppet from traveling up the incline. The experimenters then presented the babies with the puppets. "Just about all of the babies reached for the good guy,"[83] the helping puppet. The babies favored the puppet who "acted" on a "duty of benevolence," and shunned the one that violated the duty of nonmaleficence. Babies are able to distinguish nice from naughty and gravitate intuitively toward "nice." Nice is constituted by helpfulness.

Indeed, in an iteration of this experiment, the psychologists devised a scenario in which the babies could choose between rewarding the helpful puppet or punishing the mean, unhelpful one. Babies over five months preferred to punish the mean puppet.[84] They manifested precognitive awareness of the duty of justice; they did not want the mean puppet to receive any benefit. The mean puppet violated the duty of nonmaleficence. Toddlers, by sixteen months, also show a strong bias in favor of equal distribution. In another puppet experiment, ten- and sixteen-month-olds were shown a lion and a bear; each of these puppets had two multicolored disks. The lion gave one disk each to a donkey and a cow. The bear gave both to the donkey. The researchers asked the children "which is the good one?" "Please show me the good one." While the ten-month-olds chose randomly, the sixteen-month-olds chose the fair divider, the one that exemplified the duty of beneficence.[85]

The rudiments of moral consciousness, of normative orientation, thus appear in early childhood. Paul Bloom sums up his findings:

> We have talked so far about certain capacities for judgment and feeling. While perhaps not present in the first few months of life, these capacities are natural in the sense that they are a legacy of our evolutionary history, not cultural inventions. I have described these capacities throughout as *moral*. This is because they share significant properties with what adults view as moral—they are triggered by acts that affect others' well-being; they relate to notions such as fairness; they connect to feelings of empathy and anger; and they are associated with reward and punishment. Also, once toddlers learn enough language to talk about their judgments, they use terms that, for adults, are

explicitly moral, such as *nice, mean, fair*, and *unfair*. What first shows up in looking time and preferential reaching in a baby appears later as the topic of moral discourse in a toddler.[86]

What Bloom terms "judgments and feelings" may be taken as moral intuitions. The evolutionarily deep promptings of our evolved nature form of the content of moral intuition.

Babies may not know the golden rule, but, as Frans de Waal said about the chimpanzees, they sure act as if they do.

Until they don't. Young children, like chimps, can also be selfish and mean-spirited. They can act out angrily. Human children, by age six, show racial bias, showing preference for members of their own race and being willing to ascribe misbehavior more frequently to members of other races.[87] These tendencies, the taproots of xenophobia, are no less inborn than the positive ones. Indeed, as we will explore in the next chapter, aggression is evolutionarily older than love. The presence of a biological basis for vicious as opposed to virtuous action shows how moral intuitionism needs to be buttressed by other theoretical resources (and, more importantly, how moral intuitions need to be ordered by moral reflection and reasoning). Ross has already stacked the deck against negative tendencies by limiting our intuitions to the intuitions of duties, of morally positive performances. Foot, in her own virtue ethics idiom, takes natural normativity and flourishing to exclude vicious will and action; they are held to be inimical to human flourishing. For naturalist realism in general and moral intuitionism in particular to work, there must be a built-in corrective mechanism. If both virtue and vice are equally natural, there needs to be an additional natural factor for why virtue should predominate over vice. The most fruitful naturalist claim, I should think, is that, in line with our gifts of shared intentionality and empathy, the capacity for cooperation and coordination has tremendous survival value. Moral reflection and reasoning need to take that natural fact into consideration and incorporate it into human moral agency and choice. Whenever possible, we should opt for cooperation over domination, alliance over aggression. Of course, aggression, exclusion, and domination have also featured in human survival. But our reflection and reasoning can lead us to the understanding that they don't feature in human *flourishing*. Indeed, the use of them as tactical measures to ensure the survival of one's group reduces the value attaching to that survival. Survival is not the same as flourishing. For the latter to be achieved, moral means are required to contribute to an ethical end, where "ethical end" is an ordered, integrated conception of a good life for both person and community.

The general claims that I have been making are that our primate and human nature predisposes us to morality. Our survival as a lineage was promoted by our ability to feel empathy and sympathy, to cooperate, to manage conflict, to manifest altruistic behavior and attitudes, to share, to police and punish, to bond and protect. There is a continuity in some of these capacities with subrational, nonhuman life. Prerational human infants manifest some of these moral traits, suggesting that the rudiments of morality are "hardwired" rather than entirely learned. I have claimed that our moral intuitions, especially regarding principles and behaviors that have normative, authoritative force, derive from these naturally selected capacities. Nonetheless, our intuitions alone are insufficient to guide us in pursuit of a moral life. Duties conflict, as do goods. There is a gap between principle and application. Negative tendencies, such as aggression, are also basic to our nature. We need ways of ordering and applying, in reflection and judgment, the moral impulses that we feel. We need as well powerful motivations to control our aggressive tendencies and, at the cognitive level, to argue against the invidious beliefs that express and attempt to justify them. We need to bring our desires and beliefs into equilibrium, test them against standards, such as the golden rule or categorical imperative, and formulate them as justifiable reasons for choice and action. In this way, we can get from the moral intuitions embedded in our nature to a fully human morality, which can be rationally articulated and justified.[88]

I have further argued that we are capable of a perception of intrinsic good, of real value that presses upon our consciousness and focuses our sense of obligation. This should strengthen our moral intuitions and check our aggressive drives. We sense the holy in our perception of the intrinsic good of those realities most closely related to human well-being, such as our progeny in their most vulnerable state. We have an intuition of a kind of value, incarnate in real entities, that is noninstrumental, nonutilitarian, and properly basic. It signifies existential value, to use Kateb's term. It is coeval with the good, heightening it and giving it greater normative and cultural salience. Perhaps it is a sign of an infinite good expressed in a finite manner.

The feeling that the finite points to the infinite comes more easily to some than to others. But is the feeling only psychological, a matter of basic disposition or constitution? What is its cognitive status? William James thought that this "oceanic" feeling referenced a mind-independent reality, or at least that it might. He thought that our sense of the sacred had a "noetic quality" that goes beyond strong emotion to reveal and illumine something that has "intense authority" and presence.[89] Rudolf Otto, who wrote of a *sensus numinus*, agreed. Although some tentativeness about the cognitive implications of this feeling are in order, I think that we should honor it and see where the feeling or intuition takes us. To do so is to go beyond the naturalist form of realism that I have been advocating and take a transcendent turn.

There are reasons to do so. The first is that naturalism might well run out. Nature may not be enough. It might fall short of the full explanation of the holy—of our deep sense of the goodness and the holiness of life—that we seek. Even granting my claim that the holy and the good are value properties to which we respond in our experience of the world, we can't quite reach the world as a whole. The Bible's claim that the whole is "very good" will be stuck in a thicket of particulars unless we can find a language appropriate to the whole. We need an external perspective, as it were, on nature. The language of nature as God's Creation provides one, giving us at least a notional view of the whole.

Furthermore, we are finite creatures with finite lives. The microcosmic whole that each one of us is comes to an end. Our own good runs out. If we are not to despair by reason of our mortality, not let our mortality infect our conviction of the good and the holy, we need to believe that there is good beyond our own good. Even if we are not eternal beneficiaries of the good, we need the good to be eternal, to be available for as long as there are beings to avail themselves of it. Perhaps this is more a matter of moral imagination and motivation than metaphysics. But I don't know where one ends and the other begins. If holiness and goodness are not illusions, if they are more than the sports of neuronal synapses, then morals and metaphysics are natural allies. An account that puts nature— that puts you and me—within a larger frame will always be in order.

Second, if we are to treat holiness in Judaism in a way that conforms even roughly with prior Jewish religious sensibility, we are obliged to take a transcendent turn. Holiness, as I had mentioned, is a language game played by theists, and there is no discounting the robust theism of Judaism. Also true of Judaism, as the Bible's sense of holiness as a *project* shows, is that Judaism insists on incorporating holiness into its way of life. Holiness is not just about persons and objects, it is about a comprehensive *way*. Although the Bible presents this way as revealed by a commanding God, we can approach the basic idea by another route. Recall that the natural good, on Foot's account, is a chief factor in our flourishing as the kind of creatures that we are. We need to take the natural good into consideration, to incorporate it as a reason or a system of reasons in the plan of our life. The good supports the virtues. In light of a coherent scheme of virtues, we channel the good toward our own flourishing and the flourishing of all, mitigating our selfishness and allying with a common good. In theistic terms, the virtues are the imitation of God. They grow, with much tending, from the soil of our human nature. Natural goodness and holiness both constrain and enable a virtuous way of life in imitatio dei. The biblical sense of holiness as a *project* can be translated in this way: the real holiness that we discern in some beings, places, and things should be incorporated into a way of life that safeguards and expresses that holiness over its course. I had argued earlier that intuitions of duty and value do not serve as justifications *simpliciter* for moral choice. They need to be taken up as reasons; they play a role in the rational justification of a way of life. The way of life that is Judaism depends on the intuitions of goodness and holiness. But intuitions of goodness and holiness, if their nisus is to be sustained, depend on something akin to Judaism, which is an incomparably rich synthesis of morals and metaphysics, of attunement and action.

Let us then take a transcendent turn from naturalist realism toward a "theological realism" about the good and the holy.

The Holy and the Infinite Good of God

Do values come from God? Do goodness and holiness ultimately derive from the divine? Do we glimpse an infinite source in our finite encounters with the good and the holy? To ask these questions puts us at odds with most modern and contemporary moral philosophy, which is largely secular. Alice Crary notes that a principal complaint against moral realism has been its tendency to introduce a "strange metaphysic."[90] That criticism would apply here. Ordinary secular moral realists need, according to Crary, to claim that values exist objectively and that the mere encounter with these strange beasts provides reasons that prompt us to choose and act in certain ways. The belief that there are properties that are both objective and rational (in a practical sense) is what is metaphysically strange. The world of tables and chairs, colors and sounds, mountains and oceans hardly seems to contain such things. Accordingly, realists, like Crary herself, need to show that there is nothing strange about objective values. What we call values are not some metaphysically "special set of properties" but moves that we make—indeed, that we *must* make—in figuring out how best to live within an "already moralized image of the world."[91] My attempt to foreground goodness and holiness against the background of a natural history was a step in that direction.

Kant said that we are not "volunteers" to morality—that is, we don't get to decide whether to inhabit a moral outlook or not.[92] That is a given for us. Dworkin, in his assault on internal and external moral skepticism, agrees. Our image of the world is, as Crary puts it, already moralized. Our natural languages and the capacities that we acquire for using them well are already bound up with normative evaluation. In this sense, value is objective; objectivity has always to do, for beings like us, with attending to patterns of thought and action *that we cannot do without*. Within this "already moralized" world, we do get to choose how we shall live. We get to—indeed, we must—decide what purposes merit our devotion, whether we shall be loving or cruel, how we shall treat others and ourselves. We are already and ineluctably practical beings who, although not born as blank slates, come into the world with a measure of freedom within which we choose what manner of person we want to become. Crary's concern, shared by other secular realists, such as Thomas Nagel, is to give full support to the reality and objectivity of value without suffering "metaphysical embarrassment."[93] We have seen comparable moves by Putnam and Foot. But to ask our questions about God, the good, and the holy already puts us in an embarrassing place, from the strict secularist point of view. However, as any adult who has ever tried to speak a foreign language in which he or she is not fluent knows, there is no progress without embarrassment. Let us not be impeded by that. Nonetheless, questions remain. Other than fidelity to inherited Judaism, is there any rational pressure on us to go toward transcendence? Is a naturalistic realism as an account of the good and the holy necessarily insufficient?

At least two distinguished philosophers in the analytic tradition have thought that a transcendent turn is necessary— that naturalism does not suffice.[94] Iris Murdoch and Robert Adams claim that we need to speak of the Infinite Good or of Perfection in a robust metaphysical sense. Our search for understanding, especially for an understanding of how we as persons are drawn to knowledge, truth, and love cannot be satisfied by naturalistic accounts alone. Their writ runs short of explanatory adequacy.[95] We cannot underwrite virtue, excellence, moral criticism, or moral imagination on the exclusive basis of naturalism. Nor can we be true to the gravity or bliss of our human experience. These are obviously controversial claims. They are not, however, obviously false or incoherent. Although I will not offer an original argument of my own on behalf of a transcendent turn, I take its continuing appeal to rigorous thinkers to provide at least preliminary evidence for its rationality.

Both Murdoch and Adams bring a Platonic sensibility to their metaphysics and ethics. For Murdoch, "the serious attempt to look compassionately at human things . . . automatically suggests that 'there is more than this.' The 'there is more than this,' if it is not to be corrupted by some sort of quasi-theological finality, must remain a very tiny spark of insight, something with, as it were, a metaphysical position but no metaphysical form."[96] Murdoch is both tentative and convinced. For Murdoch, the window onto the "more than this" is art, and also morality. "The background to morals is properly some sort of mysticism, if by this is meant a nondogmatic essentially unformulated faith in the reality of the Good, occasionally connected with experience."[97] Murdoch is wary of the traditional God of Western theism; she is wary of the false "finality" that theology brings. But she is warier of the depletion of ethics and the diminution of human experience that results from banishing "the contemplation of the Good." There is a mystic undercurrent to her call to "look right away from self towards a distant transcendent perfection, a source of uncontaminated energy, a source of *new* and quite undreamt-of virtue."[98] The ideas of "source" and "energy" are redolent of biblical conceptions of divine presence and *kedushah*, as a force or power. Although she does not use the word "holy," it is clear that her idea of a perfect, indefinable Good would exclude negative traits. It could not license violence. Murdoch does not think that we can get to the Good in an anti-metaphysical way, and get to the Good we must. For "we are spiritual creatures attracted by excellence and made for the Good."99

Adams is an explicitly Christian philosopher, who unlike Murdoch identifies the Good with God. Like Murdoch, Adams finds intimations of the Good in our finite, local experience. Thus, "the experience I am describing [of beauty] is at least close kin to that which leads people to speak of 'seeing the glory of God' in a beautiful sunset. The glory of God here is the wonderful though fragmentary visibility of something vastly more valuable than other things, something too good for us to have more than a dim and imperfect apprehension of it. To a theism that identifies the Good itself with God, this sort of transcendence of the Good will be of utmost importance."100 The finite goods of experience are "organized around a transcendent Good.... The Good is transcendent in the sense that it vastly surpasses all other good things, and all of our conceptions of the good. They are profoundly imperfect in comparison with the Good itself."101 The Good thereby outstrips any conception that we can form of it. (Note the trace of Moore here.) Its independence from our thought warrants a "metaphysical realism" toward it. It has its own kind and level of existence about which we will always know little.

Adams uses "the Holy" to designate this metaphysically "alien" aspect of the Good. "We are not likely to be wholly comfortable with the Good itself.... It is not merely an extension and refinement of familiar values." But, if so, how can we say anything about the Good at all? Adams resists the common approach of a *via negativa*—that is, the claim that the Good (or God) is free of defect. He wants to say something positive. "The divine knowledge, love, beauty are not just free from defects we can identify; they contain a richness we can hardly name. To us this richness is bound to be alien in ways we may find uncomfortable." That alien, discomfort-causing aspect of

God and the Good he calls, rather echoing Otto, the Holy. "From a human point of view, the Holy has rough edges. It screams with the hawk and laughs with the hyenas. We cannot comprehend it. It is fearful to us, and in some ways dangerous. All of this, on the theistic view that I favor, is true of the Good itself. We are not the measure of all things and have at best a very imperfect appreciation of the full dimensions of the good."[102] The holiness of the Good makes for a breach between what we might ordinarily consider good and what is truly good.

Is it possible then, on Adams's account, for things we would ordinarily consider to be bad—such as gratuitous violence, injustice, disrespect, abuse, or violation—to count as good in God's (incomprehensibly transcendent) sight? That would seem compatible with what the "alien" aspect of holiness would allow. Adams equivocates somewhat on this point. Analyzing Abraham's near sacrifice of Isaac as a paradigm case, he endorses Kant's view as "substantially correct." Kant held that "Abraham should have replied to this supposedly divine voice: 'That I ought not to kill my good son is quite certain. But that you, this apparition, are God—of that I am not certain, and never can be, not even if this voice rings down to me from (visible) heaven.'"[103] On the other hand, Adams does not want Kant to have the last word. Simply to defer to Kant's Moral Law would make religion "safer than it is." But it would also be "less interesting and less rich as a resource for moral and spiritual growth, if it did not hold the potentiality for profound challenges to current moral opinion." Most pointedly:

> Religion's connection with the transcendent would be threatened if it could not command costly sacrifices for distinctly religious reasons, or if one's acts of faith and devotion could not be allowed to be costly in any way to anyone besides oneself. If we believe in divine commands at

all, we should not want to hold that they could never be surprising.[104]

Adams evaluates God's command to Abraham within its cultural context, where sacrifice of the firstborn child was thought exemplary. He finds moral virtue in the spirit of sacrifice, in the obedience that it demonstrates. Nonetheless, the cultural and religious meaning of child sacrifice is wholly undercut by "ethical reflections that we can hardly reject."[105] We ought not to picture God as one who would make such demands. Adams believes that it is "unimaginable" that a good God has given "such an abhorrent command." We ought therefore to dismiss any thought of God commanding such a thing as human sacrifice. The holy may sometimes be uncanny, but it should not give occasion for moral horror.

The identity of the good with God seems to preclude that manifestly bad practices, such as religiously ordained murder, could legitimately be the will of God. Significantly, although he sides with Kant on the Akedah, Adams *does* endorse the decision by Jewish martyrs during the Crusades to slay their families and themselves rather than suffer apostasy. He judges that kind of religiously motivated sacrifice, derived from the martyr's own conscience, as exemplary of holiness—that is, of the way that holiness exceeds conventional goodness. The martyrs had a stark choice: death at their own hands or being forced to betray their "sacred convictions," which would be worse. God did not command them, unlike Abraham, to slay their sons. They undertook that freely, albeit under unspeakable duress. He finds, as does the Jewish tradition that preserved the chronicles, heroic religious virtue in these tragic acts. (Indeed, if the Akedah has any redemptive meaning, it is as an example for Jews *in extremis* to make of their deaths something that affirms the strength of their faith.) Their behavior qualifies as holy, as an example of a saintliness that is more and other than intensified conventional goodness. Adams disallows that the true, good God could have asked for Isaac's murder. The God who is infinitely good could not command such a thing. That approach raises obvious interpretative problems as to how to assess the status of Genesis, chapter 22. But the Jewish reader has a more pressing problem. Whatever he or she thinks of the Akedah, a site of endless exegetical struggle and creativity, God *has* given commandments, as the tradition depicts it, that are no less challenging to moral sensitivity than the one to sacrifice Isaac. And unlike that pre-Sinaitic, private commandment to Abraham, the commandments to obliterate, for example, the seven Canaanite nations (Deuteronomy 20:16) or destroy the descendants of Amalek (Deuteronomy 25:19) are public, collective, and, at least in the latter case, enduring. These are essentially commandments to commit genocide against a group of disfavored nations for divinely mandated reasons. Adams, a Protestant Christian philosopher who endorses a view of moral obligations as divine commandments, can take "commandment" in a rather open way. But Jews must take "commandment" in the sense of mitzvah: highly specific directives given in the Pentateuch and interpreted by the rabbis, whose exegeses are accepted by the tradition as necessary and authoritative. Unlike the directive to take Isaac to Mount Moriah and offer him as a sacrifice, the mitzvot bind every Jew. Although there are no more Canaanites left to exterminate, the commandment doesn't quite lose its normative magnetic pull. It remains part of the covenant. This is even more true of the commandment to blot out the memory of Amalek. Jews have identified various implacable enemies over time as spiritual descendants of Amalek and have taken that identity to justify extreme measures, where possible, against them.[106] Adams, presumably, does not need to face this problem. His equation of God with the good, even as it makes room for the "alien" goodness of the holy, has a philosophical serenity about it that cannot fully characterize a ground-level, biblical/Jewish ethics.

Yet it would rub against the grain of Jewish thought to describe God as other than wholly good. Moses sought to know God's ways (Exodus 33:13). He also sought to encounter God's direct presence (*kavod*) (Exodus 33:18). To his second request, God replied that no man could see his "face" and live. As a substitute for his presence, God made his "goodness" pass before Moses. The biblical text itself glosses God's goodness as constituted by moral qualities:

> The LORD! the LORD! A God compassionate and gracious, slow to anger, abounding in kindness and faithfulness, extending kindness to the thousandth generation, forgiving iniquity, transgression, and sin; yet He does not remit all punishment, but visits the iniquity of parents upon children and children's children, upon the third and fourth generations (Exodus 34:6–7).

These qualities are mostly if not entirely positive. It is true that God does not always forgive and can hold children responsible for the sins of their parents. (The rabbis, hastening to correct the appearance of collective, intergenerational punishment, interpret the punishment as a just desert; if [and only if] the children continue to act as the parents did, then they will merit comparable punishment [b Berakhot 7a].) The key point is that punishment is presented as a *desert*, as an instance of justice warranted by a morally intelligible reason. God's ways, in the text's view, are merciful and just. They are coherent with a conception of a wholly good God.[107]

In Exodus, God substitutes his goodness (*tuv*) for his presence, face, or "glory," as *kavod* is sometimes translated. That substitution is made for the sake of Moses—that is, as a concession to human epistemic and existential frailty. The goodness of God is intelligible. Nonetheless, one could still ask, does the divine presence, in its utter transcendence, retain the potential for action that is not, in any straightforward sense, good? Is the identity of God and the good total or partial, provisional or permanent? Does God elide his being into goodness or do these remain, at least from a human point of view, notionally separate? At the level of the biblical text, *tuv* and *kavod*, goodness and presence, seem to remain distinct concepts. At a more philosophical level, the concepts are functionally equivalent. In my reading, that is Maimonides's view. There are reasons why it should be our view as well.

Maimonides practices the kind of "negative theology" that Adams eschews. Given the absolute gulf between God and all of Creation, humans included, nothing in our world refers to God. Nothing that one can predicate of entities familiar to us—from "red" or "hard" to "wise" or "loving"—can properly be predicated of God. Accordingly, when the Bible states that God is just or wise or compassionate or angry, we must not take these terms as properly descriptive of the divine being. We must take them, first, in a negative sense: God is not unjust or unwise. That is, God is free from defect. We must also take them in a highly restricted positive sense: God's *actions* are (what we understand to be) just or wise. Descriptive terms never apply to God as such; they apply to what we take to be actions flowing from him. God as an entity, if this term is even allowable, is unknowable and beyond characterization. What can be known and characterized are God's actions. Accordingly, when Moses asks to see God's presence, he asks to transgress an epistemic limit based on an ontological fact: God cannot be known because of the absolute difference between God and the world—that is, the sum of all those things that our minds are fit to know. Maimonides is a radically apophatic thinker. Nonetheless, Maimonides does think that Moses's request to encounter God's presence was granted. How so?

In revealing his goodness to Moses, God reveals his actions. Actions characterized as merciful or gracious, and so on, do not derive from God's putative psychological or affective states. It is not correct to say that "God is merciful" or "God is angry" at time *t* or at any time. God is impassible and simple; he has no emotions or parts. Nor is he in time at all. Any attributes that one would ascribe to God are "attributes of action"— that is, they are properly ascribed to what we take to be actions coming from God, not to their source. In this sense, then, it is a category mistake to claim that God is good. "Goodness" is an attribute of action, not of being. God's "essence" is beyond predication, including the predicate "good."

Maimonides thus takes God's revealed goodness (*tuv*) to be a response to Moses's request to understand God's "ways." But he *also* takes it to be a fitting response to Moses's request to encounter God's presence (*kavod*). He links God's *tuv*, with the "very good" (*tov meod*) of the consummated Creation (Genesis 1:31). *What it is to encounter God's presence, in Maimonides's highly intellectualist view, is to grasp the full goodness of Creation.*

> This dictum—*All my goodness*—alludes to the display to him of all existing things of which it is said: *And God saw everything that He had made, and, behold, it was very good.* By their display, I mean that he will apprehend their nature and the way they are mutually connected so that he will know how He governs them in general and in detail.[108]

The glory of God, insofar as human beings can encounter it, is a cognition. It is the cognition of the natural whole, of the universe in general and in detail. It is a deep, truthful understanding of the laws of nature, of nature's structure and internal relations. Maimonides is not a pantheist. He is not saying that to comprehend the structure and function of the cosmos is to comprehend the divine. That would contradict his entire outlook. He is saying that to understand the universe in a scientific way is to appreciate God's creation and governance of it. That intellectual appreciation and achievement is as close as we can get to knowing God. It doesn't leave the realm of discerning and describing God's actions; we cannot get to God as he is *in se*. But through achieving a cognition of the whole, we reach the outermost limit of human knowledge. We reach the edge, beyond which is the unseeable face of God, as it were.

This cognition is good; it is a cognition of goodness. Goodness consists of the governance and order of the natural whole. The whole qua cosmos has the property of being good. God perceived it as such (Genesis 1:31), and so can we, if we conceive of it rightly. This beatific metaphysical vision has consequences for Maimonides's ethics. After all, God's "attributes of action" are meant to be emulated by human beings. Maimonides would have us emulate God's graciousness and kindness in bringing life into being. Beings have no claim to be created. God acts with unmerited generosity. He acts with kindness, as he fits embryos with the developmental capacities that will allow them potentially to flourish. We call God "gracious" and "kind," but we are really remarking on natural processes that we ascribe, in an ultimate causal sense, to God. It is also the case that nature is dangerous. There are floods, storms, earthquakes; there are humanly caused catastrophes such as wars and genocides. We ascribe those to God, too, although the same philosophical distancing must obtain. God is the ultimate, ineluctably mysterious cause of causes. We ought not to say that God is angry or cruel, if some great tragedy befalls us. Rather, the actions that we ultimately trace to him have that characterization.

The upshot of this for ethics is that when the governor of a city, whose legitimate rule should emulate God's rule of the universe, needs to reward or punish a subject, he should do so without emotion. His administration of law should be based on giving persons their just deserts. If someone deserves death, the Maimonidean ruler should not show or feel anger or hatred toward that person; he should be passionless in imitation of divine impassibility. True justice in the city should have the same quality as justice in the cosmos. The whole balances and integrates the parts.

Although Maimonides wants to characterize both divine and (ideal) human justice as a desert-based affair with respect to individuals, his metaphysical perspective draws him to consider the state of the whole. In this context, he brings up the commandment to exterminate the seven Canaanite nations—to leave no man, women, or child of them alive (Deuteronomy 20:16, 18). The commandment to holy war cannot be based on a principle of individual desert. The killing of children cannot by definition be so justified (if it can be justified at all, which I doubt). Maimonides seems to sideline his desert-based criterion and move to a consequentialist one: the elimination of idolaters, of those who hate God, will improve the prospects for other human beings to reach perfection. The Torah ordains in this case that "everyone who deviates from the ways of truth should be put an end to and that all obstacles impeding the achievement of the perfection that is the apprehension of Him, may He be exalted, should be interdicted."[109] The suspension of a principle of individual desert as an essential element of justice in favor of a consequentialist principle is horrifying. From our point of view, no supposed good should ever be thought to justify mass slaughter. It is unclear whether Maimonides himself really believed this.[110] Nonetheless, it reveals the tensions between the holy and the good, even in an account such as Maimonides's in which the good is given a large and leading role.

Maimonides, Murdoch, and Adams share a Platonic sensibility. I do not, but I have tried to learn from each of them. I take from Murdoch that our full engagement as human persons with art and morality inspires us to believe in a transcendent Good. We can't easily dismiss or deride the initial feeling or the tentative belief. Neither should we rush to give it finality and solidity. I take from Adams that the good and the holy are entangled with each other—that sorting them, such that the holy has alien dimensions, is tempting but fraught. Adams himself, no less than Otto, has trouble sustaining that move. That leads back to the coeval nature of the good and the holy. Our encounter with them is simultaneous, although they develop in related but distinct ways. For both of these thinkers, the naturalist realism that I have advocated bears little weight. Unlike them, I think that naturalism and the theism of rational mysticism or contemplative piety can hold together; we should let the naturalist story take us as far as it can.

I find that harmonizing, integrating strategy descriptive of Maimonides. What I take from Maimonides is the view that the cosmos per se radiates goodness. We identify that goodness and take its true measure through disciplined inquiry and the attainment of knowledge. The perfection of knowledge is impossible but its pursuit is imperative. We get flashes of truth that we must labor to articulate and integrate. We cannot know God, but we can believe that our intuitions of value are pointers toward an unknowable source that, all things considered, acts for the good. We need to attain a perspective of contemplative piety, by the light of which the "rough edges" of the holy are smoothed through consideration of the goodness of the whole. A vision of the good may induce equanimity, even moments of bliss, but it should not induce resignation or fatalism. That natural catastrophes and human tragedies occur should not lead to a Stoic withdrawal from the activism and agency that might mitigate or prevent them. Acceptance of the goodness of Creation must not be a surrender to the status quo, for nature itself is dynamic.

It seems natural to us to want to go beyond nature. There are eminent mathematicians who believe that mathematics cannot be explained without positing a supernatural reality of mathematical entities. Mathematical thinking is noetic exploration of a supersensible world. There are Platonizing arguments to the effect that beauty is not in the eye of the beholder; it subsists in its own right.[111] We have seen similar claims on behalf of value. In general, Kant's cautions about such claims seem well-taken to me. The most secure provinces of our knowledge will be those that have some empirical warrant, some testing procedures, some means of falsifying claims ready at hand. But we should add to these our intuitions of value, our sense of our own reality as persons, and the irreducible nature of thought. For Kant, these cannot quite lead us over a notional bridge from human sense-making into genuine transcendence. (Transcendence will play a relative not an absolute role for us. That is, we can always imagine conditions or causes on account of which some feature of the world is the way it is. Those conditions transcend the current state of affairs; they are transcendent relative to the given feature. We can even imagine the totality of conditions or causes such that the whole must itself be unconditioned. Kant would urge us to see this as the way pure, unfettered reason works. It would not, however, disclose to reason anything about the way the world ultimately is, as if from an absolute point of view.) That leaves room, Kant thought, for faith.

Faith here would not mean belief in entities in the absence of evidence—far from it. I take it to mean confidence in the goodness of being, trust in the rightness of justice and peace, hope for the transience of violence and injustice. And these not as spurts of emotion or wishful thinking but as rightly formed responses to the realities of the human condition, in its wretchedness and its glory. Such faith entails that what confronts us as holy in the world, if it is compatible with our best understanding of the good, merits that we cherish and protect it. The holiness of at least some things thought sacred is real. It is as close to God as we get.

CHAPTER THREE

Holiness and Violence

AGGRESSION IS OLDER than love. The inclination to fight with other conspecifics or with members of other species is evolutionarily older than the inclination to cherish. "Equipped with the aggressive impulse alone," Eibl-Eibesfeldt writes, "we should not have advanced beyond the level of reptiles." When we fight, we enact something that goes back to the dawn of animal life. When we inhibit our aggression, and seek peaceful means of pursuing our ends, we realize a capability that came about much more recently but that is no less fundamental to our evolved human nature. Indeed, the astonishing development of human culture, which allowed human beings to become the dominant species on earth, Eibl-Eibesfeldt claims, is based on "cooperation and mutual assistance."[1] Were we not able to control our propensity for violence and substitute more pacific strategies for realizing our purposes, we would not have flourished in even a basic, biological way.

Cooperation and mutual assistance are (sometimes tenuous) human achievements, but we are far from alone in our ability to achieve them. All social species have elaborate ways of working together. Their survival is keyed to their ability to coordinate, cooperate, and share. From bees to wolves, social animals live in bonded groups with elaborate rituals and rules to govern their common life. A long evolutionary backstory informs human sociality and its constitutive virtues. Aristotle, who famously called humans social (or more precisely, *political*) animals, noticed both the continuity and the rupture. He asked what differentiated human beings from other, social species. He found the answer in speech. While other social animals may make sounds to signal one another, only humans can speak with one another about good and evil, the just and the unjust. Human beings get to choose their political constitution; they get to reason about what forms of social life best contribute to their flourishing. Most of all, they get (or fail) to achieve justice. Human beings without justice and good political order are the most "unholy and savage of animals." But when brought together in a well-functioning, political society, they are the "best of animals."² Speech and thought that lead to a just polity can secure one of the main conditions for human flourishing.

Aristotle alerts us to what distinguishes humanity. Other animals, including our close evolutionary cousins, the chimpanzees, live and work together. Chimpanzees have complex emotional lives, political alliances within their groups, friends and enemies. They have common purposes that they pursue in a coordinated fashion. They share tasks, help one another, offer emotional support. They fight and make up. They cherish their young. They can even show affection to members of other species, as when, de Waal reports, a captive chimp protected a bird with a damaged wing that had fallen into its enclosure and helped it to fly away.³ But of course there is a dark side to the solidarity of group life among chimps (and humans). Their empathy stops at the border of their own group. Beginning in the 1970s, field researchers observed how chimpanzee groups in the wild can attack other groups to the point of annihilating them. Part of their motivation, if that is not too anthropomorphic a word, was the expansion of their territory. Chimps from one group formed a raiding party, made incursions into the territory of a neighboring group, and brutally assaulted isolated members of the other group until, after multiple raids, the other group collapsed. The old idea that human beings were more beastly than other animals because only they made war and killed members of their own kind turned out to be false. Wild chimpanzees have genocide on their minds, so to speak, when it comes to other groups of chimpanzees, even if the groups had separated into two in the recent past.[4]

One distinction of humanity then is the ability to rise above an instinctual hostility toward members of other groups and to inhibit aggression. But on what basis? The human capacities for thought and speech can take us part of the way. They can lead us to discover the significant similarities between "us and them." There are innumerable reasons that can defeat this intellectual ascent—some of them credible, most not. But if we allow ourselves this cognitive and imaginative ascent, we can rise to a picture of the world in which we as individuals (and our group as a group) are not at the center. If we can imagine the world from a point of view that includes ourselves but is not limited to ourselves, then we can include others as significantly like ourselves.[5] When our moral imaginations are not entirely entrapped by our own or our group's self-interest, we can attain the possibility of empathizing with as yet unknown others. We can see us and them as if from a neutral perspective. Of course, when we realize that others are significantly like us, we might yet find reasons—sometimes good reasons—to fear them. They might after all really be a cruel and implacable enemy intent on killing us. But we can't quite efface our knowledge that they too are persons. They too came into the world in pristine innocence, sacred in their natality. If in the course of their lives they desecrated their personhood through evil deeds, we can still recognize that they were once persons but are now reduced in moral stature. (Jewish tradition refers to this as "diminishing" or "annulling" the image of God within oneself [Tosefta Yevamot 8:4].[6]) Their personhood deserves respect, albeit sympathy for them will be beyond our emotional repertoire. Kant, who defended the death penalty, thought of just punishment, even in extremis, as the legal mode by which we express *respect* for personhood.[7] We give war criminals trials when we can; we don't just throw them to the lions.

Unlike apes driven by a territorial imperative to expand their range, human beings can summon what the British philosopher Jonathan Glover calls "the moral resources" of sympathy and respect for others outside their group. It is not easy to do, particularly when groups are trapped in cultural traditions of suspicion and hostility toward one another or are in an active state of war. A famous example of summoning these moral resources comes from the front lines of World War I. On Christmas 1914, German and British soldiers emerged from their trenches and exchanged "cigarettes, schnapps, and chocolate with the enemy." A Scottish soldier produced a soccer ball and the two sides played a game. The Germans, upon discovering that the Scots wore no underwear beneath their kilts, burst into laughter. The game continued until the officers put a stop to it. At another place along the front, the Germans invited the British to share a Christmas meal with them. A participant reported the shared sentiment: "We don't want to kill you and you don't want to kill us, so why shoot?"[8] The officers on both sides worked hard to prevent these occasions of fraternization. There were instances of soldiers communicating apologies to the other side for having to follow orders and shoot at them.[9]

Viewing the enemy as a human being similar to oneself, equally caught up in world-historical events over which ordinary individuals have no control, broke through the moral sclerosis of war. A tacit form of cooperation took hold, a kind of prisoner's dilemma choice to work together to maintain an informal truce rather than relentlessly pursue self-interest. As brutal and inhuman as human beings can be, we are also beings capable of disgust at our brutality and inhumanity.[10] Intuitions of moral value, especially the sense that human life as such is precious, fuel that disgust. The intuition that life is sacred gives rise to the demand that it not be desecrated. When the other is viewed as an agent of desecration, however, our moral compass shifts. We want to be allied with the sacred. We believe that it is our sacred duty to eliminate the impure other and stop the desecration of what we know is holy.

The preparation for war, ethnic cleansing, or genocide— as well as sustaining their actual conduct—often involves the portrayal of the enemy as impure and unholy. An extreme tribalism is generated when one side sees itself as on God's side and the other side is seen as hated by God. The Nazi effort to marginalize, degrade, dehumanize (and eventually destroy) the Jews is too well known to require exposition here. But other, lesser known and more "ordinary" instances can serve to illustrate the tragic ubiquity of the practice.[11] The Puritans of New England likened the Indians to "Amalek annoying this Israel in the wilderness." God's proclamation of continuous total war against Amalek (Deuteronomy 25:19) gave the Puritans, as a self-styled biblical people, an imagined license to attempt the extermination of the Native Americans. Myles Standish "rounded up the Indians into their villages and set fire to the whole." A Puritan preacher, Herbert Gibbs, thankfully recalled "the mercies of God in extirpating the enemies of Israel in Canaan" in reference to subduing the Indians.[12]

Closer to our time, at the onset of World War I, the poet laureate of Britain Robert Bridges wrote: "I hope that our people will see that it is primarily a holy war. It is manifestly a war between Christ and the Devil. . . . There was never anything in the world worthier of extermination, and it is the plain duty of civilised nations to unite to drive it back into its home and exterminate it there." The precise referent of "it" was left vague by Bridges, as was the exact meaning of "exterminate." That he meant to dehumanize the Germans, however, is indubitable. A member of Parliament (soon to be indicted for fraud, as it turned out) called on his countrymen to reject the legitimacy of naturalized German fellow citizens. "You can't 'naturalize' an unnatural abortion, a hellish freak. But you can exterminate him."[13]

During World War II, the Japanese gained motivation from their belief that they were "the sole superior race in the world," the racially pure descendants of the gods. A nationalist publication urged its readers to "beat and kill these animals [the Americans] who have lost their human nature! That is the great mission that Heaven has given to the Yamato race for the eternal peace of the world." For "the more [Americans] are sent to hell, the *cleaner* the world will be."[14] On the Allied side, the Japanese were referred to as "beastly little monkeys," "subhuman beasts," "a cross between the human being and the ape." The journalist Ernie Pyle, who as a war correspondent was killed in a Japanese attack, wrote: "Out here I soon gathered that the Japanese were looked upon as something subhuman and repulsive; the way some people feel about cockroaches or mice." Observing Japanese prisoners, he remarked: "They were wrestling and laughing and talking *just like normal human beings* and yet they gave me the creeps. I wanted a mental bath after looking at them."[15] Similar characterizations may be found in the former Yugoslavia or Rwanda. A Croatian newspaper described Serbs as "beasts in human form," "bearded animals on two legs," and "bloodsuckers."[16] Where rhetorical dehumanization begins, a total loss of moral perspective may follow.

Some authors have laid the blame for this syndrome at the feet of biblical monotheism. The proclamation of one God, it is alleged, engenders an immediate sense of superiority and militant intolerance. Additionally, the concepts of holy and profane, pure and impure, when applied to the people of the one God and, in the negative, to their enemies, are morally toxic. Thus, the Harvard sociologist Barrington Moore Jr. writes, "[T]he invention of monotheism by ancient Hebrew religious authorities was a cruel, world-shaking event. It had to be cruel in the general sense that any group identity is liable to be formed in hostile competition with other groups." Despite Jesus's mitigating the harshness of "ancient Hebrew vindictive intolerance," Christianity "amplified it and institutionalized it." And so there is a stream of influence, according to Moore, from biblical conceptions of one God, one holy people, holy land, and holy war to twentieth-century totalitarianism. In prose as colorful as it is nasty, Moore opines:

> The long route from the ancient Hebrews to Stalinism was a river of social causation fed by many different streams and dropping floating debris all along the way. Yet despite all the twisting and turning and historical debris, the river has a clear identity and an obvious ending point (or way station?) in twentieth century totalitarian regimes. Without this long line of causation providing a readily available model of vicious behavior, it is very hard to see how these regimes could have come about. The monotheistic tradition by this time was hardly the most important cause of

Nazism and Stalinism. But it was, I suggest, an indispensable one.[17]

This is perhaps the ultimate case of blaming the victim. The Jews, in Moore's account, are responsible for Nazi totalitarianism by having brought biblical faith into the world.

Regina Schwartz espouses a kindred view. She takes monotheism to be based on a gratuitous "principle of scarcity," which incurs a heavy cost in violence:

> When everything is in short supply, it must all be competed for—land, prosperity, power, favor, even identity itself. In many biblical narratives, the one God is not imagined as infinitely giving but as strangely withholding. Everyone does not receive divine blessings. Some are cursed—with dearth and with death—as though there were a cosmic shortage of prosperity.... Scarcity is encoded as a principle of Oneness (one land, one people, one nation) and in monotheistic thinking (one Deity), it becomes a demand of exclusive allegiance that threatens with the violence of exclusion. When that thinking is translated into secular formations about peoples, "one nation under God" becomes less comforting than threatening.[18]

Schwartz sees in the identity formation of biblical Israel the source of virulent modern nationalism, a secularized extension of the culturally salient biblical narrative. Identity formed by allegiance with one exclusive God monopolizes blessing, loyalty, and worth; the Other is deprived of all of those and demonized. The promise of land and the violence of its conquest model an ongoing history of victimization. Israelite liberation from Egypt soon elides into Israelite genocide in Canaan. For Schwartz, God and Israel—the "myths" of monotheism, nationhood, and promised land—lock the West into a trap of violence of astonishing duration and perniciousness. The very notion of identity based on a relationship with God is lethal. Slightly less dismissive than Moore, however, she sees countervailing tendencies toward polytheism, pluralism, and "plentitude" in the Bible that could be nurtured to offset the dominant thrust.

Finding the unholy in the Holy Scriptures has been a live option at least since the second-century Christian heretic Marcion, who thought the Scriptures to constitute the story of a lesser god. He believed that the nascent Church should repudiate what became its Old Testament. Modern critics, such as Moore, Schwartz, Avalos, Girard, and many others, are right to be troubled by the violence enshrined in the text. It is morally jarring, radically discordant with our contemporary convictions about the worth of human life, the conduct of war, and the role of violence in human affairs more generally. Nonetheless, there is a tendentiousness to their work that is troubling. The problem for these critics is not that biblical thought can be open to abuse. The problem is that biblical thought per se is rotten. The very idea of the God of Abraham, Isaac, and Jacob has totalitarian implications. The holy leads necessarily to unholy consequences. The demand of ethics is to repudiate God and all his works. Morality requires the banishment of the holy from our cultural and conceptual vocabulary. By contrast, I want here to defend the holy and to ally it with ethics. But I also want to purge holiness of violence. Let us explore the possibility of affirming the holy without invidious consequences.

Biblical Violence

Biblical scholars often push back against such critics by pointing to the fantastical nature of the conquest narratives. Both internal (textual) and external (archaeological) evidence tell against a straightforward endorsement of the historicity of the tale of total war told in the Book of Joshua. Although Joshua, chapters 1–10, presents a picture of divinely led Israelite conquest, completely subjugating the Land of Israel and destroying all of its pagan inhabitants, as well as their livestock and possessions, the reality was likely much more partial. The archaeological evidence does not support the kind of total destruction envisioned by Joshua.[19] The Bible itself preserves multiple instances, especially in the Book of Judges, when Israel lived alongside the Canaanites, gradually gaining the upper hand. The "conquest" was likely a later invention, retrojected, perhaps by an already exiled Israel, onto the early period. The reality of Israelite settlement was likely one of gradual penetration, intermarriage, and assimilation. In this view, the shocking calls to total extermination of the aboriginal inhabitants of Canaan in Deuteronomy 7:1–2 and Deuteronomy 20 are indictments of Israel's contemporary situation of infidelity to God. Destruction of the Canaanites is a literary symbol for uprooting lingering pagan practices in a not yet fully monotheistic Israel. The imagined enemy without becomes a metaphor for the enemy within, the "uncircumcised hearts" of biblical folk.[20]

The earlier biblical material, such as Exodus 23:27–30, envisions a gradual displacement of the Canaanites—and this by divine, nonviolent means. Not only do many Canaanites remain (see, for example, Judges, chapter 3), some of them, such as Rahab, marry into Israel and become progenitors of biblical leaders, such as the prophet Jeremiah, according to rabbinic interpretation. The rabbis believed that Rahab became Joshua's wife.[21] Uriah the Hittite, a member of one of the nations that Deuteronomy proscribes, was an officer of King David's guard. The actual interaction between generations of Israelites and the native Canaanites must have been quite different from the idealized, at times genocidal fantasy retrojected by Deuteronomy and the Deuteronomistic histories. A range of interactions from expulsion or enslavement to coexistence and assimilation likely occurred.

Scholarly contextualization of the relevant biblical books goes some way toward mitigating the extreme violence commanded or depicted in those books. The same is true for post-biblical, rabbinic interpretation, where physical struggle often becomes spiritual struggle with refractory elements of one's own soul.[22] The rabbis depict Joshua as offering terms of peace to the Canaanites and warring against them only when they reject his offer.[23] They claim that the Assyrian king, Sennacharib, confused the identity of the Canaanites in antiquity. As they vanished without a trace, no ongoing valid commandment to exterminate them remains. In consequence, any attempt to identify contemporary enemies as symbolic Canaanites is misguided.[24] Scholars such as Moshe Greenberg argue that the overall vector of rabbinic thought is to subordinate violence on behalf of the holy to ethical constraints: "The rabbis adjusted its meaning [that is, of the proscription law of Deuteronomy 20] to their moral sentiment. Since Deuteronomy expressly grounds the herem in the warning 'lest you learn their evil ways and they cause you to sin to the LORD,' the rabbis concluded, reasonably enough, that if the Canaanites reformed, they should be allowed to remain."[25] Rahab is a rabbinic symbol of a penitent Canaanite. One corollary of this view, which the Bible also endorses, is that Canaanites are not objectionable on racial or biological grounds. They "merit" the harsh treatment envisioned for them on moral-religious ones. They sacrifice their children and worship idols. They will induce Israelites to apostasy and depravity if left unchecked. Indeed, the same treatment is to be meted out to Israelites if they turn against God.

A signal instance of rabbinic interpretation that tries to contextualize and minimize violence is the Talmud's treatment of Phinehas.[26] The story of Phinehas begins with the notice that the Israelites were encamped in Shittim, where the men took up with the local Moabite women. (They "profaned themselves by whoring with the Moabite women, who invited the people to sacrifices for their god" [Numbers 25:1–2].) The Israelites obligingly sacrificed to the Canaanite god, Ba'al Peor. God was incensed. He ordered Moses to slay the ringleaders, by impalement, in public "so that the LORD's wrath may turn away from Israel" (Numbers 25:4). Moses called his officials together and commanded them to slaughter those members of their tribes who fell into promiscuity and idolatry, the latter being the decisive sin but closely associated with the former. At this point, an additional provocation occurred, and the zealous Phinehas jumped into the breach:

> Just then one of the Israelites came and brought a Midian-
> ite woman over to his companions, in the sight of Moses
> and of the whole Israelite community who were weeping
> at the entrance of the Tent of Meeting. When Phinehas,
> son of Eleazar son of Aaron the priest, saw this, he left
> the assembly and, taking a spear in his hand, he followed
> the Israelite into the chamber and stabbed both of them, the
> Israelite and the woman, through the belly. Then the plague
> against the Israelites was checked. Those who died in the
> plague numbered twenty-four thousand (Numbers 25: 6–9).

The text is very compressed, and it is not clear whether God ordered Moses to slay all of the heads of the people or only to have the heads slay the "ringleaders" of the episode. Nor is it clear how the plague relates to the slaughter. Nor is it clear why the Israelite, later identified as Zimri (Numbers 25:14), a prince of the tribe of Simeon, brought the Midianite (the ethnic designation is different from but closely related to Moabite) woman before the assembled public, nor whether the place to which they retreated had cultic significance. What is clear is that Phinehas acted in a decisive, extralegal, violent way in the face of Moses's inaction and that this placated God and stilled his wrath. In the sequel, God praises Phinehas to Moses: "Phinehas . . . has turned back My wrath from the Israelites by displaying among them his passion for Me, so that I did not wipe out the Israelite people in My passion. Say, therefore, 'I grant him My pact of friendship'" (Numbers 25:11). It is thus also clear that God approves of Phinehas's violent action. His pact of friendship (*berit shalom*; literally: "covenant of peace") secures for Phinehas and his descendants the priesthood for all time. Phinehas made "expiation" for Israel (Numbers 25:13) and so is fit to conduct expiatory sacrifices in perpetuity. In the sequel to this story (Numbers 31), God instructs Moses to "avenge the Israelite people on the Midianites." Moses assembles a thousand warriors from each tribe, accompanied by Phinehas, who serves as the priest for this holy war. They destroy all of the kings of Midian, their cities, and all of the adult males, taking the women, children, livestock, and possessions as booty. On their return, Moses excoriates them for sparing the women. He commands them to slay the women, sparing only the virgins, and to slay the male children. The spoils will be distributed to God, to the warriors, and to the community. This is an example of a partial ban, rather than the total one envisioned by Deuteronomy.

What justifies—in the eyes of the tradition, at any rate—Phinehas's extraordinary, violent act? A surface reading would focus on the defection of the Israelites from God through idolatry, on the "intermarriage" with a group of Canaanites, and possibly on the promiscuous sexuality, although that is subordinated to idolatry. A deeper reading would note that both

Zimri and the Midianite woman, later identified (Numbers 25:15) as a princess of Moab, Cozbi, were political leaders. Their actions took place in public, constituting an overt *political* challenge to Moses's authority. Moses was uncharacteristically paralyzed. Phinehas's action arose from more than zealous rage; he aimed to save Mosaic authority from public denigration and collapse. Rabbinic midrash, found in the Talmud and elsewhere, develops this theme. In the rabbis' retelling, Zimri publicly challenges Moses with the taunt that he too married a non-Israelite, the Midianite Zipporah. How can he now condemn an Israelite—a prince of a tribe whose founder preceded in birth order the founder of Moses's tribe—for doing the same thing! Zimri puts the authority of Moses and ultimately the authority of God in jeopardy. Thus, Phinehas might be taken to have acted outside the normative constraints of the system of Mosaic law in order to save the system. His act is both religious and political; zeal for the Lord is also righteous defense of his polity. The midrash is keenly attuned to the political entanglements of the holy, especially in the matter of violence.

Although they rationalize this violence by the extremity of the situation, the rabbis also want to constrain the permissible scope of extraordinary, violent action. The Talmud's treatment is based on a mishnah (Sanhedrin 9:6) that teaches that one who steals a holy vessel from the Temple or one who curses another through magic or one who cohabits with a heathen ("Aramean") woman may be punished by zealots. These zealous Jews, like Phinehas, are apparently authorized by the law to intervene and kill someone guilty of such actions, but only while the malefactors are in the midst of performing them. They are not allowed to bring the accused perpetrator to trial if they fail to kill him on the spot. Their testimony would not be dispositive. God will punish the perpetrators in time. And then a crucial observation follows. If a zealot comes to the rabbis to ask for counsel, *they do not advise him to slay perpetrators.* Furthermore, had Zimri—assuming that he had parted with Cozbi—been attacked and slain by Phinehas, *Phinehas himself would have been guilty of murder and executed by the court.* Had Zimri tried to defend himself against Phinehas and succeeded in killing him, he would not have been tried as a murderer; self-defense is legitimate in Jewish law. The upshot is that the rabbis try to minimize violence on behalf of the holy; they seek to make all action accountable to law and to have law err on the side of moderation and restraint. This general tendency of rabbinic thought and law applies as well to warfare.

Let us grant then that both ancient rabbis and modern scholars have tried to bring the texts into line with their moral sensibilities through creative interpretation. These strategies, however, do not quite answer the radical challenges of Moore or Schwartz. Why does Deuteronomy or Joshua portray God as a deity who *wants* the destruction of entire peoples? Even if this is a literary fantasy retrojected onto an early period by contemporaries challenged by their own communal defections, why are such depictions legitimate within the Bible's moral universe? Even if Phinehas can be taken to have acted within a notional legal framework, why should God reward his extremism? (Is extremism in defense of the holy, with apologies to Barry Goldwater, no vice?) Regardless of whether wars of total annihilation against the Canaanites actually took place and notwithstanding the rabbis' moderating influence, formidable ethical problems remain. The text presents the Canaanites or the Amalekites as peoples who *deserve* total annihilation. The texts present a God who *desires* the complete eradication of whole nations, down to the last newborn babe (Deuteronomy 20:15–18). As in the case of Midian, whenever the Israelite fighters engage in limited, albeit deadly campaigns—of the kind that a later king of Israel, like David, might undertake—God or Moses castigates them for not being *sufficiently* genocidal. Rational calculation about tactics, strategy, and consequences should give way to war as an act of total religious devotion and trust in the divine Warrior. The text describes the extermination of an Israelite soldier, Achan, as well as his entire family, because he took some garments and silver from Jericho rather than consign them to the fire, along with everyone and everything in Jericho after its conquest (Joshua 7:19–26). After a confession, Achan and his sons and daughters, animals, and possessions, were taken to a valley, stoned to death, and immolated. No amount of traditional or scholarly interpretation relieves the pressure of the moral-theological problems such texts generate. Is God evil? Is God a "blood devourer" or "Destroyer?"[27] Does God truly demand such carnage?

As much of the moral opprobrium focuses on the institution of the ban (ḥerem), by which is meant the total destruction of the enemy and the dedication of both destroyed persons and spoils to God, let us consider how the Bible and the rabbis attempt to justify it. The case of the ḥerem confronts the demands of ethics with the demands of the holy and thus constitutes the strongest problem for the proper ordering of the two.

The first thing to note is that ḥerem is not unique to ancient Israel. The Mesha inscription, from the mid-ninth century BCE, gives an account of the conquest of an Israelite town by the Moabite king Mesha. The conquest is undertaken due to the command of the Moabite god Kemosh. Furthermore, the Israelite victims are "utterly destroyed" (a cognate of ḥerem) and thereby dedicated to the Moabite god:

And Kemosh said to me "Go seize Nebo from Israel" and I went at night and fought against her from the rising of the morning star until noon and I seized her and killed all of her seven thousand men and young men and women and young women and virgins, because for Ashtar-Kemosh I utterly destroyed her.[28]

Against Moore and Schwartz, then, monotheism is not required for holy war, nor is the totality (and cruelty) of the ban tied to any alleged Hebraic "principle of scarcity." Garden variety polytheism is capable of sanctifying war and picturing its victims as sacrificial gifts to the gods. Indeed, in diverse cultures that practice child sacrifice, it is an easy step to think of other human victims as rare and precious offerings. This is, at least, an oblique acknowledgment of the high worth of human life.[29]

The term ḥerem belongs to the semantic field of the holy. It entails consecration, dedication, sacrifice to God. It is the "negative side of the holy, the content of which is making something inaccessible to general use, whereas the better-known Hebrew expression for the holy [*kadosh*] indicates its positive qualities, those to be preserved."[30] In this view, holiness is positive and negative; holy things are set apart sometimes to be preserved and sometimes to be destroyed, albeit destroyed as a means of giving them to God. The status analysis of holiness is relevant here. A key text is Leviticus, chapter 27. This text discusses the fulfillment of vows that a person has made. Some vows that dedicate items or property to the sanctuary can be modified; one can substitute for the dedicated items. But at the highest level of consecration, proscription, no alteration is possible. One can consecrate one's animals, house, or land holdings to God; these thereby become holy (*kodesh*), as well as proscribed (ḥerem):

> But of all that anyone owns, be it man or beast or land of
> his holding, nothing that he has proscribed for the LORD

may be sold or redeemed; every proscribed thing [ḥerem] is totally consecrated [*kodesh kodashim*] to the LORD. No human being who has been proscribed can be ransomed; he shall be put to death (Leviticus 27:28–29).

That which has been given a holy status should not be returned to common use or desecrated. The process of consecration/proscription must not be undone.

Although this is not a war text, it has a disturbing, violent feature. The text implies that human beings can also be proscribed and, when so designated, must die (*mot yumat*). They cannot be redeemed. (Rabbinic interpretation rejects this reading and takes the person proscribed for death to be either a Canaanite slave or an Israelite who was convicted of a capital crime by a court. Similar to the case of Phinehas, the rabbis order morally difficult holy action to the demands of a legal system. Holiness is subordinated to justice, so to speak. Biblical scholars, however, often take the text at its literal word.[31]) Thus, some things set aside for God and designated as most holy have acquired a status, which, as Leviticus 27 indicates, is indefeasible. To return them (to sell, redeem, or ransom them) amounts to profanation or desecration. Those texts that insist on the absolute and nonnegotiable quality of the ban on the Canaanites draw from this conviction. One must not renege on what one has promised to God—or on what God demands.

In some respects, the ḥerem is a promise to God. In other respects, it is a demand of God. Both of these are attempts within biblical thought to justify the ḥerem. The need for justification, when human lives are at stake, implies that the biblical authors themselves were aware of the ethically problematic aspects of the ban. There are two strategies for justification of the ban in the Bible. The first construes the ban as sacrifice; the second thinks of it in terms of justice, of just desert. On the first construal, Israel vows that if God grants them victory in battle, they will proscribe everything—all the human beings, animals, and possessions—to God. The vow is a promise to God. Thus, Numbers 21:2: "Then Israel made a vow to the LORD and said, 'If you deliver this people into our hand, we will proscribe their towns.' The LORD heeded Israel's plea and delivered up the Canaanites; and they and their cities were proscribed [*v'yaḥarem*]. So that the place was named Hormah [*ḥormah*]." War here has a ritualized, sacramental quality. The vanquished will be given as a sacrifice to the conquering deity. But there is also something straightforwardly pragmatic about the negotiation; if God helps Israel, Israel will give to God. *Do ut des*. The conquest of Canaanite cities in Joshua, chapters 8 and 10, where the best of booty—the human beings— are given to God, reflects the justificatory strategy of the ban as sacrifice (albeit without the element of the initial human vow).[32] Although this strategy of justification seems ethically alien, Niditch finds moral irony in it: "The ban validates the enemy as human and valuable and does not turn him into a monster worthy of destruction, a cancer that must be rooted out. The enemy is not the unclean 'other,' but a mirror of the self, which God desires for himself."[33]

In the second strategy, the Canaanites who are proscribed for total destruction are thought to merit their fate; destruction is their just desert. They are morally evil—a cancer to be rooted out. Deuteronomy 7:2–5 demands that the conquered Canaanite peoples be doomed to destruction, lest you "intermarry with them." Intermarriage will lead to Israelite assimilation to Canaanite ways—to idolatrous rejection of God as the sole covenantal deity. The holiness of Israel, as a chosen, consecrated, treasured people (Deuteronomy 7:6) will be compromised. The impure Canaanites will infect Israelite purity. The Canaanites are hopelessly mired in idolatry; they must be eradicated to prevent the contagion of idolatry to Israel. (Indeed, Israel is by no means immune to idolatry. When Israelites, singly or collectively, become idolatrous, they too must be banned and destroyed [Deuteronomy 13].) The Canaanites also display a more mundane evil. When Moses asked, on behalf of the Israelites, to pass through the territory of Sihon, he refused them safe passage (Deuteronomy 2:32–35). Sihon and his people merited destruction as a matter of justice. (This suggests the counterfactual that if Sihon had granted Israel's request, he and his people would not have been subject to the ḥerem.) So too Amalek, the arch-symbol of evil in the biblical and rabbinic imaginary, earned his status as wickedness incarnate through aggression upon the most vulnerable members of the Israelite camp after the Exodus from Egypt (Deuteronomy 25:17–19). There is nothing "genetic" about Canaanite/Amalekite evil. It is an ascribed status, earned by misanthropic behavior.

By associating the ban with justice, the Bible, on the one hand, brings a moral calculus to the possible justification of violence. If the enemy deserves his fate on moral grounds, violence can be accommodated to an ethical outlook, at least in principle. Just punishment under law is not necessarily barbaric or irrational. On the other hand, as Niditch argues, "in the ban as God's justice a sharp line is drawn between us and them, between clean and unclean, between those worthy of salvation and those deserving elimination. The enemy is thus not a mere human ... but a monster, unclean, and diseased. The ban as God's justice thus allows people to accept the notion of killing other humans by dehumanizing them and the process of dehumanization can take place even within the group during times of stress, distrust, and anomie."[34] The gain in rationality—through justifying violence as a matter of administering justice—is offset by a massive failure of moral imagination.

I do not believe that the violence against the Canaanites can be justified, in a blanket way, by either strategy. I honor the biblical authors' attempts to make moral sense of these remote events, but I do not think that either they or the rabbis quite succeed in doing so. To be part of a tradition is to take on both its best and worst *tradita*; one cannot simply write them off or bracket them out. Moral reinterpretation becomes a religious obligation, as Avi Sagi puts it.[35] That is our obligation here, although the means I will propose likely go beyond what traditionalists could accept.

There are important insights in both of the biblical strategies of justification, which we can extract. The two approaches work to complement and correct one another. From the ban-as-sacrifice strategy, we infer the preciousness of human life, to which sacrifice obliquely, indeed, perversely attests. The core holiness of human persons is what makes them, again perversely, "worthy" of proscription as the ultimate gift to God. Human life belongs to God, its source and final destination. From the second justificatory strategy of the ban-as-justice, we find that, minimally, people should get, with respect to punishment, only what they deserve. The text enshrines the belief that the Canaanites deserve either extirpation or expulsion or enslavement. We need not believe that *anyone* deserves such treatment, but we can nonetheless affirm the basic norm of desert.

Because human beings are essentially sacred, moving images of the Highest One, they must be treated in the most scrupulous and just way possible. The fundamental sacredness of the human person puts persons into relationship with God. A life devoted to the Highest One suits us as the highest goal of which we are capable. But this must be chosen by ourselves alone, freely and willingly. The insight of the ban-as-sacrifice that human lives are precious and of surpassing worth is undermined by its violent misapplication, which is a desecration of justice. It is unholy and unjust to kill human beings in the name of the holy; they are not to be sacrificed on any altar whatsoever. No end, no matter how notionally exalted, can justify the means if the means involve the systematic violation of human beings. It is unjust and unholy to pervert the norms of justice by sweeping up whole groups and classes into a blanket policy of retribution. Individuals are to be judged on the basis of their individual wrongdoing and treated accordingly. Only a sensitive, rationally defensible administration of justice can honor the sacred nature of persons, who bear within them the image of God. Justice and the sacredness of persons are correlates.

Maimonides's interpretation of the ban reflects these insights. Deuteronomy, chapter 20, has a rudimentary code of war, to which Maimonides gives determinate legal form. In Deuteronomy, a distinction is drawn between towns that are "very far off from you" and towns that are "hereabout" (Deuteronomy 20:15). The latter belong to the Canaanite nations and are meant to be proscribed: "you shall not let a soul remain alive" (Deuteronomy 20:16). The former towns, however, must be given the option of surrender: "When you approach a town to attack it, you shall offer it terms of peace. If it responds peaceably and lets you in, all the people present shall serve you as forced labor" (Deuteronomy 20:10–11). If it does not surrender, upon victory, all the males are to be killed. The females, children, livestock, and other items may be taken by the Israelites as booty. Based on rabbinic precedents, Maimonides elides the distinction between the types of town.[36] He writes:

> A war is never waged against *anyone* before peace is offered. This applies both to an obligatory war and to a permitted war, as it is written "when you get near a city to

wage war against it, you must offer peace" (Deut. 20:10). If
they agree and accept upon themselves the seven mitzvot
given to the children of Noah, not a single soul is to be
harmed, and they are to pay taxes, as it is written "they will
pay taxes and serve you" (Deut. 20:11). If they accepted
taxes but not servitude, or servitude and not taxes, we don't
listen to them, until they accepted both.[37]

Maimonides holds that both towns that are far off and those
that are near—even in the case of the commanded, obligatory
wars (against the seven Canaanite nations and Amalek)—are
to be offered peace terms.[38] He effectively nullifies the ḥerem
as an absolute commandment. It becomes contingent on the
behavior of the antagonist. Had the Canaanites chosen peace
and thereby Noachide status (and enslavement), Israel need
not have exterminated them. In fact, however, they chose war
and so the provisions of the ban applied.[39]

Maimonides leaves the violence of the ban in place—it comprises biblical commandments, after all. He even attempts to
justify it on philosophical grounds in the *Guide*.[40] He doesn't
question the justice, morality, or rationality of the commandment. He cannot entirely dispose of the moral burden that
weighs upon the text. He does, however, make bold moves in
the right direction.[41] The Canaanites are treated as *rational
human beings* who can decide whether to change their ways,
repent, and accept the sovereignty of God. They are not thought
to be unclean, dehumanized others, who must simply be destroyed. Their capacity for rationality and agency; their standing as persons is implicitly recognized. Their lives are worth
something; they can redeem them by turning from their ways
and approaching the truth. They can become allies rather than
enemies through moral revolution. The choice was in their
hands; they were apprised of the consequences like the Me-

lians in Thucydides's famous dialogue. Neither the Israelites nor the Athenians come off well in these texts. Both seem cruel, but both are operating with models of justice that they think, implicitly, they can defend.[42] The Athenian defense is pure realpolitik. The biblical defense, as interpreted by Maimonides, takes moral considerations with greater seriousness.

Maimonides is also at pains to remove hatred and vengeance from the emotional disposition of the Israelites. Israelites shouldn't hate Canaanites. In his code, he writes: "there is no vengeance in the commandments of the Torah, but compassion, mercy, and peace in the world."[43] As we saw in chapter 2, he wants the administration of justice to be passionless; it ought to be based strictly on desert. The emotional responses of the ruler or soldier must be bracketed. The ruler of a city who must apply the death penalty, for example, should do so without hatred toward the offender. This is part of a larger argument about the transcendence of God. God, being beyond humanly intelligible description, cannot be said to have an emotional constitution. Terms such as "angry" or "jealous" cannot apply to him, only to the perceived effects of his action. Thus, when calamity strikes persons, nations, cities, or landscapes, we are inclined to ascribe this to divine wrath. But that is a category mistake. God is passionless. Destruction to a calamitous degree must be ordered to moral desert. Our tendency is to project the character of our minds and hearts onto God, but the tendency plays us false. We might act from base or conflicted motives. God does not. To imitate God, as behooves a ruler, is to imitate God's impassability. Glossing the commandment in Deuteronomy 20 to exterminate the seven Canaanite nations lest they cause Israelite apostasy, Maimonides comments

Do not think that this is hard-heartedness or desire for vengeance. It is rather an act required by human opinion, which considers that anyone who deviates from the ways of truth should be put an end to and that all the obstacles impeding the achievement of the perfection that is the apprehension of Him, may He be exalted, should be interdicted. *In spite of all this, it behooves that acts of mercy, forgiveness, pity and commiseration should proceed from the governor of a city to a much greater extent than acts of retaliation.*[44]

Decoupling punishment from hard-heartedness and the desire for vengeance is a gain of sorts. It goes to the independence of law from whim. It helps to ensure equality of treatment. On the other hand, the specter of dispassionate officials who suppress normal human inclinations of empathy in pursuit of "higher" purposes, especially in the light of the industrial extermination of the Holocaust, is chilling. Worse, from a democratic point of view, is Maimonides's linkage of the power of the state to an ideological program. Maimonides attempts to justify the ḥerem by, roughly, a Platonic political theory according to which the purpose of the polity is to enable the moral and spiritual perfection of its members. Whatever stands in the way of this high religious-metaphysical goal "should be interdicted." Isaiah Berlin's cautions about the dangers of positive liberty, of noble political aims that are thought to override individual rights, are apposite here. It would take a good deal of interpretative work to make Maimonides a friend of liberal democracy.

A saving grace of this text is Maimonides's insistence that God's (humanly imagined) attributes of compassion ought to guide human behavior. Although ontologically God is far from both negative and positive moral attributes, we ought to conceive of God's actions in positive terms insofar as these have the most benign pragmatic implications for our own actions.

The thirteen attributes of God, canonically described in Exodus 34:6–7, are all attributes of mercy, except for God's promise to punish, unto the fourth generation, those who reject him. Maimonides takes those who are held guilty by God to be idolaters. And in dealing with them, as we have seen, the Israelite should be open to the possibility that they might have a change of heart. Following God's "attributes of mercy" constitutes, for Maimonides, the pinnacle of moral virtue:

> For the utmost virtue of man is to become like unto Him, may He be exalted, as far as he is able; which means that we should make our actions like unto His, as the sages made clear when interpreting the verse *Ye shall be holy*. They said: *He is gracious, so be you also gracious; He is merciful, so be you also merciful.*[45]

It is well to keep this in mind as we consider the contemporary uses to which Maimonides's laws of war have been put. Maimonides's insistence on viewing the enemy as human, accountable, capable of rational choice, and, if possible, worth saving can mitigate some of the extreme positions that have emerged in Judaism under conditions of ongoing conflict in the Middle East.

Holiness and Violence in Contemporary Judaism

The legacy of biblical violence was moralized and diminished by rabbinic Judaism. Medieval thinkers and codifiers, preeminently Maimonides, considered war in an entirely theoretical way. War to reclaim the Land of Israel was a prerogative of the Messiah. War was deferred to a distant (but, the Jews prayed, not too distant) future. Without the power of a state, Jews could neither engage in war nor, alas, defend themselves against host societies turned hostile. With the rise of modern Jewish settlement in the Land of Israel in the nineteenth and twentieth centuries, organized self-defense became both possible and imperative. The ancient stories of Jewish warriors inspired the secular Zionists, who sought a model for a new, postexilic kind of Jew. Their inspiration was not a religious ratification of "holy war" but a modern nationalist assertion of self-respect. Within religious Zionist circles, however, especially with the success of Israeli arms in 1967, a messianic reading of war began to develop. Religious Zionist thinkers began to see Israel's wars as providential, part of an eschatological process of messianic redemption. The State of Israel as such began to be considered holy or at least part of God's plan for the consummation of history. So too its wars. The unification of Jerusalem and the conquest of the historic ancient territories of Judea and Samaria were considered miracles. (Whoever does not believe in miracles, Chief Rabbi Shlomo Goren said, is not a realist.[46]) The language of the Israeli Rabbinate's official prayer that acknowledged Israel as the "beginning of the flowering of our redemption" was, it seemed, ever more accurate.

The conquest of the territories stirred the religious Zionist movement to an energizing, radical interpretation of the meaning of contemporary history. Long a junior partner in the Zionist project, outflanked on one side by the secular majority and on the other by an anti-Zionist fervently Orthodox stream, religious Zionism came into its own after 1967. A staple of its ideology became the holiness of the Land of Israel. The holiness of the land, which we considered in chapter 1, is subject to several interpretations. Some, such as Halevi, saw its holiness as intrinsic or ontological. Others, such as Maimonides, saw its holiness as a legal artifact, an enabling condition for the performance of land-dependent commandments. The legal tradition itself raised unresolved questions of how the land acquired its sanctity, whether sanctity (*kedushat ha-aretz*) was permanent or transient, how much of the land was or remains holy, and what sanctity entails vis-à-vis choice of residence.[47] These long-standing questions took on new urgency in light of the Six-Day War. The religious Zionist answer increasingly stressed settlement of the conquered lands. One of the classical views was that the land acquired its *kedushah* from Joshua's conquest (and then lost it with the demise of the First Temple), only to reacquire it with the return of the Jews in the days of Ezra and Nehemiah.[48] Both conquest and settlement can consecrate. Link that to the eschatological urgency of the times, and a formidable rationale for settlement in Judea, Samaria, and Gaza emerges. For the first time, religious motives for retaining holy ground competed with the practical political approach of using land as a bargaining chip in a future peace process. Holiness was put on a collision course with *raison d'état*. Fifty years on, and innumerable social, cultural, and political developments later, the tension between these two ideals remains. Add to this the moral considerations that weigh in favor of compromise and peacemaking between Israelis and Palestinians—a two-way street, to be sure—and holiness and ethics are again in tension.

In addition to a militant, religious valorization of war among some thinkers, there has been a dehumanization of the enemy. The way has been paved by those mystical elements of the religious tradition that see non-Jews as lesser beings, as well as by the doctrine of Yehuda Halevi. Drawing on the teachings of Halevi, a leading religious Zionist rabbi, Shlomo Aviner, writing in a magazine intended for the troops, formulates the alleged difference between gentiles and Jews. He makes a strong ontological distinction in the context of a halakhic discussion

about why corpses do, or in the case of gentiles do not, convey
ritual impurity:

> Death is impurity. Therefore, its essence is the diminution
> of the divine vitality [found in] what has been created. The
> degree of impurity corresponds to the degree of withdrawal
> of this divine vitality. The graves of gentiles under a "tent"
> do not convey impurity as a matter of law *because their
> souls are not so holy and the difference between their bodies
> without a soul and with a soul is not that great.* Therefore,
> the withdrawal of their souls does not bring about such a
> terrible crisis. Contrariwise, the graves of righteous Jews
> [*tzadikim*] do not convey impurity (according to many
> views but not as a matter of practical halakha) because
> *their bodies are holy* and therefore there is no diminution
> of the divine phenomenon with the withdrawal of the soul.
> The graves of (ordinary) Jews convey impurity because al-
> though their souls are holy, their bodies without souls are
> not holy. The withdrawal of the soul constitutes a terrible
> crisis of the separation of divine vitality from the body—
> and this is the impurity of death [*tumat ha-mavet*].[49]

Rabbi Aviner has a concept of holiness as a property, a feature
of the (highly reified) soul and also, in the case of *tzadikim*, of
the body. The holiness of their bodies remains after death, so
no impurity issues from them. Not so the case of the ordinary
Jew. The departure of the holy soul leaves a now impure corpse
behind. The radical claim is that gentile bodies do not defile
because *there was nothing holy in them to depart in the first
place*; death, from a certain point of view, doesn't make a difference. If impurity results from the departure of a divine element, conceived as a property of the soul, there can be no
impurity if there is no antecedent divinity. Aviner posits an
insuperable ontological distinction, in the manner of Halevi,

between Jews and gentiles. This clearly goes beyond the resources of halakhah as such. Discussions about *tumah* and *taharah* are not conducted in these terms. A metaphysical perspective has been imported that functions as a "meta-halakhic" context for Aviner's halakhic analysis. Kellner sees in Aviner's view not just the leaven of Yehuda Halevi but traces of nineteenth-century German Romanticism as well.[50]

Rabbi Aviner, a child survivor of the Holocaust with advanced degrees from the Sorbonne, is aware that this view might be considered racist. He is therefore at pains to defend himself against the charge. He argues that if racism has something to do with biological characteristics—the color of one's skin, for example—he should not be considered a racist. For there are Jews of all skin colors. What he points to, he claims, is the higher nature of the Jewish soul (*ha-teva ha-nishmati shelanu*), which distinguishes the Jew from all other peoples. Lest that be taken as pure chauvinism, however, this higher spiritual nature is for the sake of the nations. It brings blessings to all of the other peoples.[51]

Contemporaries such as Rabbi Aviner do not jettison moral considerations but rather subordinate them to what they take to be the comprehensive normative teaching of the Torah. In their view, morality does not have an independent foundation; there is no cogent morality outside of halakhah.[52] Thus, Aviner writes of the commandment to conquer the land of Israel: "[it] is above and beyond any moral, humanistic considerations and national rights of the gentiles to our land . . . because all ethics and justice in the hearts of man have no existence whatsoever if not for their having been drawn from the word of God. God, as the source of ethics, instructs us to ignore human ethical considerations in conquering the land."[53] Holiness is unhinged from the good; holiness is the only good. It sponsors a higher ethic, discontinuous with ordinary considerations of competing rights, interests, potentially legitimate claims, and so on. Aviner, similar to how he justifies the divine paternalism of Jewish spiritual superiority, asserts that the world is blessed by the Jewish conquest and settlement of the whole land of Israel:

> Fortunate is the world in which the Jewish people return to health and a normal settlement of their entire land. Thus declares the *musar elyon* [higher ethics] not the lower ethics that are detached from their Divine source and bring suffocation to the spirit of the King Messiah.[54]

The text shows that ethics cannot be abandoned. Holiness cannot quite float free of morality. The two must be recast and effectively bent to the religiously inspired interests that Jews pursue. By no means can ethics have independent critical force. But holiness too must be justified in terms of an alleged "higher ethics." The persistence of the normative is revealing. If there are no good reasons to think that normal moral considerations can be subordinated to "higher" ones, then claims such as Aviner's fail.

There are no good reasons to think that normal moral considerations should be subordinated to allegedly higher ones. Apologists such as Aviner cannot rely on religious metaphysical claims alone. They use moral arguments, but their use of them is self-undermining. A moral point of view involves taking the interests of the other into account, respecting the rationality, agency, and personhood of the other. Morality is premised on a responsibility toward the other, on not treating the other in a way that he or she does not deserve or accept. Paternalism, instrumentalization, humiliation, and disrespect are incompatible with a moral point of view. An alleged higher ethics that sanctions such attitudes and attendant conduct is not higher but lower than morality. It is not holy. It is merely immoral. Thomas Scanlon writes: "[R]especting the value of human (rational) life requires us to treat rational creatures only in ways that would be allowed by principles that they could not reasonably reject."[55] I very much doubt that non-Jews could accept as a principle their supposed spiritual and moral inferiority vis-à-vis Jews.

The loss of a moral perspective independent and potentially critical of halakhah is acutely evident in *Torat ha-Melekh* (*The King's Torah*). As mentioned in the introduction, this 2009 compendium of halakhic rules bearing on loss of gentile life in peacetime and wartime caused a scandal in the Israeli public sphere. Although the book was endorsed by some prominent rabbis, closer inspection of its contents upon publication led to a massive rebuke. Prominent religious Zionist rabbis, including Rabbi Aviner, rejected the book. One leading rabbi, Yaakov Meidan, called for one of the book's authors, Rabbi Shapira, to be prevented from teaching. A group of citizens, religious and secular alike, formed to oppose the work and to demand that the government indict the authors for racial incitement. The Israeli government launched an investigation into whether the authors should be indicted. The defense of the authors was that they were investigating a field of religious law, not encouraging anyone to act according to their findings. The attorney general ultimately decided not to indict the authors or the rabbinic supporters of the book. The Israel Defense Forces (IDF) did remove the book, however, from all IDF-based synagogues in the territories.[56]

There is no question that the authors value the lives of Jews over those of gentiles. If the killing of a gentile can save the life of a Jew, then a gentile should be killed.[57] There is no prohibition against a Jew killing a gentile if the gentile is violating the Seven Commandments of the Sons of Noah and the Jew is concerned to enforce them.[58] Most notoriously, the authors argue

that gentile children may be preemptively killed if there is reason to believe that they will harm Jews when they grow up.[59]
What is striking about these—and many other morally offen-
sive opinions—is that the authors attempt to justify them on
the basis of kabbalistic doctrines about the superiority of the
Jewish soul, the unique redemptive role of Jews in the world,
and so on. They are convinced that the holiness of the Jew excuses, indeed, demands behavior that on principle should dis-
regard ordinary ethics.[60]

As Ariel Finkelstein, a leading critic of *Torat ha-Melekh*
contends, the authors come to their low view of the worth of
non-Jewish lives by characterizing those lives as essentially
animalistic—categorically other than (truly human) Jewish
lives.[61] What orders the moral lives of non-Jews is the Seven
Commandments of the Sons of Noah. But most non-Jews,
according to the authors of *Torat ha-Melekh*, do not practice
them. This leaves these gentiles in an inhuman state, where
the brutish nature of their souls has free rein and their lives
have lost value.[62] This view relies on the kabbalistic metaphysics we surveyed in chapter 1, but it also requires the rejection of natural reason and morality. If all normativity is bound
up with the Seven Commandments of the Sons of Noah and,
more expansively and definitively, with the Torah, then nothing can remain to those in a "state of nature," unaware of divine revelation. Rabbi Finkelstein, arguing incisively against
Torat ha-Melekh, shows how such leading Jewish thinkers as
Naḥmanides in the thirteenth century and Rav Kook in the
twentieth century conceive of the Torah as built upon the normative legacy of the Seven Commandments. For Naḥmanides,
the gentiles have a full range of moral and legal norms, which
their courts—set up under the Seven Commandments—are responsible to enforce.[63] Gentiles are not morally impoverished
or animalistic; their normative world is comparable to that of

the Jews. For Rav Kook, the higher, holy morality of the Torah builds upon the natural morality (*ha-musar ha-tivi*) given to human reason and formulated in the "Torah of the Sons of Noah."[64] "Natural morality is the vestibule to the banquet hall of the splendor of the holy."[65]

Thinkers such as Naḥmanides and Kook, who resist the dehumanization of non-Jews, draw from the same kabbalistic materials that the authors of *Torat ha-Melekh* deploy. But they do so to achieve the opposite ends. The counterexample, emanating from the same universe of Jewish texts, shows that the moral resources of the tradition are able to correct the moral defects that can emerge from a failure of moral imagination. The influence of *Torat ha-Melekh*'s perverse moral outlook on its halakhic analysis is exposed and countered in detail by *Derekh ha-Melekh*. Finkelstein shows, among other things, that it can never be a matter of halakhah alone. Decision making takes place within a moral framework. When that framework rests on gratuitous and morally perverse notions, the practical consequences that follow show the underlying taint.

The critics of *Torat ha-Melekh* resist the dehumanization of the enemy—indeed, they resist categorizing non-Jews in a blanket way *as* enemies. They recognize that Jews and non-Jews (an absurdly parochial categorization in itself!) share a common world, even if they do not share a common life-world. All properly functional persons share the capacities for agency, responsibility, deliberation, and choice. All yearn for the good, however they conceive it. All have a sacred dimension to their personhood that is expressive of their basic human worth. The holy should be allied with the good. One of the chief goods is a just society in which all persons are treated according to their deserts and none are humiliated.[66] Being open to the humanity of the other is crucial for the just society. Acknowledging the other's legitimate particularity, trying to understand her perspective, showing empathy toward her projects and interests—these moral resources are needed even to understand what others deserve. Attentiveness to persons, not just scrupulousness about rules, is crucial to a decent, let alone a just and good society.

A desecration of personhood occurs when individual human beings are forced into a box of identity at odds with their self-conception. To be seen only as a Jew, as a Muslim, as a Buddhist, as an Asian or a German, as black or white, or to be seen only as a factory worker or a teacher is to be deprived of the richness of one's self-understanding in whatever forum where the narrow categorization prevails. It is inevitable that societies make these reductions for specific legal or administrative purposes. But at the level of personal ethics, we can do better. No small part of the violence of *Torat ha-Melekh* is its sweeping invidious categorization of Jew/non-Jew, made essential because of a story about the nature of the soul and the role of Jewish ritual/redemptive action in the metaphysical repair of the world. To an extent, the distinction between Jew and non-Jew is an artifact of Jewish law. The metaphysical deepening of that categorization comes from another stream of tradition. But none of this excuses the contemporary uses to which these distinctions are put if the uses are immoral. Respect for the holiness of persons requires great sensitivity to the ascriptions of identity that we make. Coercive and reductive identification is a seedbed of violence.[67]

Maimonides's Razor

If, as I have argued, the holy grows from the same response to the world as our perception of the good, then the holy and the good work in tandem. The holy intensifies the good; the good contextualizes the holy within a broadly normative framework. The holy is not an exception to the moral order. It is a moment of value within that order, affording clarity and perspective on the ground and height of the whole. Violence in the name of the holy turns on itself, desecrating what it seeks to preserve or protect. Violence there must sometimes be, for there are real, holy goods that need protection against genuine threats. But violence should not be confused with holiness, nor should a moral excuse for violent conduct, under highly specific circumstances where pacific means of resolution have failed, be taken for a blanket justification of violence. If we must march off to war, we should be chary of marching off with "Gott mit uns" on our belts.[68]

Well, what of God? Does God want the genocide of the Canaanites and Amalek? Does monotheism underwrite the worst excesses of human belligerence? Maimonides moves in the right direction by demythologizing God. The radical gulf between Creator and Creation implies that the reach of language, which touches reality as human beings experience and know it, can never extend to God. God is past the edge of language. Maimonides deprives us of our ability to make direct statements about the divine will (so the question, "Does God want x?" is ill formulated) and about the divine nature (so the assertion that God is x is also ill formulated). Maimonides's "distant God," in Kenneth Seeskin's phrase, is impossibly abstract and unsatisfying for some, perhaps for most theists.[69] It appeals to a contemplative piety more than to an emotive one. In my view, if the cosmos is more than a lucky accident, if value is more than a species-specific utility, if there is a highest explanation that our thought can touch rather than an infinity of proximate ones, then contemplative piety is the right response. Or at least the right modality for reflecting on these hunches. A contemplative piety, which sees in God sheer Goodness, shears violence from the divine. Call this critical demythologization, with apologies to William of Occam, "Maimonides's razor."

Applying Maimonides's razor, we can say that God's violence is on loan from nature. The ancient Near East abounded in storm gods and others that traded on the majesty and frequent virulence of nature. As mentioned in the introduction, Burke was not wrong to find the sublime in nature and to depict it as a substitute for the awesome uncanniness of God. He was returning the symbols to where they began and belong. The violence of God belongs to the language of poetry. It is a mythic projection of power. The power that poetry and myth depict is not only that of nature—nature does that well enough on her own and does not need the pictorial representation provided by theistic myth—it is also that of value. To emphasize the awe-inspiring otherness of a God whose theophany overwhelms with its power is to evoke the compelling force of value. The poet thinks that values, such as fidelity, devotion, love, submission, dedication, need the sound and fury of a demanding, commanding Power. In truth, they would be better served by the still, small voice. They align better with quiet focus, reflection, and meditation rather than with thunder and lightning. We intuit them. They insinuate themselves into our conscience, if we let them. We stabilize and heighten them with reason, incorporating them into our plans of life. Nonetheless, the power ascribed to God befits the force of the values that the concept of God works to project. A contemporary theist's task is to parse the values, and the holy way of life they order, from the poetic form in which the Bible makes them manifest in the world. The holiness of God and all its human instantiations is made manifest in the awareness that the world is alive with sacred value. Our quickening of consciousness in its presence, our alliance with it, our delight in our service to all that it enshrines is at the heart of holiness.

The harshness of God, as depicted in the Bible, especially with respect to the ḥerem, is a poetic way of capturing the imperative of justice. Justice need not be harsh, but depicting it as implacable underscores its centrality to a good social and political order—indeed, to a well-ordered life. What we should take from the divine insistence on justice is not the image of a jealous or avenging God but a sense that justice should "well up like water, righteousness like a mighty stream" (Amos 5:24). We should not shunt or block its flow. Impeding or defeating justice swamps and drowns human life. An insistent, demanding, jealous God is a harsh image of something that is not harsh; justice is a life-giving virtue for communities and for the individual soul. But justice is also the value in the name of which we sometimes take lives, both through judicial means and in the moral fog of war. It is well that justice be linked to the holy, for the administration of justice can both advance or, when we judge wrongly, curtail the sacred value of human life. The close association of God with justice in Jewish thought expresses this axiological nexus. Holiness reminds us of what is at stake.

Some object to the association of justice with the God of monotheism. For Stuart Hampshire, for example, the harshness of God represents the exclusive claim of a single, substantive way of life. "The primary enemy is monotheism and after that moral universalism."[70] Like Rawls, he rejects any single, commanding, comprehensive conception of the good. No substantive concept of justice can aspire to universality. Rather, justice as fairness—as listening to every side—is the best we can do. Justice is procedural; its model is the give and take of rational reflection we find within our own souls, the oscillation of thesis and antithesis. Justice is dialectical, local, and conflictual. We must do the best we can with adjudicating conflicting claims both in public and *in foro interno*. Argument, not logical deduction, is the best image of reason. Monotheism's promise of transcendence, absoluteness, and universal authority is both illusionary and pernicious.

Such views founder on their subtraction of holiness from the equation. Why should justice as fairness, as procedural or instrumental rationality, be normative in the first place if human life were not universally and absolutely such as to require just treatment? Hampshire, more than Rawls, appeals to Hobbesian grounds: we want to avoid the *summum malum*, the great evils that can come with social existence.[71] As indeed we do. But we could do so by slaughtering some powerless others as easily as by respecting their claims. What gives their claims the standing to compel our consideration? Surely more than the thrust and parry of reason attentive to its own internal dialogue.[72] I fail to see how a purely secular, contractual account of justice, severed from its anchorage in a sense of the sacred nature of the subjects of just treatment, can succeed.

Monotheism has, as its critics unceasingly remind us, wrought its share of moral havoc. Applying Maimonides's razor, shearing the mythological covering from the mystery of divine transcendence can go some way toward saving what is best and most needful in monotheism. It can help control the violent tendencies in the Jewish imaginary as well. For these should not be allowed to discredit the beauty of holiness that Judaism otherwise embodies.

NOTES

Introduction

1. Jonathan Fine, *Political Violence in Judaism, Christianity, and Islam: From Holy War to Modern Terror* (Lanham, MD: Rowman & Littlefield, 2015), 135–36. Robert Eisen, *The Peace and Violence of Judaism: From the Bible to Modern Zionism* (New York: Oxford University Press, 2011), 154.

2. Holy things, such as temples, that the gods retain for themselves are *hieron* (sacred). Greek thought thus recognizes two types or domains of holiness: a human sphere, where pious actions affect a holy way of life, and a divine sphere, where gods own places, persons, and things and where humans must respect their ownership or presence. See Thomas G. West and Grace Starry West, trans., *Four Texts on Socrates* (Ithaca, NY: Cornell University Press, 1998), 45.

3. Mark L. McPherran, *The Religion of Socrates* (University Park: Pennsylvania State University Press, 1999), 27. See also Lenn E. Goodman, "Ethics and God," *Philosophical Investigations* 34, no. 2 (2011): 135–50.

4. *The Complete Plays of Sophocles*, trans. Richard Claverhouse Jebb (New York: Bantam Books, 1967), 131.

5. Edmund Burke, *A Philosophical Enquiry into the Origin of Our Ideas of the Sublime and the Beautiful*, part II, sect. 1. For an excellent discussion of the significance of the sublime in its historical context, see Charles Taylor, *A Secular Age* (Cambridge, MA: Belknap Press of Harvard University Press, 2007), 335–44.

6. Taylor, *A Secular Age*, 338.

7. Excerpts from Isaiah 6:1–8. All biblical citations, unless otherwise noted, are from the New Jewish Publication Society (NJPS) Tanakh translation, as found in Berlin and Brettler, eds., *The Jewish Study Bible*, and are used with permission of the publisher. I shall follow the older convention of using "He," "His," and so on to refer to God when this tracks the original Hebrew. Where opportunities arise to use gender-neutral formulations, I will take advantage of them.

8. Rudolf Otto, *The Idea of the Holy*, trans. John Harvey (New York: Oxford University Press, 1973 [1923]), xvii, 51.

9. Adi Ophir sees God's violence as pervasive and constitutive of God's claim to rule. Insofar as God is presented by the biblical text as essentially a ruler, God is presented as essentially violent. See Adi Ophir, *Divine Violence* [Hebrew] (Jerusalem: Van Leer Institute/Hakibbutz Hameuchad Publishing House, 2013). Ophir's reduction of God's role to an exclusively political one is reminiscent of Max Weber's treatment of God in his *Ancient Judaism*. This

opens Ophir to the same kind of criticism that Julius Guttmann directed against Weber. Guttmann's critique in brief is that religious experience has its own integrity vis-à-vis political exigency and power. For a treatment of the Weber-Guttmann discussion of the political significance of the biblical God, see Alan Mittleman, *The Scepter Shall Not Depart from Judah* (Lanham, MD: Lexington Books, 2000), 59–68.

10. Even Robert M. Adams, who finds in God only infinite, transcendent Good, nonetheless states that, "from a human point of view, the Holy has rough edges. It screams with the hawk and laughs with the hyena. We cannot comprehend it. It is fearful to us and in some ways dangerous." Robert M. Adams, *Finite and Infinite Goods: A Framework for Ethics* (New York: Oxford University Press, 1999), 52. We consider Adams's views more fully in chapter 2.

11. There are, of course, proposals to find the sacred in nature—to make science soulful, so to speak—or to find human persons sacred. Some contemporary writers do use terms such as "sacred" or "holy" while making a clean break from biblical faith and the religious traditions descended from it. See, for example, Stuart Kaufman, *Reinventing the Sacred: A New View of Science, Reason, and Religion* (New York: Basic Books, 2010), or Ronald Dworkin, *Life's Dominion* (New York: Vintage Books, 1994), especially chapter 3. See also Ronald Dworkin, *Religion without God* (Cambridge, MA: Harvard University Press, 2013). Another (and quite profound) work in this genre is Mark Johnston, *Saving God: Religion after Idolatry* (Princeton, NJ: Princeton University Press, 2009). The bibliography could be indefinitely extended. These books either assume or argue that traditional theism is a failure but that its insights into the holiness of aspects of reality ought to be given a new expression commensurable with the scientific and humanistic outlook of our age. They are somewhat parasitic on their robustly religious, traditional predecessors. Insofar as this is an essay on Jewish philosophy, I do not want to sever religious concepts, such as holiness, from their roots in the tradition. I do take an unorthodox stance toward traditional theism, however.

12. For an example of a contemporary biblical theology that takes seriously a personal, passionate God, including a God capable of anger and of being placated, see Yohanan Muffs, *The Personhood of God: Biblical Theology, Human Faith, and the Divine Image* (Woodstock, VT: Jewish Lights, 2005), 30–33.

13. For extensive documentation of this claim in the Jewish mystical tradition, see Elliot Wolfson, *Venturing Beyond: Law and Morality in Kabbalistic Mysticism* (New York: Oxford University Press, 2006).

14. An exponent of this view is the late philosopher Michael Wyschogrod, who claimed that "ethics is the Judaism of the assimilated." Even he, however, was unable to do without the concept. See Michael Wyschogrod, *The Body of Faith* (San Francisco: Harper & Row, 1989), 181.

15. Yitzhak Shapira and Yosef Elitzur, *Torat ha-Melekh* (Yitzhar: Yeshivat Od Yosef Ḥai Press, 2010), 45 n. 57, 198.

16. Ariel Finkelstein, *Derekh ha-Melekh: Racism and Discrimination against Gentiles in Halakha: An Alternative Halakha and Meta-Halakha to Torat ha-Melekh* [Hebrew] (Netivot: Yeshivat Ahavat Yisrael, 2010).

17. The philosopher Lenn Goodman, who makes extensive use of this strategy, refers to it as "chimneying." Chimneying is a technique in rock climbing where one climbs by pushing back and forth against two opposing walls to ascend. See Lenn Goodman, *Love Thy Neighbor as Thyself* (New York: Oxford University Press, 2008), vii.

18. This is, in fact, the premise of a fine book on Judaism and violence: see Eisen, *The Peace and Violence of Judaism*. As a historian, Eisen does not want to argue that an anti-violence stance in Judaism is any more basic than a pro-violence stance. He simply describes the robust plurality of views. One significant distinction then between a historical-descriptive work and a philosophical-constructive one is the commitment to take a normative stance and argue for it. Nonetheless, in Jewish, as opposed to general philosophy, the philosopher must take diverse historical-textual evidence into account. One must be faithful both to the logic of the argument and to the sources of the tradition, a daunting responsibility. On the inaptness of the term "religion" to Judaism, at least in premodern times, see Leora Batnitzky, *How Judaism Became a Religion* (Princeton, NJ: Princeton University Press, 2013).

19. Abraham Isaac Ha-Cohen Kook, *Orot ha-Torah* [*The Lights of Torah*] (Sderot: Sderot ha-Torah Institute, 2016), 175.

20. For the distinction between thin and thick terms in ethics, see Bernard Williams, *Ethics and the Limits of Philosophy* (Cambridge, MA: Harvard University Press, 1986), 129, 140.

21. George Kateb, *Human Dignity* (Cambridge, MA: Belknap Press of Harvard University Press, 2011), 12.

22. See b Sotah 14a; Tanhuma Va-Yishlakh 10. These ancient rabbinic texts ask how humans can imitate God insofar as God is "a consuming fire." The *Tanhuma* text in particular enumerates violent aspects of God, which would exceed the human ability to imitate. The answer to the rhetorical question in both texts is that humans are to emulate only the loving, kind, patient, forgiving, truth-seeking attributes of God, not the terror-inducing ones. For a discussion, see David S. Shapiro, "The Doctrine of the Image of God and Imitatio Dei," in *Contemporary Jewish Ethics*, ed. Menachem Marc Kellner (New York: Hebrew Publishing, 1978), 126–51.

23. For the history of the euphemism "ethnic cleansing" (the Serbo-Croatian *etnicko ciscenje*), see www.theguardian.com/notesandqueries/query/0,,-2894,00 .html (accessed February 24, 2016). The term recalls the Nazi term *Judenrein*, "clean of Jews," as if the Jews were something dirty that needed to be scrubbed away. It also recalls the Nazi euphemism *Kristallnacht*, which focuses attention on the broken glass of the November 9–10, 1938, pogrom rather than on the broken lives.

24. Jonathan Glover, *Humanity: A Moral History of the 20th Century* (New Haven, CT: Yale University Press, 2012), 130.

25. The IDF Code of Ethics is a highly secular document, although one could argue that, similar to how just war norms in international law reflect a millennial Christian background, so too does the IDF Code reflect traditional, humane Jewish ideals.

Chapter 1: Holiness and Judaism

1. Although "holy" and "sacred" have different etymologies as English words, I shall use them interchangeably. English language studies of holiness often use words such as "sacred," "sancta," "sanctify," "consecrate," and "desecrate" in addition to "holy," "holiness," and so on. As all of these are appropriate to a study of holiness, an artificial distinction between "holy" and "sacred" based on etymology would be pedantic and run afoul of contemporary English language usage.

2. Emile Durkheim, *The Elementary Forms of the Religious Life*, trans. Joseph Ward Swain (New York: Free Press, 1965), see especially 52–53, 56, 107, 172–73, 488.

3. Mircea Eliade, *The Sacred & The Profane: The Nature of Religion*, trans. Willard R. Trask (New York: Harcourt Brace Jovanovich, 1987), 11.

4. See Eliade, *The Sacred & The Profane*, 203–9, on the lingering presence of the sacred in modernity—despite humanity's strenuous efforts to liberate itself from religion. The duality of sacred and profane persists despite modern efforts to desacralize all of reality and render it homogenously profane.

5. Jean Jacques Rousseau, *The Social Contract* (book IV, chapter 8), in *Jean Jacques Rousseau: The Basic Political Writings*, ed. and trans. Donald Cress (Indianapolis: Hackett Publishing, 1987), 220–27. A contemporary application of Rousseau's basic approach may be found in the late Edward Shils's essay, "Center and Periphery." Shils dwells on the connections between the sacred and authority, as well as the sacred and transcendence within the context of society. See Edward Shils, *The Constitution of Society* (Chicago: University of Chicago Press, 1982), 96.

6. Otto's classic, which I will consider in chapter 2, is *The Idea of the Holy*, trans. John W. Harvey (New York: Oxford University Press, 1973).

7. Pascal Boyer, *Religion Explained: The Evolutionary Origins of Religious Thought* (New York: Basic Books, 2001), 309. Boyer is no less a debunker of the integrity of religious claims and experience than the neuroscientists he describes. He merely thinks that they are going about it the wrong way. For a sympathetic (and nonreductionist) view of contemporary neuroscience research on religious experience, see Barbara Bradley Hagerty, *Fingerprints of God: The Search for a Science of Spirituality* (New York: Riverhead Books, 2009).

8. Having a brain is at least a *necessary* condition for religious experience! No one should be entirely dismissive of brain science in the study of religion.

9. Mary Midgley, *Evolution as a Religion* (New York: Routledge, 2002), 35.

10. Hilary Putnam following John Dewey distinguishes between a "dichotomy" (or "dualism") and a "distinction." Distinctions are perfectly serviceable ways of distinguishing matters in context. Dichotomies or dualisms tend to be metaphysical, reified generalizations about the way the world is. The sacred-profane distinction in Judaism is, as the following analysis will show, more of a distinction than a dichotomy. See Hilary Putnam, *The Collapse of the Fact/Value Dichotomy and Other Essays* (Cambridge, MA: Harvard University Press, 2002), 9.

11. In the Pentateuch, *ḥol* ("profane") occurs only at Leviticus 10:10. As a verb, however, it occurs elsewhere. The master exegete, Jacob Milgrom, prefers to translate *ḥol* as "common" rather than "profane." Although it occurs only once in the Torah, Milgrom gives "the common" a somewhat larger role than I, following Dan and Jenson, do here. See Jacob Milgrom, *Leviticus 1–16*, Anchor Bible, vol. 3 (New York: Doubleday, 1991), 615–17. That the prophet Ezekiel uses and amplifies the distinction of Leviticus motivates Milgrom's argument. See Ezekiel 44:23.

12. Joseph Dan, *On Sanctity: Religion, Ethics and Mysticism in Judaism and Other Religions* [Hebrew] (Jerusalem: Magnes Press, 1998), 14. Philip Peter Jenson, *Graded Holiness: A Key to the Priestly Conception of the World* (Sheffield, UK: Sheffield Academic Press, 1992), 43–45.

13. See Dan, *On Sanctity*, 26. Dan points out that in the ritual that declares the end of the Sabbath, *havdalah* ("separation"), the blessing distinguishes the holy from the profane. To say that non-Sabbath time is "profane" (*ḥol*), however, does not mean that it is wholly unlike sacred time. It is the medium in which continued holy activities take place. Time is not fallen, as it were. It is common and available for consecration when the appropriate moment arrives.

14. For a thorough study of how the term "religion" comes to describe the life of the Jews in the early modern West, see Leora Batnitzky, *How Judaism Became a Religion*. The basic idea is that the modern state, in order to accept Jews as citizens, needed to construe the Jews as having a religion rather than being a nation, a status with political implications. Historic exilic Judaism was something of a state within a state—an exiled nation trying to live under its own laws to whatever extent was allowed. Jettisoning the comprehensive legal-national modus vivendi of the Jews and transforming their tradition into a spiritual, "religious" matter, along the lines of a Protestant denomination, made their entry into the modern Westphalian state easier. Central and Western European Jews were willing participants in their transformation. The development of national or communal ideologies in the nineteenth century, such as Zionism or Autonomism, indicates the shortcomings of the Judaism-as-religion project. It is important to note that the concept of religion itself underwent a transformation during the Enlightenment. See Wilfred Cantwell Smith, *The Meaning and End of Religion* (Philadelphia: Fortress Press, 1963).

15. Dan, *On Sanctity*, 9, 26. This thesis would profit from exposure to Ernst Troeltsch's distinction between church and sect. Dan makes Christianity into a

sect and deprives it of the opportunity to be a church, in Troeltsch's terms. To use H. Richard Niebuhr's language, he allows the church to be only against the world.

16. Dan, *On Sanctity*, 29.

17. The sacred space that accompanies the Israelites during their forty-year wandering in the wilderness is variously referred to as a *mikdash* ("sanctuary"), *mishkan* ("dwelling"—that is, Tabernacle), and *ohel mo'ed* ("tent of meeting"). *Mikdash* refers to the whole structure, including the inner sanctum, outer courtyard, and walls. *Mishkan* and *ohel mo'ed* may sometimes refer to the whole but more typically refer to the covered structure within it. See Berlin and Brettler, eds., *The Jewish Study Bible*, 165.

18. For the idea of holiness as a field comprising God and all that belongs to him, see *Enzyklopedia Mikra'it* [Hebrew] (Jerusalem: Bialik Institute, 1976), vol. VII, entry *"kodesh, kadosh, kedushah,"* 43–62.

19. *Kedushah* ("holiness") "is the concept in Israelite faith which parallels *abstraction* in philosophical religion." See Israel Knohl, *The Sanctuary of Silence: The Priestly Torah and the Holiness School* (Minneapolis: Fortress Press, 1995), 147, n. 91. This idea is not original to Knohl; he derives it from Yehezkel Kaufmann and Walther Eichrodt. Levine, by contrast, claims that k-d-sh words very seldom indicate abstractions; they almost always have concrete meanings, which must be understood in context. In Levine's view, we should not generalize about what "kodesh," "kadosh," and so on mean. See Baruch Levine, "The Language of Holiness: Perceptions of the Sacred in the Hebrew Bible," in *Backgrounds for the Bible*, ed. Michael Patrick O'Connor and David Noel Freedman (Winona Lake, IN: Eisenbrauns, 1987), 252.

20. For an illuminating essay on different systems of thought about the divine in the Bible, see Steven Geller, "The God of the Covenant," in *One God or Many? Concepts of Divinity in the Ancient World*, vol. I, ed. Barbara Nevling Porter (n.p.: Transactions of the Casco Bay Assyriological Institute, 2000), 277–81. It is interesting that Ronald Dworkin, in his attempt to define a suitably nonpersonal God, looks to Tillich, Einstein, and Spinoza, never imagining that resources for such a theology exist in the Bible itself. Ronald Dworkin, *Religion without God* (Cambridge, MA: Harvard University Press, 2013), 31–43.

21. Jenson, *Graded Holiness*, 48. God's "static" presence is his dwelling in the *mishkan*; "dynamic presence" refers to encounters between God and humans. Ibid., 113–14.

22. For a review of the sources of ritual impurity, see Jonathan Klawans, *Purity, Sacrifice, and the Temple: Symbolism and Supersessionism in the Study of Ancient Judaism* (New York: Oxford University Press, 2006), 53–56.

23. Jenson, *Graded Holiness*, 111.

24. Nahum Sarna, *Exploring Exodus: The Heritage of Biblical Israel* (New York: Schocken Books, 1986), 213–14. For a premodern comparison of Tabernacle with Creation, see *Exodus Rabbah*, Terumah 33:4.

25. Schwartz points out that k-d-sh can also apply to things set apart or designated for a special purpose without regard to divine ownership. In Jeremiah 22:7, for example, "I will appoint [*kidashti*] destroyers against you." Also Jeremiah 51:27, "appoint [*kadeshu*] nations against her." God is speaking here, but there is nothing "holy" about the adversaries that he is preparing for Judah. They are simply set aside for a designated purpose and so have a unique status. Subsequently, in rabbinic Hebrew, when a man weds (*mikadesh*) a woman, he dedicates her for himself. She acquires the status of being set aside for him, not available to any other man. For other examples, see Baruch J. Schwartz, *The Holiness Legislation* [Hebrew] (Jerusalem: Magnes Press, 1999), 253.

26. For the concept of social reality, see John R. Searle, *The Construction of Social Reality* (New York: Free Press, 1995). For an application of Searle's view to holiness, see Alan Mittleman, "The Problem of Holiness," *Journal of Analytic Theology* 3 (2015), 29–46; available at http://journalofanalytictheology.com/jat/index.php/jat (accessed March 20, 2016).

27. Benjamin D. Sommer, *The Bodies of God and the World of Ancient Israel* (New York: Cambridge University Press, 2009), 64.

28. See Milgrom's analysis of *ma'al*, the technical term for desecration or sacrilege, which parallels *ḥillail* in Milgrom, *Leviticus 1–16*, 320, 345–56.

29. This is evident from Exodus 16:21–26. God does not shower manna on the Israelites on the seventh day. He continues to rest, as on the first Sabbath after Creation.

30. The opening of Hilary Putnam's famous essay, "Brains in a Vat," comes to mind. Putnam presents an ant who improbably traces an image of Winston Churchill in the sand. We don't think that the image, produced unintentionally and randomly, "represents" Churchill in the way that human acts of representation do, but why not? What makes representation possible? Putnam opts for an explanation that takes a shared, social world seriously. Nonetheless, the point that nature per se does not represent stands. See Hilary Putnam, *Reason, Truth, and History* (Cambridge, MA: Cambridge University Press, 1981), 1–21.

31. For an extensive analysis of the construction materials of the sanctum and their grade of holiness, based on value and complexity, see Menahem Haran, *Temples and Temple-Service in Ancient Israel: An Inquiry into the Character of Cult Phenomena and the Historical Setting of the Priestly School* (Oxford, UK: Clarendon Press, 1978), 149–88. See also H. Mueller, "qdš," in Ernst Jenni and Claus Westermann, *Theological Lexicon of the Old Testament*, vol. 3, trans. Mark Biddle (Peabody, MA: Hendrikson Publishers, 1994), 1103–18.

32. Although some hold that separation is the main sense of holiness, it is more accurate to say that separation is a consequence of holiness, not its criterion. Holiness has a positive content, which the mere condition of separation does not imply. See Jensen, *Graded Holiness*, 48. Schwartz claims, to the contrary, that separation is one of the two primary senses of k-d-sh, the other being cleanness, purification. Schwartz, *The Holiness Legislation*, 251–54.

33. Baruch A. Levine, *The JPS Torah Commentary: Leviticus*, (Philadelphia: Jewish Publication Society, 1989), 257.

34. Jacob Milgrom, *Leviticus: A Book of Ritual and Ethics, A Continental Commentary* (Minneapolis: Fortress Press, 2004), 9.

35. Ibid., 12. Klawans is critical of Milgrom for associating all of the impure substances with death. He avers that both death and sex are in play. The focus on fluids connected with sexuality suggests this. Symbolically, the point is that God neither dies nor reproduces. To be careful about contact with blood and seminal discharge is, in Klawans's view, a kind of imitatio dei. Death and sex are what is furthest from God. Klawans, *Purity, Sacrifice, and the Temple*, 57–58.

36. One of the exegetical issues here is what *kol* (normally "all" or "every") means. Should it be translated as "whoever" or "whatever" or both depending on context, as in the New Jewish Publication Society (NJPS) version here? The rabbis opt for "whatever," excluding persons from the category of recipients of contagious holiness.

37. Berlin and Brettler, eds., *The Jewish Study Bible*, 218.

38. Medieval exegetes such as Rashi, ibn Ezra, and even Rashbam, who sometimes dispenses with rabbinic tradition and reads the text according to its apparent, plain sense, try to see the concerns about holiness in these texts as admonitions to prepare to be in contact with the holy items, not as descriptions of "holiness contagion." See Martin Lockshin, "Is Holiness Contagious?" in *Purity, Holiness, and Identity in Judaism and Christianity*, ed. Carl Ehrlich, Anders Runesson, and Eileen Schuler (Tübingen: Mohr Siebeck, 2013). Milgrom argues that the rabbis do endorse holiness contagion but to a very limited extent; only the most sacred altar and vessels communicate holiness and then only to already sacred offerings placed on or in them. See Milgrom, *Leviticus 1–16*, 446.

39. Levine, *The JPS Torah Commentary: Leviticus*, 37.

40. Levine, ibid., 38 (emphasis added). Note that the prophetic text is from Haggai, not Malachi, as erroneously given in *The JPS Torah Commentary: Leviticus*.

41. Milgrom, *Leviticus 1–16*, 446. Menahem Haran also endorses contagious holiness in the Priestly Source (P) and elsewhere: "[Holiness] is conceived of as being virtually tangible, a physical entity, the existence and activity of which can be sensorially perceived. Any person or object coming into contact with the altar (Exodus 29:37) or any of the articles of the tabernacle furniture (Exodus 30:29) becomes 'holy,' that is, contracts holiness and like the tabernacle appurtenances themselves becomes consecrated." Haran, *Temples and Temple-Service*, 176.

42. Transporting the most holy altar and appurtenances of the movable Tabernacle is an acute concern. In Numbers, chapter 4, the Tabernacle has to be dismantled by Aaron and his sons, who have access to the sancta. Only then can the Levite clan of the Kohathites transport the holy items. If the Kohathites were to have direct contact with or even view the holy items, they would die (Numbers 4:15, 20).

43. Haran, *Temples and Temple-Service*, 187.

44. Mary Douglas, *Purity and Danger: An Analysis of the Concepts of Pollution and Taboo* (London: Routledge, 1989), 50.

45. Milgrom, *Leviticus 1–16*, 453–55.

46. Milgrom's speculation about the reason for the diminution of the importance of contagious holiness has to do with the ancient idea that murderers could take refuge in the sanctuary (Exodus 21:12–14). By holding onto the altar, they would come under divine protection. The priests "were probably deeply disturbed by the stream of murderers, thieves, and assorted criminals who flocked to the altar and resided on the sanctuary grounds on the basis of hoary, venerable tradition that the altar 'sanctifies.'" They therefore took the radical step of limiting the sanctifying ability of the altar to communicate holiness to the sacrifice, not to persons. The authorities could then apprehend criminals with impunity. Fascinating, but highly speculative! See Milgrom, *Leviticus 1–16*, 455–56.

47. Israel Knohl, *The Divine Symphony: The Bible's Many Voices* (Philadelphia: Jewish Publication Society, 2003), 65. Knohl's more extensive and technical presentation of what he terms the "Priestly Torah" and the "Holiness School" can be found in Knohl, *The Sanctuary of Silence*, especially 124–98.

48. Knohl, *The Sanctuary of Silence*, 209. The chronological relation of P and H, Knohl notwithstanding, is a matter of ongoing controversy. See Klawans, *Purity, Sacrifice and the Temple*, 49–52.

49. Schwartz, *The Holiness Legislation*, 249.

50. Ibid., 247.

51. See Alan Mittleman, *A Short History of Jewish Ethics* (Malden, MA: Wiley-Blackwell, 2012), 29, 31, from which this paragraph has been adapted.

52. Klawans, *Purity, Sacrifice, and the Temple*, 55.

53. Ibid.

54. See comments of Marc Brettler to Psalms 15, in Berlin and Brettler, eds., *The Jewish Study Bible*, 1297.

55. Douglas, *Purity and Danger*, 132.

56. This point is made by Jacob Neusner in such books as *The Idea of Purity in Ancient Judaism* (Leiden: Brill, 1973). For a digest and analysis of Jacob Neusner's extensive scholarship on this point, see Susan Haber, *"They Shall Purify Themselves": Essays on Purity in Early Judaism* (Atlanta: Society for Biblical Literature, 2008), 31–40.

57. See b Megillah 29a, where the presence or ten men, or even fewer, in a synagogue is accompanied by God's presence in the form of the *shekhinah*, God's indwelling. See also *Mekhilta d'Rabbi Ishmael*, B'Ḥodesh 11.

58. Tzvi Nozick, "Holiness in the Rabbinic Period," in *Holiness in Jewish Thought*, ed. Alan Mittleman (Oxford, UK: Oxford University Press, 2018), 42.

59. Note, however, that in some rabbinic texts Israel is promised by God that it will be holy forever, despite its backslidings and defections. See, for example, *Vayikra Rabbah* 24:2.

60. *The Mishnah*, trans. Herbert Danby (London: Oxford University Press, 1933), 605. The opening chapter of Kelim is structured so that it begins with ten

degrees of uncleanness (*tumah*) and then details ten degrees of holiness (*kedushah*). The structural symmetry nicely illustrates the spectrum concept.

61. *Bereshit Rabbah* 96:5; see parallels at *Tanḥuma* I, chapter 12, midrash 3, and *Pesikta Rabbati* I:4.

62. For these and other miraculous qualities of Israel, see *Mekhilta d'Rabbi Ishmael*, Bo, introduction.

63. M Yoma 5:2; b Yoma 54b.

64. For an analysis and constructive theological response to this ambivalence regarding the holiness of the land of Israel, see Joseph Isaac Lifshitz, "Holiness and *Eretz Yisrael*," in *Holiness in Jewish Thought*, ed. Mittleman, 75–79.

65. *Tanḥuma*, ed. Buber, 3:37a, cited in Hannah K. Harrington, *Holiness: Rabbinic Judaism and the Graeco-Roman World* (New York: Routledge, 2001), 162. I have revised the Jeremiah passage by using the NJPS translation.

66. *Mekhilta d'Rabbi Ishmael*, Shirata, 3; available at http://babel.hathitrust .org/cgi/pt?id=hvd.hwnmuh;view=1up;seq=156 (accessed April 13, 2016).

67. Assessing the literature, Wolfson goes so far as to claim that "we may not be far off the mark by describing the rabbinic attitude as affirming the Jewish people as the incarnation of God on earth, the full embodiment of the divine image, the physical site of God's indwelling in the mundane." Elliot Wolfson, *Venturing Beyond: Law and Morality in Kabbalistic Mysticism* (New York: Oxford University Press, 2006), 39–40.

68. *Sifra*, Kedoshim 1:1; available at www.sefaria.org/Sifra,_Kedoshim,_Sec tion_1.1?lang=he-en&layout=heLeft&sidebarLang=all (accessed April 14, 2016).

69. For a comparable statement of radical mutuality, see *Sifre: A Tannaitic Commentary to the Book of Deuteronomy*, trans. Reuven Hammer (New Haven, CT: Yale University Press, 1986), 346, a favorite text taken up by the modern thinkers Franz Rosenzweig and Abraham Joshua Heschel. The source text in Isaiah (43:12) reads: "You are My witnesses—declares the LORD—and I am God." In the midrash, Rabbi Shimon bar Yoḥai makes bold to say: "If you are my witnesses, then I am God. If you are not my witnesses, then I am not God."

70. Cited in Harrington, *Holiness*, 163.

71. Text taken from the Soncino translation of the Talmud Tractate Avodah Zarah, ed. I. Epstein (London: Soncino Press, 1935); available at http://halakhah .com/pdf/nezikin/Avodah_Zarah.pdf (accessed October 19, 2017). An older, slightly different version of this progression of virtues is found in the Mishnah, Sotah 9:15.

72. That is Solomon Schechter's view. Schechter drives holiness in an ethical direction and then subordinates it to saintliness, with its purely moral resonances. See Solomon Schechter, *Aspects of Rabbinic Theology: Major Concepts of the Talmud* (New York: Schocken Books, 1961 [1909]), 209.

73. A fascinating study of the superman/*Übermensch* theme in medieval Jewish thought is Isaak Heinemann, "Der Begriff des Übermenschen in der jüdischen Religions-Philosophie," *Der Morgen* 1 (1925): 3–17.

74. Kuzari I:11–13. Judah Halevi, *The Kuzari: An Argument for the Faith of Israel*, trans. Hartwig Hirschfeld (New York: Schocken Books, 1964), 44–45. The Arabic original was translated into Hebrew in the Middle Ages by Judah ibn Tibbon. References to the Hebrew follow the ibn Tibbon translation; available at www.sefaria.org/Sefer_Kuzari.1?lang=he-en&layout=heLeft&sidebarLang=all (accessed October 19, 2017).

75. Kuzari I:65 (Hirschfeld translation, 53).

76. Alexander Altmann, "Judah Halevi's Theory of Climates," *ALEPH* 5 (2005): 215–46. This is a translated version of Altmann's classic article "Torat ha-'aqlimim le-rabbi Yehuda Ha-Levi," *Melilah* 1 (1944): 1–17.

77. Kuzari I:95, II:10 (Hirschfeld translation, 64–67, 88).

78. All references in this paragraph are from Kuzari I:95.

79. Personal communication with Prof. Lenn Goodman, who offered the translation of *safwatuhu* (April 20, 2016).

80. Kuzari I:27 (Hirschfeld translation, 47). The convert will derive benefit from his conversion, but not equality. Halevi uses a particularly ugly example to "prove" his point: just as the white man and the black, although both created by God, are not equal, neither are Jews and non-Jews. Racialist thinking of this kind was common in antiquity and under Islam. See, for example, Bernard Lewis, *Race and Color in Islam* (New York: Harper Torch Books, 1971). See also Abraham Melamed, *The Image of the Black in Jewish Culture: A History of the Other*, trans. Betty Sigler Rozen (New York: RoutledgeCurzon, 2003). There is an argument to be made for not imposing contemporary moral views upon thinkers of the past. However that may be, there is no case to be made for using ancient and medieval views uncritically today. We may not be wise to impose our moral views on our ancestors, but we should not hesitate to impose them on ourselves.

81. Kuzari II:14 (Hirschfeld translation, 89).

82. Kuzari III:53 (Hirschfeld translation, 180–83). Performing mitzvot brings about material changes, comparable to the processes of nature. God has created both nature and Torah with intelligence and intent. Religious action in performance of commandments is efficacious in elevating the soul, for example, not in a mechanical way but because such actions are decreed by God and are integral to his overall design of the cosmos.

83. James Kugel, "The Holiness of Israel and the Land in Second Temple Times," in *Texts, Temples, and Traditions: A Tribute to Menachem Haran*, ed. Michael V. Fox and Edward L. Greenstein (Winona Lake, IN: Eisenbraun, 1996), 28. Kugel's line refers to the view of Israel of the *Book of Jubilees*, not in Halevi, but the same point mutatis mutandis applies to the Kuzari.

84. Kugel argues that the language of seed and mingling allude to the biblical prohibitions of planting mixed seed (Leviticus 19:19; Deuteronomy 22:9). This violation of "cultic law" now means that Israel impugns its sacred status by mixing with gentiles in marriage. Kugel, "The Holiness of Israel," 24.

85. Kugel, "The Holiness of Israel, 26. See Jubilees 2:30–31.

86. Menachem Kellner, *Maimonides on Judaism and the Jewish People* (Albany: State University of New York Press, 1991), 92. Kellner writes: "[I]t is the rational appropriation of metaphysical truths about God that constitutes Israel 'a kingdom of priests and a holy nation.'" For Maimonides's own interpretation of Exodus 19:5–6, see Guide III:32. Kellner's fully developed reading of Maimonides on holiness can be found in Menachem Kellner, *Maimonides' Confrontation with Mysticism* (Oxford, UK: Littman Library of Jewish Civilization, 2006), 85–126, and more recently in Menachem Kellner, *They Too Are Called Human: Gentiles in the Eyes of Maimonides* [Hebrew] (Ramat Gan: Bar Ilan University Press, 2016).

87. Kellner, *Maimonides' Confrontation with Mysticism*, 28.

88. Wolfson, *Venturing Beyond*, 27. See also Moshe Hallamish, *An Introduction to the Kabbalah*, trans. Ruth Bar-Ilan and OraWiskind-Elper (Albany: State University of New York Press, 1999), 267–71.

89. Hallamish, *An Introduction to the Kabbalah*, 173. Alternatively, the "husks" protect the fruit but must eventually be cast away. The husks have a role in the economy of holiness. Their evil serves a purpose, albeit a temporary one. Ibid., 174.

90. Wolfson, *Venturing Beyond*, 51. On the Second Temple origins of the myth of Eve's progeny, other than Abel and Seth, being fathered by the serpent, see ibid., 40–41.

91. *Sefer ha-Rimmonim*, 211–12, quoted in Wolfson, *Venturing Beyond*, 74.

92. Cited in Hartley Lachter, *Kabbalistic Revolution: Reimagining Judaism in Medieval Spain* (New Brunswick, NJ: Rutgers University Press, 2014), 97.

93. See Wolfson, *Venturing Beyond*, 45n115, for textual references.

94. For a study of the complex, dialectical theology of Ḥabad Hasidism, see Rachel Elior, *The Paradoxical Ascent to God: The Kabbalistic Theosophy of Habad Hasidism*, trans. Jeffrey M. Green (Albany: State University of New York Press, 1993), especially 115–29 on the soul.

95. The concept of klipot, as it develops in Kabbalah, becomes part of a cosmogonic myth innovated by the mystical circles of Safed in the sixteenth century. God's creation of the world was actually catastrophic. The world is made up of shards and fragments of divinity. God's pure energy poured into vessels, which shattered and scattered into the world as we know it. Elements of divinity are trapped within materiality. Jews must do spiritual work to raise the sparks of divinity and restore the unity of God. The klipot are outer shells, the deceptive material manifestations of divinity within. See Hallamish, *An Introduction to the Kabbalah*, 173–82, for a treatment of the klipot in the context of the Zohar and Safed Kabbalah.

96. See, for example, *Tanya*, part I, chapters 1:17, 6:1, 8; available at www .sefaria.org/Tanya,_Part_One,_The_Book_of_the_Average_Men.7?lang=he &layout=lines&sidebarLang=all (accessed May 2, 2016).

97. *Tanya*, part I, chapter 7.

98. Lenn Goodman comments, in an oral communication: "What marks them as superstition is the coloration of nature with the hopes and fears of those who subscribe to such beliefs and the practices they underwrite."

99. See, for example, Lachter's presentation of kabbalistic portrayals of Jewish-gentile difference as inversions of Christian anti-Judaism in Lachter, *Kabbalistic Revolution*, 73, 91–92.

100. Biur to Exodus 19:6; available at https://books.google.com/books?id =0ZosAQAAIAAJ&pg=PA1&dq=%D7%A0%D7%AA%D7%99%D7%91%D7 %95%D7%AA%20%D7%94%D7%A9%D7%9C%D7%95%D7%9D&hl=en&ei =lmdHToi5NIO5tgf-joH5BQ&sa=X&oi=book_result&ct=result&resnum =4&ved=0CEMQ6AEwAw#v=onepage&q&f=false (accessed May 9, 2016). See also Mendelssohn's characterization of the Jews as a priestly nation to teach God's ways and truths to those nations in whose midst it lives. Moses Mendelssohn, *Jerusalem*, trans. Allan Arkush (Lebanon, NH: Brandeis University Press, 1983), 118.

101. Biur to Leviticus 19:2; available at https://books.google.com/books?id =8qpAAAAAYAAJ&printsec=frontcover&dq=%D7%97%D7%95%D7%9E %D7%A9%20%D7%9E%D7%A7%D7%95%D7%A8%20%D7%97%D7%99 %D7%99%D7%9D&hl=en&ei=2WlHTsW3I4G6tgfZ2eDnBQ&sa=X&oi =book_result&ct=result&resnum=1&ved=0CDAQ6AEwAA#v=onepage&q&f =false (accessed May 9, 2016).

102. Compare the commentary of Malbim, a century later than Mendelssohn, on Leviticus 19:2. The old, metaphysically inflated claims remain. For Malbim, controlling our natures through practicing the mitzvot parallels God's control of Creation. It allows us to transcend the laws of nature. Malbim wants to shore up the traditional framework against the Reformist tendencies in part unleashed by Mendelssohn's work in the eighteenth century.

103. For an overview and analysis, see Henry E. Allison, *Kant's Theory of Freedom* (New York: Cambridge University Press, 1990), 171–79. For studies that are highly sensitive to the religious dimension of Kant's ethics, see John E. Hare, *The Moral Gap: Kantian Ethics, Human Limits, and God's Assistance* (Oxford, UK: Oxford University Press, 1996) and *God and Morality* (Malden, MA: Wiley-Blackwell, 2009).

104. Allison, *Kant's Theory*, 171.

105. Ibid., 172.

106. Immanuel Kant, *Critique of Practical Reason* (Upper Saddle River, NJ: Prentice Hall, 1993), 129 (book II, chapter IV:123).

107. Hermann Cohen, *Religion of Reason out of the Sources of Judaism*, trans. Simon Kaplan (Atlanta: Scholars Press, 1995), 111.

108. Ibid., 103.

109. Ibid., 109.

110. Ibid., 109.

111. Ibid., 111.

112. Martin Buber, *I and Thou*, trans. Walter Kaufmann (New York: Simon and Schuster, 1996), 62. For Israel's encounter with God at Sinai as a "holy event," see Martin Buber, *The Prophetic Faith* (New York: Harper Torchbooks, 1949), 46.

113. Heschel's view will be taken up more fully in chapter 2.

114. Abraham Joshua Heschel, *The Sabbath* (New York: Farrar, Straus, and Giroux, 2005 [1951]), 78.

115. Joseph B. Soloveitchik, *Halakhic Man*, trans. Lawrence Kaplan (Philadelphia: Jewish Publication Society, 1983), 150 n. 51.

116. Ibid., 46–47.

117. For insight into the relation between halakhah and ethics in Soloveitchik's thought, I am indebted to my colleague, Prof. Yonatan Brafman.

118. Franz Rosenzweig, *The Star of Redemption*, trans. Barbara E. Galli (Madison: University of Wisconsin Press, 2005), 318.

119. Ibid., 324 (emphasis added).

120. Ibid., 323.

121. Ibid., 327.

122. Ibid., 438.

123. Ludwig Wittgenstein, *Philosophical Investigations*, trans. G.E.M. Anscombe (New York: Macmillan, 1968), 32 (para. 67).

124. Comparison of dispositional properties such as color to moral properties is a trope of realist metaphysics of value. See, for example, John McDowell, "Values and Secondary Qualities," in *Essays on Moral Realism*, ed. Geoffrey Sayre-McCord (Ithaca, NY: Cornell University Press, 1988), 166–80.

Chapter 2: Holiness and Ethics

1. The translation is Milgrom's in Jacob Milgrom, *Leviticus 17–22: A New Translation and Commentary* (New York: Anchor Bible/Doubleday, 2000), 1791.

2. Milgrom comments that "the fact that she 'sprang from the loins' of a priest means that she partakes of his holiness, which she diminishes, as would a priest (v. 7) by her promiscuity. Indeed, as a member of a priest's family, she literally absorbs holiness by partaking of her father's portion of holy (but not most holy) sacrifices." He also speculates that her transgression was premarital sex. Milgrom, *Leviticus 17–22*, 1810.

3. Abraham Joshua Heschel, "The Meaning of Observance," in *Understanding Jewish Theology: Classical Issues and Modern Perspectives*, ed. Jacob Neusner (Binghamton, NY: Global Publications, 2001), 95. Heschel repeats the observation in his major work *God in Search of Man* (New York: Farrar, Straus, and Giroux, 1983 [1955]), 17. The text there reads: "to the Bible the idea of the good is penultimate; it cannot exist without the holy. The holy is the essence, the good is its expression. Things created in six days He considered good, the seventh day

He made *holy*." Heschel thus takes the logic of the Book of Genesis to imply that the holy is the telos or fulfillment of the good.

4. Heschel, *God in Search of Man*, 290.

5. Ibid., 285–87.

6. John Reeder Jr., "The Relation of the Moral and the Numinous in Otto's Notion of the Holy," in *Religion and Morality*, ed. Gene Outka and John Reeder Jr. (Garden City, NY: Anchor Books, 1973), 290.

7. Some writers treat "ethics" and "morality" as synonyms, differing mainly in their etymology but bearing the same semantic load. Others take "morality" to refer to first-order normative behavior and "ethics" to refer to second-order reflection on norms, typically within a larger context of human flourishing. On this view, ethics is to morality what aesthetics is to art. I shall largely use "ethics" in this way, as roughly synonymous with moral philosophy, taking "morality" as its subject matter.

8. Donald E. Brown, *Human Universals* (Philadelphia: Temple University Press, 1991), 90.

9. This is a central thesis of Susanne K. Langer in her classic work *Philosophy in a New Key: A Study in the Symbolism of Reason, Rite, and Art*, 3rd ed. (Cambridge, MA: Harvard University Press, 1979), 144–70. For an updating of the case, see Kenan Malik, *Man, Beast and Zombie* (New Brunswick, NJ: Rutgers University Press, 2000), 214–21.

10. Do chimpanzees use symbols or do they use only signs? To the extent that symbols convey complex ideas, such as the relations of similarity and dissimilarity, chimpanzees, arguably, can be trained to use symbols and think symbolically. Chimpanzees naturally group like objects (shoes with shoes, for example) but can be trained to group pairs of like objects with different pairs of like objects. For example, they can group two apples with two hammers, excluding a third pair consisting of a shoe and a flower. Given a large circle and a small circle, and then a large square; they can pick out a small square and add it to the second set. Given a lock and a key, they can compose a can and a can opener as the equivalent. Thus, they can grasp, albeit in a limited way, the relation of similarity and dissimilarity—that is, a relation not just of objects (A = A) but of relations (A:A = B:B). Does this constitute symbolic thought or is it a prerequisite for such thought? What is clear is that the chimps' training in analogical thought leads nowhere. It remains a laboratory demonstration. The human ability by contrast underwrites broad swaths of our intelligence and mental life. See David and Ann Premack, *Original Intelligence* (New York: McGraw Hill, 2003), 184–99. Cf. Terrence W. Deacon, *The Symbolic Species: The Co-Evolution of Language and the Brain* (New York: W. W. Norton, 1997), 22. For Kenan Malik's dissent, see Malik, *Man, Beast and Zombie*, 217.

11. This and the preceding quote are from Langer, *Philosophy in a New Key*, 176.

12. Brown, *Human Universals*, 69, 94.

13. Mary Douglas, *Natural Symbols: Explorations in Cosmology* (London: Routledge, 1996), 78.

14. Douglas, *Purity and Danger*, 115.

15. Paul Bloom, *Just Babies: The Origins of Good and Evil* (New York: Crown Publishers, 2013), 31.

16. See, for example, Frans de Waal, *Our Inner Ape* (New York: Riverhead Books, 2005). See also Patricia Churchland, *Braintrust* (Princeton, NJ: Princeton University Press, 2011).

17. Bloom, *Just Babies*, 64, 98–99.

18. For a categorical (too categorical?) statement of the difference, see Christine Korsgaard, *The Sources of Normativity* (Cambridge, UK: Cambridge University Press, 2006), 13–16.

19. For a magisterial argument on behalf of the independence of morality—essentially an advocacy of Hume's fact/value distinction, see Ronald Dworkin, *Justice for Hedgehogs* (Cambridge, MA: Harvard University Press, 2011), 23–87.

20. For a major contemporary synthesis of ethical theory and evolutionary theory, see Philip Kitcher, *The Ethical Project* (Cambridge, MA: Harvard University Press, 2011). For an overview of the evolutionary ethics project and philosophical debates surrounding it, see Scott M. James, *An Introduction to Evolutionary Ethics* (Malden, MA: Wiley-Blackwell, 2011).

21. An illustrative study is Robert B. Louden, *Kant's Human Being: Essays on His Theory of Human Nature* (New York: Oxford University Press, 2011).

22. Kitcher, *The Ethical Project*, 112. One immediate problem with Kitcher's view is that the early history of gods and other unseen forces reveals their moral ineptitude, stupidity, or lack of ethical concern. He generalizes the ethicized divinity of the Western monotheisms onto the cultural history of religion per se. For a corrective, see Robert Wright, *The Evolution of God* (New York: Little, Brown, 2009), 17–26.

23. Kitcher, *The Ethical Project*, 114.

24. In Otto's foreword to the first English translation of his work (1923), he laments that his thesis has been taken to justify "irrationalism." His plea is for holism. No one should concern himself with God as "Numen ineffabile" unless he has already "devoted serious and assiduous study" to God as "Ratio aeterna." See Otto, *The Idea of the Holy*, xxi.

25. The term "veneer theory" is Frans de Waal's. See Frans de Waal, *Primates and Philosophers: How Morality Evolved* (Princeton, NJ: Princeton University Press, 2009), 6.

26. Otto, *The Idea of the Holy*, 5. William James does something similar in the *Varieties*, strongly separating religion from morality and giving religion, in the sense of religious experience, greater power, primacy, and authenticity. See citations and discussion in Hans Joas, *The Genesis of Values*, trans. Gregory Moore (Chicago: University of Chicago Press, 2000), 47.

27. Otto, *The Idea of the Holy*, 6–7.

28. Ibid., 12–13 (emphasis added).

29. Reeder, "The Relation of the Moral and the Numinous," 264.

30. Otto, *The Idea of the Holy*, 109.

31. Ibid., 51–52.

32. For ancient antecedents, especially Xenophanes, see Eric J. Sharpe, *Comparative Religion: A History* (LaSalle, IL: Open Court, 1986), 1–7.

33. David Hume, *Dialogues and Natural History of Religion* (Oxford, UK: Oxford University Press, 1993), 140, 143.

34. Sarah Hrdy, *Mothers and Others: The Evolutionary Origins of Mutual Understanding* (Cambridge, MA: Harvard University Press, 2009), 33, 51, 52.

35. My treatment in this section is indebted to Robert Bellah in Robert N. Bellah, *Religion in Human Evolution* (Cambridge, MA: Belknap Press, 2011, 44–116.

36. Premack and Premack, *Original Intelligence*, 145.

37. De Waal, *Our Inner Ape*, 194.

38. Sarah Hrdy, cited in Bellah, *Religion in Human Evolution*, 70.

39. Frans de Waal, cited in Bellah, *Religion in Human Evolution*, 72. For the development of empathy, compassion, and helping behavior in human toddlers, see Bloom, *Just Babies*, 33–57.

40. Michael Tomasello writes, "the crucial difference between human cognition and that of other species is the ability to participate with others in collaborative activities with shared goals and intentions." This, Hrdy notes, is the new dividing line "separating our natures from those of other apes." Tomasello, quoted in Hrdy, *Mothers and Others*, 9.

41. Bloom, *Just Babies*, 45.

42. De Waal, *Our Inner Ape*, 195.

43. Irenäus Eibl-Eibesfeldt, *Love and Hate: The Natural History of Behavior Patterns*, trans. Geoffrey Strachan (New York: Aldine de Gruyter, 1996), 130–55.

44. Ibid., 152.

45. De Waal, *Our Inner Ape*, 108.

46. Korsgaard, in her criticism of moral realism, accuses the realist of stipulating primitive goods or rights and wrongs and then believing, with undue confidence, that they can overcome all skeptical challenges. On that view, my insistence that the human infant is an undeniable locus of extraordinary value, value such as to be called sacred, is just so much special pleading. I do not deny the always available possibility of the open question. I do deny that the exercise of cognitive skepticism is a value-neutral one. I do not see how acting on one's skepticism about the value of human life is anything other than immoral. See Korsgaard, *The Sources of Normativity*, 41. For a view that is far more sympathetic to the one taken here, see Robert M. Adams, *Finite and Infinite Goods—* for example, "[t]o explicate our sense of the sanctity of certain objects, and particularly of human life, in terms of images of God, is to explicate it in terms of what the objects *are*," 121.

47. See Pinker's "The Stupidity of Dignity," *New Republic*, May 28, 2008; available at https://newrepublic.com/article/64674/the-stupidity-dignity (accessed June 19, 2016).

48. I follow Dworkin's distinction between external and internal skepticism in the next two paragraphs. See Dworkin, *Justice for Hedgehogs*, 30–39.

49. Even as resolute a secular philosopher as Ronald Dworkin finds the concept of sacredness crucial to his depiction of the worth of human life. Indeed, he chooses to use the word "sacred," which for him connotes inviolability and dishonoring "what ought to be honored." Perhaps "sacred" lends itself a bit more readily to purely secular interpretation along the lines of intrinsic value than does "holy," which retains its religious resonance. See Ronald Dworkin, *Life's Dominion*, 74.

50. Hannah Arendt, *The Human Condition* (Chicago: University of Chicago Press, 1958), 247.

51. I owe the reference to the cherubim to Rabbi Moshe Grussgott of Congregation Ramath Orah. For the symbolism of the cherubim, see *Encyclopedia Judaica*, vol. 5 (Jerusalem: Keter, 1972), 397–99, s.v. "Cherub." Note also that a parallel is made between the baby Moses, whose mother "sees that he is good [*ki-tov*]" (Exodus 2:3) and the Creation story, where God sees that his work is good (*ki-tov*). See Midrash Shemot Rabbah 1:20 and exegetes such as Nachmanides and Rashbam on Exodus 2:3.

52. For the idea that common human experiences form the base that supports symbolic and metaphorical thought and expression, see George Lakoff and Mark Johnson, *Metaphors We Live By* (Chicago: University of Chicago Press, 1980), 19.

53. Sarah Hrdy, *Mothers and Others*, 69.

54. Ibid., 73.

55. Ibid., 78–79.

56. Clifford Geertz, "Ethos, World View, and the Analysis of Sacred Symbols," in Geertz, *The Interpretation of Cultures* (New York: Basic Books, 1973), 127.

57. Clifford Geertz, "Religion as a Cultural System," in Geertz, *The Interpretation of Cultures*, 112.

58. Catherine Bell, *Ritual: Perspectives and Dimensions* (New York: Oxford University Press, 1997), 82. I am indebted to my daughter-in-law, Amy Levin, for bringing this work to my attention.

59. Bellah, *Religion in Human Evolution*, 81–82.

60. See ibid., 91–92. The idea that human play and, eventually, ritual constitutes a good in itself may be compelling, but it is questionable whether this applies to animals. Eibl-Eibesfeldt discusses "tournaments" among fish, reptiles such as marine iguanas, birds, and mammals. Among the cold-blooded animals, these combative tournaments seem to be precursors to mammalian play. They evidently serve to discharge aggression, constitute or reconstitute social hierarchies (among social creatures), and so on. See Eibl-Eibesfeldt, *Love and Hate*, 64–69.

61. Bell, *Ritual*, 157.

62. A sophisticated version of the "make-believe" thesis is found in Samuel Lebens, "The Epistemology of Religiosity: A Jewish Perspective." Lebens argues for the necessity of make-believe to a properly religious life. It is insufficient to

believe in God, say, as a deist might. A Jew must make that belief consequential in every waking moment. Make-believe, in the sense of making a belief occurrent and giving it practical weight, is essential. Lebens goes beyond this, however, to claim that make-believe must employ the imagination as well. (He doesn't connect this explicitly with play but it does no violence to his thesis to do so.) The participants in a Seder, say, must believe that were it not for God's ancient deliverance, they would still be slaves today. They must take an as-if stance, imagining what the world would be like under their counterfactual conditions. Religiosity on the whole requires such an as-if perspective. Holiness, in his view, is an attitude of awe that follows from seeing the world as if it were full of the divine presence. This has the additional benefit of ensuring good morality. Holiness seems to be an emergent characteristic, in this account, of human intention and action. It is a "relational property" (a "status" in my typology) rather than a substantive one. This is an attractive view, but it still lacks, in my judgment, realist grounding. Available at www.theapj.com/wp-content/uploads/2011/08/Lebens-1-Epistemology_of_Religiosity.pdf (accessed June 21, 2016).

63. For an attack on the physicalist claim that the world is made up solely of facts, such that values have no explanatory role in a proper scientific account of nature, see Adams, *Finite and Infinite Goods*, 63–70.

64. Jon Levenson, *Creation and the Persistence of Evil* (Princeton, NJ: Princeton University Press, 1994). For a full development of the meaning of "goodness" in biblical thought, see Alan Mittleman, "The Durability of Goodness," in *Judaic Sources and Western Thought: Jerusalem's Enduring Presence*, ed. Jonathan Jacobs (Oxford, UK: Oxford University Press, 2011), 21–48.

65. Christine Korsgaard, *The Sources of Normativity* (Cambridge, UK: Cambridge University Press, 2006), 2–4.

66. The arguments among different trends in Anglophone philosophy over cognitivism, noncognitivism, realism, naturalism, and so on are vast, ramified, dense, and technical. I am stepping very lightly and selectively here. For useful overviews of issues and thinkers with respect to realism, see Jonathan Jacobs, *Dimensions of Moral Theory* (Malden, MA: Blackwell Publishers, 2002), 110–50, and Geoffrey Sayre-McCord, *Essays on Moral Realism* (Ithaca, NY: Cornell University Press, 1988), 1–23.

67. Putnam, *The Collapse of the Fact/Value Dichotomy*, 21.

68. Ibid., 31. As Polkinghorne puts the same point: "It is an actual technique for discovery in fundamental physics to seek theories that are formulated in terms of equations possessing the unmistakable character of mathematical beauty.... [Mathematical beauty] involves qualities such as elegance and economy and the property of being 'deep'; that is to say, extensive and surprisingly fruitful consequences are found to derive from an apparently simple starting point." John Polkinghorne, ed., *Meaning in Mathematics* (Oxford, UK: Oxford University Press, 2011), 32–33.

69. For a full explication of these issues, see Hilary Putnam, "Objectivity and the Science/Ethics Distinction," in Hilary Putnam, *Realism with a Human Face*

(Cambridge, MA: Harvard University Press, 1990), 163–78. A nontechnical, highly accessible analysis of the same problem may be found in Kwame Anthony Appiah, *Cosmopolitanism* (New York: W. W. Norton, 2006), 33–44.

70. Putnam, *The Collapse of the Fact/Value Dichotomy*, 44. (Note also Hilary Putnam, *Ethics without Ontology* (Cambridge, MA: Harvard University Press, 2004).

71. Philippa Foot, *Natural Goodness* (Oxford, UK: Oxford University Press, 2001), 38.

72. Ibid., 35.

73. Ibid., 47, 51.

74. Ibid., 44–45.

75. Other standard bearers for intuitionism include Sidgwick, Prichard, and Broad. For an analysis of British intuitionism, see Robert Audi, *The Good in the Right: A Theory of Intuition and Intrinsic Value* (Princeton, NJ: Princeton University Press, 2004), 5–39. Audi's project is to reclaim and defend intuitionism.

76. G. E. Moore, *Principia Ethica* (Cambridge, UK: Cambridge University Press, 1994), 68.

77. Jacobs, *Dimensions of Moral Theory*, 5.

78. W. D. Ross, *The Right and the Good* (Oxford, UK: Clarendon Press, 1973), 29–30.

79. Audi, *The Good in the Right*, 59.

80. Implicit in this claim is the realist idea that there is moral knowledge; morality is cognitive. Intuitions are not just feelings about right and wrong, and so on. They are noninferred knowledge claims. See Jonathan Jacobs, *Dimensions of Moral Theory*, 86.

81. All quotations have been taken from Ross, *The Right and the Good*, 21–22.

82. Rawls quoted in Jacobs, *Dimensions of Moral Theory*, 88.

83. Bloom, *Just Babies*, 18–26.

84. Ibid., 98–99.

85. Ibid., 63.

86. Ibid., 99.

87. Ibid., 113.

88. See Korsgaard's response to de Waal in Frans de Waal, *Primates and Philosophers*, 98–119. Korsgaard shows how one can accept the evolutionary claim of continuity with respect to moral capacities between subrational primates and humans but at the same time insist on the uniquely human role of assessing our intentions and desires. A chimpanzee may "choose" to suppress his desire to mate out of fear of infringing on a more powerful male's prerogatives. The chimp has intentions but cannot "adopt and assess" them; he cannot exercise normative self-government—or what Kant calls "autonomy." This tracks the same distinction that Harry Frankfurt makes with the concept of the wanton. See Harry G. Frankfurt, *The Importance of What We Care About* (New York: Cambridge University Press, 1998), 16.

89. Joas, *The Genesis of Values*, 50.

90. Alice Crary, *Beyond Moral Judgment* (Cambridge, MA: Harvard University Press, 2007), 12.

91. Ibid., 39.

92. Immanuel Kant, *Critique of Practical Reason*, trans. Lewis White Beck (Upper Saddle River, NJ: Prentice Hall, 1993), 86 (para. 83).

93. See Thomas Nagel, *The View from Nowhere* (New York: Oxford University Press, 1986), 139, and, more recently, *Mind and Cosmos* (New York: Oxford University Press, 2012), 97–126. Nagel seems much less concerned in this volume to avoid "metaphysical embarrassment." See, for example, 123, where he claims that life as such has come into existence in order for value to be realized.

94. A third, whom I will not treat here, is in agreement. See two remarkable books by Roger Scruton: *The Soul of the World* (Princeton, NJ: Princeton University Press, 2014) and *The Face of God* (London: Bloomsbury Press, 2012).

95. John F. Haught, *Is Nature Enough? Meaning and Truth in the Age of Science* (New York: Cambridge University Press, 2006), 148. A thinker who is very much concerned to discern the work that the concept of God can do in ethics is John E. Hare. Hare sees the divine as our ally in overcoming the "moral gap" between the absoluteness of moral demands and our incapacity to meet them. See John E. Hare, *The Moral Gap* (Oxford, UK: Oxford University Press, 2002), and other works by the same author.

96. Iris Murdoch, *The Sovereignty of Good* (London: Routledge, 1971), 71.

97. Ibid., 72. For a further development (and complication) of these views, see Iris Murdoch, *Metaphysics as a Guide to Morals* (London: Penguin Books, 1992), especially 481–91.

98. Murdoch, *The Sovereignty of Good*, 99.

99. Ibid., 100.

100. Adams, *Finite and Infinite Goods*, 51.

101. Ibid., 50.

102. Both the two previous quotations and this one are in ibid., 52.

103. Kant quotation from *The Conflict of the Faculties*, cited in Adams, *Finite and Infinite Goods*, 284.

104. All quotations from Adams, *Finite and Infinite Goods*, 285.

105. Ibid., 289.

106. For an overview, see Reuven Firestone, *Holy War in Judaism: The Fall and Rise of an Idea* (New York: Oxford University Press, 2012), 103.

107. The Talmudic discussion of this passage at b Berakhot 7a entertains other explanations for God's infliction of punishment, but none deviate from a framework of justice that can be rationally explicated.

108. Moses Maimonides, *The Guide of the Perplexed*, trans. Shlomo Pines (Chicago: University of Chicago Press, 1963), 124 (book I, chapter 54, 64b).

109. Maimonides, *Guide*, 127.

110. Maimonides's phrasing of his justification for the commandment is complex. After citing Deuteronomy 20:18, he writes: "Thus it [the Torah] says: do not

think that this is hard-heartedness or desire for vengeance. It is rather an act required by human opinion, which considers that everyone who deviates from the ways of truth should be put an end to." The qualifying phrase "required by human opinion" may mitigate the force of the divine commandment. Perhaps he considered the commandment a concession to human weakness, as with the laws of sacrifice. At any rate, Maimonides claims in his code that even in a commanded war such as this one, the enemy is to be given terms of surrender in advance of the battle. If the enemy, presumably including the seven Canaanite nations, accepts servitude, they are allowed to live and become a subject people. See *Mishneh Torah*, "Kings and Their Wars," chapter 6:1. He furthermore stipulates that "acts of mercy, forgiveness, pity and commiseration should proceed from the governor of a city to a much greater extent than acts of retaliation." Maimonides, *Guide*, I:54, 127.

111. See Barry Stroud, *Engagement and Metaphysical Dissatisfaction* (New York: Oxford University Press, 2011), 8–17.

Chapter 3: Holiness and Violence

1. Eibl-Eibesfeldt, *Love and Hate*, 93.

2. Aristotle, *Politics*, book I, chapter 2, 1253e.

3. Frans de Waal, *Primates and Philosophers: How Morality Evolved* (Princeton, NJ: Princeton University Press, 2006), 30–31.

4. Richard Wrangham and Dale Peterson, *Demonic Males: Apes and the Origins of Human Violence* (New York: Houghton Mifflin, 1996), 5–27.

5. Thomas Nagel, *The View from Nowhere* (New York: Oxford University Press, 1986), 187.

6. See Yair Lorberbaum, *The Image of God* [Hebrew] (Jerusalem: Schocken, 2004), 292.

7. Immanuel Kant, *The Metaphysics of Morals*, trans. Mary Gregor (New York: Cambridge University Press, 1996), 106.

8. Jonathan Glover, *Humanity: A Moral History of the 20th Century* (New Haven, CT: Yale University Press, 2012), 159.

9. Ibid., 161.

10. Ibid., 41.

11. I do not mean here to diminish the uniqueness of the Shoah, which taken as a total "event" is a radical rupture, even with other genocides. I mean only to call attention to an aspect of the process of dehumanization. As the following citations show, dehumanization can be promoted even by those who are fighting a justified war.

12. Three citations from Roland Bainton, *Christian Attitudes toward War and Peace* (Nashville, TN: Abingdon Press, 1960), 168.

13. Both citations from Glover, *Humanity*, 174.

14. Cited in ibid., 175 (emphasis added).

15. Cited in ibid., 176 (emphasis added).

16. Cited in ibid., 130.

17. Barrington Moore Jr., *Moral Purity and Persecution in History* (Princeton, NJ: Princeton University Press, 2000), 26.

18. Regina Schwartz, *The Curse of Cain: The Violent Legacy of Monotheism* (Chicago: University of Chicago Press, 1997), xi.

19. David A. Bernat and Jonathan Klawans, eds., *Religion and Violence: The Biblical Heritage* (Sheffield, UK: Sheffield Phoenix Press, 2007), 8.

20. Steven Geller sees holy war as a fantasy retrojected onto the "supposed 'conquest' of Canaan" but actually serving as a prophetic metaphor for God's "fight against his own sinful people." See Geller, "Prophetic Roots of Religious Violence," in Bernat and Klawans, *Religion and Violence*, 51.

21. Pesiqta d'Rav Kahana 13:5, cited in Reuven Kimmelman, "The Seven Nations of Canaan"; available at http://seforim.blogspot.com/2015/07/the-seven -nations-of-canaan.html (accessed August 21, 2016).

22. Robert Eisen, *The Peace and Violence of Judaism* (New York: Oxford University Press, 2011), 89. Yitzchak Blau, "Ploughshares into Swords: Contemporary Religious Zionists and Moral Constraints," *Tradition* 34, no. 4 (2000): 42.

23. Leviticus Rabba 17:6; Deuteronomy Rabba 5:13–14, cited in Kimmelman, "The Seven Nations of Canaan." Maimonides, in his codification of the laws of war, will follow the same strategy.

24. Rabbi Abraham Isaac Kook draws this normative implication. See Kimmelman, "The Seven Nations of Canaan," for sources.

25. Moshe Greenberg, "On the Political Use of the Bible in Modern Israel," in *Pomegranates and Golden Bells: Studies in Biblical, Jewish, and Near Eastern Ritual, Law and Literature in Honor of Jacob Milgrom*, ed. David P. Wright, David Noel Freedman, and Avi Hurwitz (Winona Lake, IN: Eisenbrauns, 1995), 469.

26. The treatment of Phinehas in the next several paragraphs is taken from Alan Mittleman, "The Problem of Religious Violence," *Political Theology* 12, no. 5 (2011): 722–26, and used here with permission. Available at www.tandfonline .com/loi/ypot20 (accessed June 13, 2017).

27. Susan Niditch, *War in the Hebrew Bible: A Study in the Ethics of Violence* (New York: Oxford University Press, 1993), 30, 46.

28. Cited in Bernat and Klawans, *Religion and Violence*, 28.

29. John J. Collins, "The Zeal of Phinehas: The Bible and the Legitimation of Violence," *Journal of Biblical Literature* 122, no. 1 (2003): 3–21.

30. Gerd Lüdemann, *The Unholy in Holy Scripture*, trans. John Bowden (Louisville, KY: Westminster John Knox, 1997), 40. In place of the bracketed term, which I have inserted, the original had the root letters *qds*. As I am transcribing the Hebrew letter *kuf* with a k, not a q, I altered Lüdemann's text.

31. See Niditch, *War in the Hebrew Bible*, 29–30. Levine takes the verse as an intrabiblical reference to Exodus 22:19, where anyone who worships a foreign god is proscribed (*yoḥeram*) for death. See Levine, *The JPS Torah Commentary: Leviticus*, 199. For rabbinic interpretations, see Rashi, Rashbam, Ramban, on

Leviticus 27:28–29, based on the rabbinic source text b Arakhin 6b. Milgrom takes the rabbinic approach to be warranted by the biblical text; see Milgrom, *Leviticus 23–27* (New Haven, CT: Yale University Press, 2001), 2395–96.

32. Niditch, *War in the Hebrew Bible*, 37.

33. Ibid., 49–50.

34. Ibid., 77.

35. See Avi Sagi, "The Punishment of Amalek in Jewish Tradition: Coping with the Moral Problem," *Harvard Theological Review* 87, no. 3 (1994): 323–46.

36. A classical source supporting Maimonides is Sifre Devarim on Deuteronomy 20:15 (=Piska 202): "If they repent, they are not to be slain." See *Sifre: A Tannaitic Commentary on the Book of Deuteronomy*, trans. Reuven Hammer (New Haven, CT: Yale University Press, 1986), 218. For other rabbinic sources that support the need to offer peace terms to all enemies, see Numbers Rabba 19:27, Tanhuma Tzav 3:2, and Deuteronomy Rabba 13–14, cited in Eisen, *The Peace and Violence of Judaism*, 91. See also Tanhuma Shofetim 5:5.

37. Maimonides, *Mishneh Torah*, Book of Judges, Laws of Kings and Their Wars, 6:1 (emphasis added); available at www.sefaria.org/Mishneh_Torah,_Kings _and_Wars.6.4?lang=en&with=all&lang2=en (accessed August 21, 2016).

38. Despite rabbinic basis for offering peace terms to the Canaanite nations, treating Amalek in this manner seems to be a Maimonidean innovation. Maimonides's critic, R. Avraham ben David of Posquières, dissented from his lenient ruling. See Sagi, "The Punishment of Amalek in Jewish Tradition," 342.

39. Maimonides infers the Canaanite rejection of peace terms from Joshua 11:19–20, which notes that "apart from the Hivites who dwelt in Gibeon, not a single city made terms with the Israelites; all were taken in battle. For it was the LORD's doing to stiffen their necks to give battle to Israel, in order that they might be proscribed without quarter and wiped out, as the LORD commanded Moses." He thereby infers that since the Canaanite group that made peace was not wiped out, had the others done so, they would not have been wiped out either. However, Maimonides also has a tendency to understand the Canaanites and Amalekites symbolically and so to universalize the commandment as an ongoing war against idolatry. See Reuven Firestone, *Holy War in Judaism*, 118–26, for a nuanced discussion.

40. Maimonides, *Guide* I:54, 127. For analysis, see Eisen, *The Peace and Violence of Judaism*, 125.

41. Avi Sagi has a much stronger reading of Maimonides's accomplishment than I have. He sees Maimonides as having subordinated the commandment to blot out the memory of Amalek as fully domesticated to moral norms. "Religion depends on morality rather than morality on religion. God's command, as well as the norms flowing from it, are now reinterpreted in this light." Sagi, "The Punishment of Amalek," 345. Nonetheless, although Maimonides and others have domesticated the commandment to morality, they still believe that a moral justification could exist for the destruction of an entire people. This severely limits the accomplishment, in my view.

42. Thucydides, *The History of the Peloponnesian War*, trans. R. Crawley (New York: E. Dutton, 1948), 300–306.

43. Maimonides, *Mishneh Torah*, Book of Seasons, Laws Concerning the Sabbath, 2:3, cited in Sagi, "The Punishment of Amalek," 344.

44. Ibid., I:54, 127 (emphasis added).

45. Ibid., I:54, 128.

46. I heard Rabbi Goren say this—a remark of which he was apparently quite fond—at a talk that he gave at Brandeis University. David Ben Gurion spoke similarly.

47. For a discussion, see Firestone, *Holy War in Judaism*, 238–44.

48. b Megillah 10a, Ḥagigah 3b, and elsewhere.

49. Rabbi Aviner, cited in Menachem Kellner, "What Is a Jew As Opposed to Who Is a Jew? Yehuda Halevi and Maimonides in Those Days, Rabbi Aviner and Rabbi Kapah in Ours," in *Mesora L'Yosef*, ed. Yosef Parhi [Hebrew] (Netanya: Machon MSH"H, 2016), 102–3 (translation my own, emphasis added). On the general topic of gentile versus Jewish impurity, see Christine Hayes, *Gentile Impurities and Jewish Identities: Intermarriage and Conversion from the Bible to the Talmud* (New York: Oxford University Press, 2002), 115. On the halakhic background, see Maimonides, *Mishneh Torah*, Order of Purities, Book of Corpse Impurity, 1:13–15.

50. Kellner, "What Is a Jew," 120.

51. Ibid., 102. For a full analysis of the various, sometimes conflicting strands of the place of non-Jewish inhabitants of the Land of Israel, conceived in terms of the category of the biblical Canaanites, see Dov Schwartz, "The Conquest of Eretz Israel and the Seven Canaanite Nations," in *The Gift of the Land and the Fate of the Canaanites in Jewish Thought*, ed. Katell Berthelot, Joseph E. David, and Marc Hirschman (New York: Oxford University Press, 2014).

52. The classic article for the claim that there are—for Jews at least—no ethics outside the halakhic framework is Aharon Lichtenstein, "Does Jewish Tradition Recognize an Ethic Independent of Halakha?" in *Contemporary Jewish Ethics*, ed. Menachem Marc Kellner (Brooklyn: Hebrew Publishing, 1978), 102–23.

53. Aviner, cited in Yitzchak Blau, "Ploughshares into Swords: Contemporary Religious Zionists and Moral Constraints," in *Tradition* 34, no. 4 (2000): 50.

54. Blau, "Ploughshares into Swords," 51.

55. T. M. Scanlon, *What We Owe to Each Other* (Cambridge, MA: Belknap Press of Harvard University Press, 1998), 106.

56. Fine, *Political Violence in Judaism, Christianity and Islam*, 139–141. See also *Jerusalem Post*, May 28, 2012; available at www.jpost.com/National-News/A-G-Torat-Hamelech-authors-will-not-be-indicted (accessed May 28, 2012).

57. Yitzhak Shapira and Yosef Elizur, *Torat ha-Melekh* (Lev Ha-Shomron: Od Yosef Hai, 2009), 179, 216.

58. Ibid., 73.

59. Ibid., 206.

60. Ibid., 40–45.

61. Ariel Finkelstein, *Derekh ha-Melekh* (Netivot: Yeshivat Hesder Ahavat Yisrael, 2010), 32.

62. Shapira and Elizur, *Torat ha-Melekh*, 174; Finkelstein, *Derekh ha-Melekh*, 33, 93.

63. See Naḥmanides on Genesis 34:13; Finkelstein, *Derekh ha-Melekh*, 27.

64. Kook, quoted in Finkelstein, *Derekh ha-Melekh*, 31–32.

65. Kook, quoted in Finkelstein, *Derekh ha-Melekh*, 32.

66. For a powerful defense of the idea that a decent society is one that does not humiliate its members, see Avishai Margalit, *The Decent Society* (Cambridge, MA: Harvard University Press, 1996).

67. See Amartya Sen, *Identity and Violence: The Illusion of Destiny* (New York: W. W. Norton, 2006).

68. This is a view that Maimonides does not share. In his authoritative codification of the laws of war, see, for example, "he who fights with all his heart, without fear, and with the sole intention of sanctifying the Name [*l'kadesh et-Hashem*], is assured that no harm will befall him and no evil overtake him." See Maimonides, *Mishneh Torah*, Book of Judges, Laws of Kings and Their Wars, 7:15, cited in *A Maimonides Reader*, ed. Isadore Twersky (West Orange, NJ: Behrman House, 1972), 220.

69. Kenneth Seeskin, *Searching for a Distant God: The Legacy of Maimonides* (New York: Oxford University Press, 2000).

70. Stuart Hampshire, *Justice Is Conflict* (Princeton, NJ: Princeton University Press, 2000), 52.

71. Ibid., 43.

72. Ibid., 16–17. As we saw at the outset in considering the *Euthyphro*, Socratic *elenchus* (roughly, "dialectical reason") was not an end in itself but a means to reach truth and purify the soul.

ACKNOWLEDGMENTS

Many persons helped me in the writing of this book. First and foremost, I owe a debt of gratitude to the Herzl Institute in Jerusalem for providing me with a research fellowship that supported a yearlong leave from teaching. I thank Yoram Hazony, Josh Weinstein, and Gavriel Lakser for including me among the 2015–16 grantees of the Institute as a Herzl Fellow, as well as for their ongoing engagement with my work. I also thank my academic home, the Jewish Theological Seminary (JTS), for its continued support during my leave. Without JTS's strong commitment to supporting its faculty's research and writing, I could not have written this book in a timely manner. As this project brought me into a number of areas where I cannot pretend to have expert knowledge, I turned to colleagues and friends for advice and expertise. These include Alan Cooper, Ben Sommer, Hartley Lachter, Alan Wiener, Isaac Lifshitz, Elias Sacks, Lenn Goodman, Jim Diamond, Yoni Brafman, Marc Herman, Liz Cunningham, and Robert Eisen. I thank as well my graduate student, Paul Steiner. I presented my work at the initial stage of writing and again toward the end of the project to the other Herzl fellows in Jerusalem. They gave me helpful, constructive criticism. I remember our meetings fondly. I am also grateful to Fred Appel of Princeton University Press for his continued interest in my work and to the anonymous readers of my manuscript for their very helpful remarks. I thank, as ever, my wife, Patti Mittleman, without whose love and support my life would be much diminished. I dedicate this book to my sons and their wives, Ari Mittleman and Tara Brown, and Joel and Amy Mittleman-Levin. When I think about them, their love for one another, and the work to which they've dedicated their lives, I have confidence that the good and the holy can yet flourish in the world.

INDEX

Aaron, 35–37, 165, 200n42
Abraham, 54, 67; Isaac and, 8, 60,
    143–45; Isaiah and, 7–8
Adam and Eve, 66–67, 71, 204n90
Adams, Robert M., 140–47, 151,
    194n10, 209n46
adultery, 90
aggression, 106, 134–36, 156, 173;
    Eibl-Eibesfeldt on, 108, 154,
    210n60
altruism, 96–97, 135
Amalekites, 3, 145, 158, 168, 173, 189;
    Maimonides's view of, 216n39,
    216nn38–41
Amir, Yigal, 2
angels, 7, 35, 60, 68–69, 113
anthropomorphism, 33, 156
Antigone (Sophocles), 5
Arendt, Hannah, 112–13
Aristotle, 70, 121; on the good, 126;
    on the good life, 97; on human
    nature, 155
augustus (supreme value), 101
Avalos, Hector, 162
Aviner, Shlomo, 181–85
axis mundi, 60
Aztecs, 86

Batnitzky, Leora, 197n14
Beethoven, Ludwig van, 27
Bell, Catherine, 118
Bellah, Robert, 116–17
beneficence, 5, 114, 131–33
Bereshit Rabbah, 59, 60
Berlin, Isaiah, 178
bikhorim (first fruits), 57–58
Bloom, Paul, 133–34
Bosnia, 19–20
Boyer, Pascal, 27, 196n7

Bridges, Robert, 159
Buber, Martin, 79–81
Buddhism, 20, 188
Burke, Edmund, 5–6, 190
Burma, 20

Cain and Abel, 67
Camus, Albert, 122
Canaanites, 172–77; genocide of, 3,
    12, 145, 150, 161, 163, 189; inter-
    marriage with, 68, 163–64, 166,
    172, 203n84; Maimonides's view
    of, 176, 216nn38–39; "symbolic,"
    164
capital punishment, 48, 90, 150–51,
    157, 168
cherubim, 35, 113. *See also* angels
chimpanzees, 96, 103–4, 155–56,
    212n88; maternal care by, 104–9,
    114; murder by, 156; play among,
    116; symbolic thought and,
    207n10; sympathy among,
    106–7, 134
Christianity, 30–32, 75, 91, 159, 162,
    205n99; Adams on, 142, 145; Dan
    on, 31, 32, 197n15; Halevi on, 65;
    Lazarus on, 80; Moore on, 160;
    Otto on, 99; Rosenzweig on, 84
Cohen, Hermann, 77–81, 84
corpses, impurity of, 44–47, 181–83,
    200n35
Cozbi, Moabite princess, 167, 168
Crary, Alice, 139–40
Croatia, 19–20, 160, 195n23
cruelty, 3, 6, 101, 124, 150, 160

Dan, Joseph, 28, 31, 32, 40, 197n13,
    197n15
Darwinism, 98; social, 127

A NOTE ON THE TYPE

{⊶⊷}

THIS BOOK has been composed in Miller, a Scotch Roman typeface designed by Matthew Carter and first released by Font Bureau in 1997. It resembles Monticello, the typeface developed for The Papers of Thomas Jefferson in the 1940s by C. H. Griffith and P. J. Conkwright and reinterpreted in digital form by Carter in 2003.

Pleasant Jefferson ("P. J.") Conkwright (1905–1986) was Typographer at Princeton University Press from 1939 to 1970. He was an acclaimed book designer and AIGA Medalist.

The ornament used throughout this book was designed by Pierre Simon Fournier (1712–1768) and was a favorite of Conkwright's, used in his design of the *Princeton University Library Chronicle*.